Presidential Campaigns

DOCUMENTS DECODED

The ABC-CLIO series **Documents Decoded** guides readers on a hunt for new secrets through an expertly curated selection of primary sources. Each book pairs key documents with in-depth analysis, all in an original and visually engaging side-by-side format. But *Documents Decoded* authors do more than just explain each source's context and significance—they give readers a front-row seat to their own investigation and interpretation of each essential document line-by-line.

Presidential Campaigns
DOCUMENTS DECODED

Daniel M. Shea
and
Brian M. Harward

Documents Decoded

 ABC-CLIO

Library of Congress Cataloging-in-Publication Data

Shea, Daniel M.
     Presidential Campaigns: Documents Decoded / Daniel M. Shea and Brian M. Harward.
            pages cm. — (Documents decoded)
     Includes index.
     ISBN 978-1-61069-192-5 (hardcover : alk. paper) — ISBN 978-1-61069-193-2 (ebook)
    1. Political campaigns—United States—History.   2. Presidential candidates—United States—Language.
3. Presidents—United States—Election—History.   4. Speeches, addresses, etc., American—History and
criticism.   5. Communication in politics—United States—History.   6. United States—Politics and government—
Sources.   7. Mass media—Political aspects—United States—History.   8. Rhetoric—Political aspects—United
States—History.   9. English language—United States—Discourse analysis.   I. Harward, Brian M.
II. Title.
     JK2281.S495   2013
     324.70973—dc23   2013006048

ISBN: 978-1-61069-192-5
EISBN: 978-1-61069-193-2

17 16 15 14 13   1 2 3 4 5

This book is also available on the World Wide Web as an eBook.
Visit www.abc-clio.com for details.

ABC-CLIO, LLC
130 Cremona Drive, P.O. Box 1911
Santa Barbara, California 93116-1911

This book is printed on acid-free paper ∞
Manufactured in the United States of America

Every reasonable effort has been made to trace the owners of copyright materials in this book, but in some instances this has proven impossible. The editors and publishers will be glad to receive information leading to more complete acknowledgments in subsequent printings of the book and in the meantime extend their apologies for any omissions.

Contents

ELECTION OF 1960

ELECTION OF 1964

ELECTION OF 1968

ELECTION OF 2000

ELECTION OF 2004

ELECTION OF 2008

Introduction: Crisis Points in Modern Presidential Elections

Most observers knew that the 1960 race for the White House would be close. Democrats had an advantage in national voter registration numbers as well as in control of a majority of state and local elected offices. The New Deal Coalition—the bundle of groups that had created a Democratic majority since the election of Franklin D. Roosevelt in 1932—had a few cracks, but it was still strong. The Democrats were the majority party in 1960, yet Republicans seemed to have an advantage with the foremost issue, the ongoing struggle against communism, as the Cold War between the United States and the Soviet Union was at its height. Many voters believed that the Democrats were stronger on domestic policy matters and therefore wished to leave Congress in their hands, but they also thought that Republicans were stronger on foreign affairs and national defense.

Taking a bit of a gamble, the Democrats settled on John F. Kennedy as their nominee. He was a young, dynamic senator from Massachusetts who had shown party leaders his tenacity in his aggressive campaigning. If elected, he would be the first Catholic president, which seemed to give these leaders pause in the early phase of the nomination process but did not seem to be a major issue as the campaign progressed. As his vice presidential running mate, Kennedy selected the Senate majority leader, Lyndon Johnson of Texas. Many thought the so-called Boston-Austin ticket would be formidable.

On the Republican side, Dwight Eisenhower's vice president, Richard Nixon, secured his party's nomination after a divisive battle. Nixon had honed foreign policy experience and was also a good campaigner. He was perhaps a bit less charismatic than Kennedy but had been in the White House for eight years. Nixon also came from a critically important state for the electoral college—California. Nixon then chose former Massachusetts senator and United Nations ambassador Henry Cabot Lodge Jr. as his vice presidential running mate. Together, Nixon and Lodge suggested experience, continuity, and a steady hand.

As the autumn campaign progressed, polling revealed that several states were going to be too close to call. As with all modern presidential elections, candidates focus their attention on swing states as the race comes to an end. Rather than aim to win more total votes than the opponents, candidates and their managers realize that the electoral college compels a focus on winning particular states. This is because of the unit rule, where the winner of the state is granted all that state's electors (a system also called winner take all). The strategy is to amass, state by state, 270 electoral votes. Conversely, it makes little sense to spend resources campaigning in states where the outcome is more or less certain. In most presidential elections, candidates focus the lion's share of their effort in about a dozen states. The same was true in the final weeks of the 1960 election.

But that is not the whole story. Two months earlier at the Republican National Convention in Chicago, Nixon had offered a pledge to the delegates: "I announce to you tonight, and I pledge to you, that I, personally, will carry this campaign into every one of the 50 states of this nation between now and November the 8th." At the time it seemed to make sense, and the crowd cheered with approval. Nixon would be a president for all Americans, not just particular interests in particular states. He and his aides also thought that this pledge would build unity after a fractious nomination battle in Chicago. But by early November, it became clear that the pledge was a colossal mistake, as Nixon had neglected to visit a number of far-flung states scattered across the nation, including Alaska and Hawaii. Even with airplanes, visiting these states would take days and draw his attention away from the all-important swing states at a critical time. But because of his commitment to carry the campaign to each of the 50 states, Nixon had no choice. It was not until November 6—just two days before the election—that Nixon visited Alaska, officially completing his tour and living up to his 50-state pledge.

In the end, 1960 proved to be one of the closest elections in American history. Kennedy topped Nixon with 303 electoral votes to 219. But in the national popular vote, Kennedy defeated Nixon by just a 10th of 1 percent. More important, Kennedy had won a dozen states by less than 3 percentage points. In several states, such as Missouri, New Mexico, New Jersey, and Texas, Kennedy had won by less than 1 percentage point. In Illinois, Kennedy beat Nixon by a scant 9,000 votes out of 4.75 million cast—or a margin of 0.2 percent.

By the tiniest of margins in a handful of states, John Kennedy would move to the White House, and Richard Nixon would move back to private life. Had Nixon not made the 50-state pledge—if he had instead spent those critical hours in swing states—it is likely that the outcome would have been different. So too would our nation's history.

PRESIDENT BILL CLINTON SERVED TWO FOUR-YEAR TERMS, the maximum length of service permitted by the U.S. Constitution, so he could not seek reelection in 2000. As with the 1960 contest, polls during the campaign indicated that the election between the two major party candidates, Vice President Al Gore, the Democrat, and the Republican candidate, George W. Bush, the governor of Texas, would be close—perhaps very close. Other candidates—Ralph Nader of the Green Party and Patrick Buchanan of the Reform Party—posed the threat of drawing enough votes away from Gore and Bush to sway the outcome of the election.

The Democrats were determined to continue the course that they believed Clinton had set during his eight years: a strong record of job creation, a balanced budget, environmental protection, advancements in civil rights, support for working men and women, and prudent use of American aid to help developing countries. Surely Gore would do much the same if given the chance.

The Republicans, however, were anxious for change. In their view, Clinton had raised taxes, undermined the nation's military preparedness, pulled the country into conflicts worldwide while neglecting concerns at home, and, perhaps most important, allowed the moral fabric of the nation to wither. Americans had been battered by one scandal after another. Bush was the successful governor of the nation's second-largest state and was known for working with Democrats in Texas on issues that reflected his campaign slogan of compassionate conservatism. For Republicans, his candidacy held the promise of a restoration of dignity to the presidency and no small measure of conservative policies.

When Americans awoke on the day following the election, they discovered that the issue of which candidate would serve as the next president of the United States was not settled. Vice President Gore received about 500,000 more votes than Governor Bush nationally, but in the complicated electoral college system, Gore did not gain majority support in enough states to capture the presidency outright. Despite support from fewer total voters, Bush had won enough states to be neck-and-neck with Gore in the electoral vote count. The entire decision hinged on the results in the state of Florida, where election controversies and a tight race created a chaotic situation. In several counties, there were problems with ineffective voting punch card machines, inaccurate voter registration lists, and a ballot designed in a confusing manner. Such problems also appeared within counties in other states, yet the race was generally not as close as the vote in Florida. The stakes were unimaginably high; whoever won the popular vote in Florida would win the election. The nation waited with growing anxiety.

For more than five weeks after the election, teams of lawyers did battle in county circuit courts in Florida, federal district courts in Florida, the U.S. Court of Appeals, the Florida Supreme Court, and the U.S. Supreme Court. Thirty-six days after the election, the U.S. Supreme Court put an end to the election controversy. In a narrow 5-to-4 decision in a case titled *Bush v. Gore,* the majority of justices effectively ordered an end to ballot recounts and preserved Bush's narrow 537-vote victory. Many Americans were unhappy with the result of the election. Public opinion polls at the time of the decision revealed a deep division among voters regarding the legitimacy of the Court's action. As Bush was inaugurated, protesters lined Constitution Avenue decrying the Court's decision and casting a sense of illegitimacy over the initial days of the new administration. In a statesman-like gesture, Gore sought to dampen the protesters' resentment. As sitting vice president, he presided over the joint session of Congress where the official tally of the electoral votes took place and repeatedly ruled out of order those who sought to challenge the legality of the recount decision. At the time, Gore was quoted as saying that "While I strongly disagree with the Supreme Court's decision, I accept it." When the principal protagonist in the most contentious general election in the modern era decided to put the event behind him, so too did most other Americans.

THE IDEOLOGICAL TENSIONS THAT EMERGED IN THE 2000 ELECTION and the red state–blue state electoral map that so clearly marked the divergent preferences of many in the American electorate had lasting effects. Four years later, Democratic candidate John Kerry was a sitting senator from Massachusetts challenging the Republican incumbent, George W. Bush, in the general election.

Because of the terrorist attacks of September 11, 2001, and the engagement of U.S. military forces in Afghanistan and Iraq, national security, foreign policy, and counterterrorism played a large role in the general election campaign. Consequently, the candidates' own military service records as young men during the Vietnam War became relevant to voters.

During the Vietnam War era, George W. Bush had stayed in the United States, opting to serve in the Air National Guard. Reporters had uncovered evidence that Bush received preferential treatment in receiving a posting to the National Guard unit in Texas. Such a posting was coveted because it meant that by being on active duty stateside, he would not have to go overseas to serve in Vietnam. The allegations that Bush did not live up to the obligations of his National Guard service were met with counterallegations regarding Kerry's service.

Kerry served as a commander of a U.S. Navy swift boat in Vietnam. He was a decorated combat veteran, having received several medals for valor. Nonetheless, he was targeted by a group of swift boat veterans who objected to the account that Kerry had given of his meritorious service. The group also objected to Kerry's critique of U.S. policy in Vietnam during his congressional testimony when he returned from his tour of duty.

The swift boat campaign against Kerry was funded by a so-called 527 group called Swift Boat Veterans for Truth. Such groups were organized under the authority of Section 527 of the Internal Revenue Code and could finance issue ads and target candidates so long as their activities were not coordinated with a campaign.

The smear campaign by the Swift Boat Veterans for Truth included three ads that targeted Kerry in key swing states such as Ohio, Pennsylvania, and Michigan. In addition, Swift Boat Veterans for Truth produced a book and hosted numerous public appearances by the people affiliated with the group. As reporters investigated the group's claims, it appeared that many of them were simply untrue or provided an incomplete picture of Kerry's actions in Vietnam. Nonetheless, the negative ads were successful in raising concerns among voters and diverting Kerry's attention away from issues that would have favored the Democrat.

The ads effectively took questions regarding Bush's own record during Vietnam off the public's radar and also made the central question of the campaign not Bush's decision to go to war in Iraq (an issue that Kerry sought to make his core critique of the Bush years) but instead Kerry's character. Kerry's attention was so diverted by the attack ads that his campaign brought forward many others who had served with the senator in Vietnam to corroborate his version of events. In addition, his acceptance speech at the 2004 Democratic National Convention was punctuated by a sharp salute and the words "I'm John Kerry and I'm reporting for duty." By obligating Kerry to attend to defending himself from smears, the Bush campaign was able to limit the traction that Kerry could gain from offering voters a compelling critique of the war in Iraq and Bush's handling of national security issues generally. Bush, of course, ultimately won reelection in another very close vote.

The Weight of Crisis Events

The stories of Richard Nixon's 50-state pledge, the U.S. Supreme Court's ruling in *Bush v. Gore,* and the emergence of a powerful advertising campaign against John

Kerry are on one level unique. They involve vastly different circumstances and distinctive electoral dynamics. One involves the actions of a candidate (an ill-advised pledge), another involves the action of a governmental institution (a Supreme Court case), and the third involves the efforts of a noncandidate organization (a well-funded interest group). They all, however, share the common characteristic of being perceived as critical to the outcome of a presidential election.

It would seem that in most presidential elections, if not every presidential election, there are critical moments, key events during campaigns that weigh heavily on the outcome of the contest. These crisis points sometimes become the stuff of legend, but they appear to shape the contest in important ways. These events alter voter attitudes, campaign strategies, media perceptions, candidate behavior, and much more. This book provides students of electoral politics and general-interest readers a detailed account of key events in modern presidential elections since 1952. As you will find in the pages to follow, our aim has been to provide the actual transcript of events as well as discussion of their context and its implications.

There is a widespread notion, particularly among journalists and campaign strategists, that key candidate choices, critical events, revelations, and unintended incidents shape the outcome of most elections. By making a particular move instead of a different one or by responding to an event in one fashion rather than another, elections are won or lost.

For journalists, this perspective makes sense because it is their job to sell excitement, suspense, and intrigue and cover the horse-race character of a campaign. As noted by a team of election scholars, "Strategy has become a preeminent fixation of political journalists in the United States, with reporters usually zeroing in on each new charge, unflattering revelation, fundraising downturn, lost endorsement and sagging poll number."[1] Practitioners, such as campaign consultants and party activists, insist that these events are critical because they probably believe it—and because their very livelihood depends on selling their expertise, knowledge, and skill to navigate through moments of crisis and other predicaments. For this group, continuous readjustment is necessary because every campaign confronts unexpected obstacles that have consequence for the ultimate outcome. There is no formula for success, no mathematical algorithm that can predict the winner of every election. No scientific procedure will highlight all the variables on which triumph might depend.[2] Crisis points will always occur, leading to conflicting interpretations and uncertainty among campaigns. Smart candidates hire savvy consultants because they can respond effectively when those crises occur.

Yet scholars are less sure that these events really matter. Prior to recent presidential elections, scholars have made forecasts about the outcomes of those elections. At the center of these statistical models are so-called systemic forces, such as the state of the economy, the unemployment rate, inflation, presidential approval ratings, and perceptions of whether our nation is headed in the right direction. Not only are these predictions accurate, but they are typically quite accurate more than one year in advance of the election. In other words, researchers can usually predict the outcome of a presidential contest by a few percentage points well in advance of the campaign. Unexpected developments, or what we call crisis points, are not known and therefore are not part of the researchers' models. If these events are significant, how can scholars predict elections without them?

The notion that campaign events are of little consequence—or what is called the minimal effects argument—is rooted in scholarly work done some 70 years ago. Paul F. Lazarsfeld, Bernard R. Berelson, and Helen Gaudet wrote *The People's Choice* in 1944.[3] They found that systemic forces, such as religion, socioeconomic status, and place of residence could be used to place the voter on an index of political predisposition. Conversely, campaign flyers, political events, and news stories had negligible effect on the final outcome. Other books highlighted the importance of party identification. Political parties, it was argued, give voters a framework for understanding the issues and events. Voters pay attention to these events, but their analysis of the importance of each event is filtered through their partisan lens. For example, a debate gaffe such as Michael Dukakis's ill-advised response to a death penalty question in 1988 was deemed serious by Republican voters but was viewed as a minor mistake by Democratic supporters of the Massachusetts governor.

But the partisan lens argument has not been the last word. A growing number of scholars have begun to look at campaign effects, and many have developed a deeper appreciation for the weight of crisis events. Samuel Popkin, for example, in his 1991 book *Reasoning Voter,* suggested that voters are quite deliberative, thereby providing evidence that campaign events do matter. Perhaps most notably, Thomas Holbrook in his aptly titled 1986 book *Do Campaigns Matter?* found that "Election outcomes and voting behavior are easily explained with just a few variables, none of which are related to the campaign." And yet, curiously, he argues that campaign dynamics matter. Holbrook maintains that attitudes about systemic forces create a predicted equilibrium, the outcome that would be expected without dramatic campaign effects. But when crisis point events occur, skillful campaign strategists respond in ways that seem to push the outcome back to the predicted equilibrium. Campaign effects are minimal, he reasons, but they do exist.

Finally, through a comprehensive exploration of vote totals, trial-heat polls, and individual-level survey data, another scholar, James Campbell, concluded that precampaign fundamentals in presidential elections—such as incumbency and the election-year economy—frame the predicted equilibrium but do not always determine the outcome.[4] In every election, idiosyncratic campaign events, such as candidate gaffes, and strategic blunders occur. In postwar presidential elections, Campbell found that the net impact of idiosyncratic campaign effects is roughly 1.5 percent of the popular vote. Given that many elections are very close, these events are indeed significant.

The Pages to Follow

It is probably a mistake to assume that in every election there is an event that shifts the outcome. There have been instances when a massive crisis occurred, but this has not happened often. And of course, as Campbell notes, systemic forces often set the stage for a very close election. A shift of a few thousand votes in a handful of states can tip the balance. Thus, election outcomes are not preordained; candidates, issues, and the nature of the times provide a backdrop against which certain key events are brought to the fore. We can imagine, too, that key moments, while not shifting the outcome, broaden or narrow a candidate's victory. These events merge with other forces—elements perhaps below the surface—and shape the final outcome.

This volume is designed to chart many of the crisis points in presidential elections since 1952. The reader should appreciate that consensus among scholars, pundits, or average citizens regarding a list of key events in a given election is unlikely—particularly for a list of events from the past 14 presidential elections. There have certainly been really big happenings, and we have included them in the pages to follow. But beyond the standouts, the matter gets admittedly subjective. Here we have relied on media accounts, scholarly assessments, and, to be frank, a good dose of our own recollections as well as conventional wisdom. Some crisis points make the list because of the mythology that surrounds them. We did not select events based on a preset agreed-upon list or on objective measures regarding their impact (such as a shift in poll numbers). There is no such agreed-upon list of crisis points—we do not offer the pages that follow as an effort to fill such a void.

It is also probably true that particular events are more widely known and written about than others. Untold numbers of personal decisions by candidates, consultants, and members of the media likely helped to shape these elections. An insider might have had a very different view of a crisis event than those on the outside looking in. Thus, we may have missed very important events but are not likely to have included unimportant events.

Rather than merely provide the reader with an assessment of a particular crisis point, we include original documents, transcripts, and news accounts in addition to annotations about context that surrounds the event and the eventual implications. It would seem important for students of electoral politics to read the debate transcript where a gaffe occurred to see for themselves how a candidate handled an important interview with a journalist or to read the actual words given at an important convention address. It should be noted that the source documents are presented in their original versions and not tidied up for publication here.

Finally, instead of reading the pages to follow as a collection of interesting, isolated events, the reader might consider these stories as patches in the broader fabric of American politics. We begin with the effect that Harry Truman's order to desegregate the U.S. Army had on Dwight Eisenhower's prospects in the 1952 election and end with several events surrounding Barack Obama's ascendance to the White House in 2008 and reelection in 2012. Many of these stories speak to changing party alignments, the issue of race in American electoral politics, the rise of candidate-centered politics, the importance of money in elections, and a host of dramatic changes in the role of media in elections.

In a very real sense, the vignettes that follow are often not separate, discrete crisis points. They can be read as key markers along an arc of presidential elections in the modern era. We see in the racial politics of 2008, for example, a direct connection to the so-called Southern Strategy that arose as a consequence of the Civil Rights era a generation earlier. To understand the importance of Ronald Reagan in 1980 or George W. Bush in 2000, we must also recognize the allure of Barry Goldwater in 1964. And we see that the turbulence of 1968 has a profound effect on elections and campaign strategy 40 years hence.

To read the accounts of these crisis points is to engage larger questions and themes of American politics. We come to understand elections, our presidents, other institutional actors, and voters through the lens of the original documents. But we have the advantage of a perspective granted by time. We know what has happened—we can identify a key event and speculate on its consequence and moment.

The challenge—and the fun—is to recognize the event in our own time and draw important lessons from this history of our modern presidential campaigns.

Notes

1. Michael John Burton, Daniel M. Shea, and William Miller, "Campaign Strategy," in *The Electoral Challenge: Theory Meets Practice,* edited by Stephen Craig and David Hill (Washington, DC: Congressional Quarterly Press, 2011), 33.

2. Ibid., 37.

3. Paul F. Lazarsfeld, Bernard R. Berelson, and Helen Gaudet, *The People's Choice: How the Voter Makes Up His Mind in a Presidential Campaign* (New York: Columbia University, 1944).

4. James Campbell, *The American Campaign* (College Station: Texas A&M University Press, 2008).

Election of 1952

Truman on Civil Rights

President Harry Truman's Special Message to Congress on Civil Rights

February 2, 1948

INTRODUCTION

When many Americans think about the Civil Rights Movement, the 1960s springs to mind. This makes good sense, given that many of the most important demonstrations and public events occurred during this decade in which important legislation was passed. Martin Luther King Jr.'s "I Have a Dream" speech was delivered in August 1963, the Civil Rights Act was passed in 1964, and the Voting Rights Act was affirmed one year later. The 1960s was indeed a critical decade in the fight for racial equality in America.

Yet the battle for equality moved slowly for decades before these important changes, and on inspection we find that 1948 was a critical year and that its impact would be felt in the 1952 presidential election. A few significant things happened that year. First, President Harry Truman offered the nation a stern, frank assessment on the state of race relations in America in a message delivered to Congress in February. The following is an excerpt from that speech.

Second, a bit later that year, Truman issued an executive order requiring the integration of the armed forces.

Finally, in the summer of 1948 at the Democratic National Convention, a powerful address was delivered by Minnesota senator (and future vice president) Hubert Humphrey on race relations. He called for legislation to end lynching, job discrimination on the basis of skin color, and school segregation in the South. So again, 1948 was an important year in the struggle to end racial discrimination.

From an electoral vantage, the focus on civil rights by Democrats, such as Truman and Humphrey, drove a wedge in the party. Simply stated, the South, a key part of the New Deal Coalition and the key to success for Democratic presidential candidates, began to shift toward the Republican Party because of efforts of this sort. This address is noted here—in a collection of pieces on the 1952 election—because it propelled that breakup.

TO THE CONGRESS OF THE UNITED STATES:

In the State of the Union Message on January 7, 1948, I spoke of five great goals toward which we should strive in our constant effort to strengthen our democracy and improve the welfare of our people. The first of these is to secure fully our essential human rights. I am now presenting to the Congress my recommendations for legislation to carry us forward toward that goal.

This Nation was founded by men and women who sought these shores that they might enjoy greater freedom and greater opportunity than they had known before. The founders of the United States proclaimed to the world the American belief that all men are created equal, and that governments are instituted to secure the inalienable rights with which all men are endowed. In the Declaration of Independence and the Constitution of the United States, they eloquently expressed the aspirations of all mankind for equality and freedom.

These ideals inspired the peoples of other lands, and their practical fulfillment made the United States the hope of the oppressed everywhere. Throughout our history men and women of all colors and creeds, of all races and religions, have come to this country to escape tyranny and discrimination. Millions strong, they have helped build this democratic Nation and have constantly reinforced our devotion to the great ideals of liberty and equality. With those who preceded them, they have helped to fashion and strengthen our American faith—a faith that can be simply stated:

We believe that all men are created equal and that they have the right to equal justice under law.

Few even in the South disputed this notion. However, many still believed that keeping the races apart was best for the nation. As such, the doctrine of separate but equal was accepted.

We believe that all men have the right to freedom of thought and of expression and the right to worship as they please.

We believe that all men are entitled to equal opportunities for jobs, for homes, for good health and for education.

We believe that all men should have a voice in their government and that government should protect, not usurp, the rights of the people.

These are the basic civil rights which are the source and the support of our democracy.

Today, the American people enjoy more freedom and opportunity than ever before. Never in our history has there been better reason to hope for the complete realization of the ideals of liberty and equality.

We shall not, however, finally achieve the ideals for which this Nation was founded so long as any American suffers discrimination as a result of his race, or religion, or color, or the land of origin of his forefathers.

Unfortunately, there still are examples—flagrant examples—of discrimination which are utterly contrary to our ideals. Not all groups of our population are free from the fear of violence. Not all groups are free to live and work where they please or to improve their conditions of life by their own efforts. Not all groups enjoy the full privileges of citizenship and participation in the government under which they live.

We cannot be satisfied until all our people have equal opportunities for jobs, for homes, for education, for health, and for political expression, and until all our people have equal protection under the law.

One year ago I appointed a committee of fifteen distinguished Americans and asked them to appraise the condition of our civil rights and to recommend appropriate action by Federal, state and local governments.

The committee's appraisal has resulted in a frank and revealing report. This report emphasizes that our basic human freedoms are better cared for and more vigilantly defended than ever before. But it also makes clear that there is a serious gap between our ideals and some of our practices. This gap must be closed.

This will take the strong efforts of each of us individually, and all of us acting together through voluntary organizations and our governments.

The protection of civil rights begins with the mutual respect for the rights of others which all of us should practice in our daily lives. Through organizations in every community—in all parts of the country—we must continue to develop practical, workable arrangements for achieving greater tolerance and brotherhood.

"The protection of civil rights is the duty of every government which derives its powers from the consent of the people."

The protection of civil rights is the duty of every government which derives its powers from the consent of the people. This is equally true of local, state, and national governments. There is much that the states can and should do at this time to extend their protection of civil rights. Wherever the law enforcement measures of state and local governments are inadequate to discharge this primary function of government, these measures should be strengthened and improved.

The Federal Government has a clear duty to see that Constitutional guarantees of individual liberties and of equal protection under the laws are not denied or abridged anywhere in our Union. That duty is shared by all three branches of the Government, but it can be fulfilled only if the Congress enacts modern, comprehensive civil rights laws, adequate to the needs of the day, and demonstrating our continuing faith in the free way of life.

I recommend, therefore, that the Congress enact legislation at this session directed toward the following specific objectives:

1. Establishing a permanent Commission on Civil Rights, a Joint Congressional Committee on Civil Rights, and a Civil Rights Division in the Department of Justice.

2. Strengthening existing civil rights statutes.

3. Providing Federal protection against lynching.

4. Protecting more adequately the right to vote.

5. Establishing a Fair Employment Practice Commission to prevent unfair discrimination in employment.

6. Prohibiting discrimination in interstate transportation facilities.

7. Providing home-rule and suffrage in Presidential elections for the residents of the District of Columbia.

8. Providing Statehood for Hawaii and Alaska and a greater measure of self-government for our island possessions.

9. Equalizing the opportunities for residents of the United States to become naturalized citizens.

10. Settling the evacuation claims of Japanese-Americans. . . .

Source: Harry S. Truman, "Special Message to the Congress on Civil Rights," February 2, 1948, *Public Papers of the Presidents of the United States: January 1 to December 31, 1948* (Washington, DC: U.S. Government Printing Office, 1964), n. 20.

Many of these provisions were contentious, but those dealing with what many southerners believe was the usurpation of state police powers were especially so. They believed that they did not need federal protections for local crimes.

While the Fifteenth Amendment had granted blacks the right to vote after the Civil War, the federal government had turned a blind eye to states that disenfranchised blacks. For example, several southern states required would-be voters to take literacy tests or to pay a poll tax. Exceptions were given to those citizens whose parents and grandparents had previously voted—dubbed a "grandfather clause." White citizens did not have to pay the tax or take the test. Collectively, these restrictions were called Jim Crow Laws. The outcome was that very few blacks voted in the South.

As noted above, this was an important step toward racial equality in America. But there were also important political reverberations. Primarily, the northern Democratic Party seemed to take on the mantle of racial equality. This was an important shift, given that Abraham Lincoln was a Republican and that Democrats held a near monopoly in the South during this period. The outcome was a fractured Democratic Party whereby those in the North pushed for change and those in the South struggled to maintain the status quo. It was, as political scientists would note, the year when the New Deal Coalition began to unravel. Later, Republican presidential candidates would find that their ticket to the White House was strong support in most southern states. This became known as the Southern Strategy.

McCarthy at the 1952 Republican National Convention

Senator Joseph McCarthy's Address to the Republican National Convention

July 9, 1952

INTRODUCTION

Not long after World War II, America entered into a period known as the Cold War. This was a state of anxiety and distrust between the United States (and its Western allies) and the Soviet Union (and its satellite states). On one level, these hostilities centered on the proper nature of government. The United States was a democracy and supported a free-market economy. The Soviet Union, on the other hand, was a communist government, which meant governmental control of the economy.

On another level, tension arose over world politics after World War II. While the Soviet Union sought to expand communism through the world, American policy was directed at controlling the spread of communism. Direct military confrontations between the two superpowers were limited, but this did not mean that military might was unimportant. The Korean War (1950–1953), for example, pitted the global North, backed by the Soviets, against the global South, which was supported by the United States. The same sort of dynamic occurred in Vietnam (1950–1975) and in other regions of the world until the late 1980s.

In domestic politics, by the late 1940s there was a growing fear among some Americans that communism would take hold. They believed that slowly and covertly, a growing pool of Americans would become communists, secretly spread their views to others, and eventually take over the government and the economy. As odd as this might sound, this fear was palpable among some citizens. Likely a big part of the fear of the spread of communism in the United States was wrapped up in the threat of nuclear war. This period has been called the Second Red Scare. There was a concerted effort to find communists and prosecute them.

At the very front of the anticommunist movement in the 1950s was Senator Joseph McCarthy, a Republican from Wisconsin. Although relatively unknown during much of his early career, he garnered widespread recognition in 1950 by making claims that he had information on the widespread infiltration of communists in key institutions, such as the entertainment world, education, the State Department, and even the military.

McCarthy's claims would later be discredited, and the Second Red Scare (also known as the McCarthy Era and McCarthyism) would be remembered as a sad chapter in our history, given the witch-hunting nature of investigations and the blacklisting of suspected communists. But in 1952 at the dawn of McCarthy's prominence, candidates worried about not being tough on communism. After much internal debate, the leaders of the Republican National Committee agreed to allow McCarthy to speak at their 1952 convention. Presented here is an excerpt of that speech.

SENATOR MCCATHY: As we approach the all-important November elections, all Americans, Democrats and Republicans alike, must keep in mind all the facts as they are and not the facts as we would wish them to be. Even though those facts may be well at heart.

Fact number one, we are at war today, war in Korea, but the Korean War was merely a small phase of the great [world] war with the atheistic Communist.

Fact number two, for the past 7 years we have been losing that world war, at the rate of nearly one hundred million people a year. Not one hundred thousand, but losing nearly one hundred million people a year to atheistic Communist.

He was referring mostly to the spread of communism in Asia. Communism was spreading in other regions of the globe, but the big change came in China. After a civil war, the Communist Party of China came to power in 1949.

Fact number three, the day of July 9th 1952, the same man, the same men who delivered nearly half of the world to Communist Russia, are still in control in Washington.

This was a radical statement, to say the least. He was saying that President Harry Truman and his administration somehow simply allowed Russia to become communist.

There has been no change; the same men are doing your planning. The same planners who were in control before 1945, 1945 when we were the most powerful nation on earth, 1945 when all we needed was our unlimited military and economic power, with enough brains, enough loyalty to have restored a decent and peaceful world.

His reference here is to the Yalta Conference, where the victors of World War II, namely the leaders of the Big Three—the United States, the Soviet Union, and England—met to discuss the reestablishment of nations and boundaries in war-torn Europe. The Soviet Union would be given control of many of the nations in Eastern Europe.

But what happened, instead, instead we have allowed Communism to spread its dark shadow over half of Europe, and almost all of Asia, and for the first time, for the first time they are appearing on the pages of America's history. Words such as "stalemate," "retreat," "compromise," well Truman says, Truman says that the Democratic Party must run on its record. To that I say amen, so they must.

Many have concluded that both Winston Churchill, who represented the British Empire, and Franklin Roosevelt, representing the United States, stood up against Joseph Stalin (who represented the Soviet Union) on the most extreme demands. Churchill and Roosevelt did, however, concede much of Eastern Europe and the Far East to Stalin. Truman, by the way, was still vice president at the time.

Now why ladies and gentlemen, why has this administration deliberately built up Russia, while tearing down the strength of America? I have been proving that this was because of combination, a combination of abysmal stupidity and treason, and if I am wrong, if I am wrong, if no treason is involved, if the last traitor left, if the last traitor left is Alger Hiss, then the only answer, the only answer for our loss and for Russia's gain, is that those in power are guilty of stumbling, fumbling incompetence.

Suggesting that Truman was deliberately building up Russia and that his administration was stupid and treasonous was, by any standards, beyond the limits of acceptable discourse in American politics. McCarthy had crossed a line.

Perhaps fearful that he might lose the state if he did not join forces with McCarthy, Eisenhower agreed to tour Wisconsin with the senator after the election—which Eisenhower did. However, they did not get along. Eisenhower also had a close relationship with George Marshall, secretary of state under Harry Truman, and Marshall was verbally attacked by McCarthy on several occasions. After the election, Eisenhower would take pains to distance himself from McCarthy. Within two years—by 1954—McCarthy's Senate colleagues would censure him for his reckless, unfounded attacks and for his bombastic verbal assaults. McCarthy remained in the Senate for two more years, finishing out his term. But his career was ruined, and he played no role in the 1956 election.

But in either event, whether we are losing because of treason or because of stupidity, if America and her sons are to live, and that Yalta around, [unintelligible] and [unintelligible] must go my young friends. My good friends, I say one communist, one Communist the defense plants is one Communist too many.

Source: "McCarthy Speaks at the 1952 Republican National Convention." NBC Learn K–12, http://archives.nbclearn.com/portal/site/k-12/flatview?cuecard=1719. Used by permission of the Republican National Committee.

Eisenhower at the 1952 Republican National Convention

General Dwight D. Eisenhower's Address Accepting the Presidential Nomination at the Republican National Convention

July 11, 1952

INTRODUCTION

In some respects, Geneneral Dwight D. Eisenhower was the perfect Republican candidate in 1952. That year, as with all of the previous two decades, most Americans aligned with the Democrats. Most governors at the time were Democratic, and most state legislatures had large Democratic majorities. There was a brief period of Republican control of Congress at the end of Harry Truman's term, but most agree that this had more to do with Truman than it did with a growing affinity for the Republican Party. Simply stated, the Democratic New Deal Coalition that had taken over at the dawn of the Great Depression continued to dominate electoral politics in 1952.

So why was Eisenhower a perfect candidate? For one thing, he was a war hero. General Eisenhower had commanded the Allied Forces in World War II and of course secured victory. Second, he was generally considered an ideological moderate, perhaps even nonpartisan. There were even some reports that Democrats tried to persuade him to run under their banner in that election. Finally, his calm, even temperament seemed to find the mood of the nation. Coming off the Great Depression and World War II, Americans were looking for stability and calm. Eisenhower seemed to fit the bill perfectly.

Yet, he was not a politician and was not known for great oratory. This speech, his nomination acceptance speech, was watched closely by Democrats and Republicans alike. What would the general have to say, and how would it go over with average Americans?

Mr. Chairman, my Fellow Republicans:

May I first thank you on behalf of Mrs. Eisenhower and myself for the warmth of your welcome. For us both this is our first entry into a political convention and it is a heartwarming one. Thank you very much.

And before I proceed with the thoughts that I should like to address briefly to you, may I have the temerity to congratulate this convention on the selection of their nominee for Vice-President. A man who has shown statesmanlike qualities in many ways, but as a special talent an ability to ferret out any kind of subversive influence wherever it may be found and the strength and persistence to get rid of it.

Eisenhower was giving a nod to Senator Richard Nixon, his pick for vice president. Nixon had made a name for himself in 1948 as an outspoken member of the House Un-American Activities Committee. This was the dawn of a period of growing worries—some would say paranoia—about the threat of communism in America. Eisenhower's line about ferreting out subversive influences is a reference to his anticommunist efforts.

Ladies and Gentlemen, you have summoned me on behalf of millions of your fellow Americans to lead a great crusade—for Freedom in America and Freedom in the world. I know something of the solemn responsibility of leading a crusade. I have led one. I take up this task, therefore, in a spirit of deep obligation. Mindful of its burdens and of its decisive importance. I accept your summons. I will lead this crusade.

Eisenhower's recurrent use of the word "crusade" is interesting—and perhaps telling. Was he attempting to draw a religious connection to his candidacy? Generally, this term is linked with a holy war.

Our aims—the aims of this Republican crusade—are clear: to sweep from office an administration which has fastened on every one of us the wastefulness, the arrogance and corruption in high places, the heavy burdens and anxieties which are the bitter fruit of a party too long in power.

Much more than this, it is our aim to give to our country a program of progressive policies drawn from our finest Republican traditions; to unite us wherever we have been divided; to strengthen freedom wherever among any group is has been weakened; to build a sure foundation for sound prosperity for all here at home and for a just and sure peace throughout our world.

Again, most elected positions in the United States at this time were controlled by Democrats. It is also interesting, given contemporary politics, that Eisenhower would make a direct reference to the full Republican ticket. He understood that his popularity might not trickle down to the rest of the ticket, thus putting the Republican agenda in jeopardy.

To achieve these aims we must have total victory; we must have more Republicans in our state and local offices; more Republican governments in our states; a Republican majority in the United States House of Representatives and in the United States Senate; and, of course, a Republican in the White House.

Today is the first day of this great battle. The road that leads to Nov. 4 is a fighting road. In that fight I will keep nothing in reserve.

Before this I stood on the eve of battle. Before every attack it has always been my practice to seek out our men in their camps and on the roads and talk with them face to face about their concerns and discuss with them the great mission to which we were all committed.

In this battle to which all of us are now committed it will be my practice to meet and talk with Americans face to face in every section, every corner, every nook and cranny of this land.

I know that such a momentous campaign cannot be won by a few or by divided or by uncertain forces. So to all those from the precinct level up who have worked long hours at difficult tasks in support of our party—and for our party's candidates—I extend an earnest call to join up; join up for longer hours and harder work and even greater devotion to this cause. I call on you to bring into this effort your neighbors next door and across the street. This is not a job for any one of us or for just a few of us.

Since this morning I have had helpful and heartwarming talks with Senator Taft, Governor Warren and Governor Stassen. I wanted them to know, as I want you to know, that in the hard fight ahead we will work intimately together to promote the principles and aims of our party. I was strengthened and heartened by their instant agreement to support this cause to the utmost. Their cooperation means that the Republican party will unitedly move forward in a sweeping victory.

Eisenhower was making reference to his two primary nomination opponents. Robert Taft was from Ohio, and Earl Warren was from California. Eisenhower would later name Warren chief justice of the U.S. Supreme Court, where he would pen, among other decisions, *Brown v. Board of Education*.

We are now at a moment in history when, under God, this nation of ours has become the mightiest temporal power and the mightiest spiritual force on earth. The destiny of mankind—the making of a world that will be fit for our children to live in—hangs in the balance on what we say and what we accomplish in these months ahead.

We must use our power wisely for the good of all our people. If we do this, we will open a road into the future on which today's Americans, young and old, and the generations that come after them, can go forward—go forward to a life in which there will be far greater abundance of material, cultural, and spiritual rewards than our forefathers or we ever dreamed of.

We will so undergird our freedom that today's aggressors and those who tomorrow may rise up to threaten us, will not merely be deterred but stopped in their tracks. Then we will at last be on the road to real peace.

The American people look to us to direct our nation's might to these purposes.

As we launch this crusade we call to go forward with us the youth of America. This cause needs their enthusiasm, their devotion, and the lift their vision of the future will provide. We call to go forward with us the women of America; our workers, farmers, businessmen. As we go to the country, Americans in every walk of life can have confidence that our single-minded purpose is to serve their interest, guard and extend their rights and strengthen the America that we so love.

The noble service to which we Republicans summon all Americans is not only for one campaign or for one election. Our summons is to a lifetime enrollment. And our party shall always remain committed to a more secure, a brighter and an even better future for all our people.

We go out from here with unbounded trust in the American people. We go out from here to merit their unbounded trust in us.

Wherever I am, I will end each day of this coming campaign thinking of millions of American homes, large and small; of fathers and mothers' working and sacrificing to make sure that their children are well cared for, free from fear; full of good hope for the future, proud citizens of a country that will stand among the nations as the leader of a peaceful and prosperous world.

While somewhat thin on policy specifics, most media pundits agreed that Eisenhower's speech was a success. He had crossed an important barrier and was off and running in the general election.

Ladies and gentlemen, my dear friends that have heaped upon me such honors, it is more than a nomination I accept today. It is a dedication—a dedication to the shining promise of tomorrow. As together we face that tomorrow, I beseech the prayers of all our people and the blessing and guidance of Almighty God.

Source: "Dwight D. Eisenhower: Address Accepting the Presidential Nomination at the Republican National Convention in Chicago, July 11, 1952." The American Presidency Project, http://www.presidency.ucsb.edu/ws/?pid=75626.

A Promise: Dwight D. Eisenhower and Earl Warren

Memorandum from President Eisenhower to Attorney General Herbert Brownell Jr.

August 5, 1953

INTRODUCTION

Accounts of the promise made by Dwight D. Eisenhower to Governor Earl Warren to give Warren a position on the U.S. Supreme Court differ. Warren reported not giving much thought to the remark made by Eisenhower in a personal communication. Warren's view seemed to be that politicians often promise but rarely deliver. For his part, Eisenhower rejected the idea that he had made any kind of binding agreement with the governor. Nonetheless, when he handily won the 1952 election against Adlai Stevenson, Eisenhower soon had an occasion to make a decision regarding the appointment of a chief justice of the Supreme Court when the sitting chief justice, Fred Vinson, died.

Warren had been a three-term Republican governor of California, was a former vice presidential candidate (with Dewey), and had been Eisenhower's principal opponent for the Republican presidential nomination in 1952. At the convention, as in the subsequent general election, Eisenhower was an exceedingly popular choice. He was a war hero and a nonpolitician. In that sense, he was uniquely suited for the political context of the time: a nonideological candidate with experience in foreign affairs and strong anticommunist credentials. It is clear, then, that he did not need Warren's support for his campaign, nor did he feel like he owed Warren anything. Eisenhower did, however, know that Warren would be interested in a judicial post if one was offered.

Memorandum to the Attorney General: I have just received a handwritten letter from Governor Warren in which appears this expression, "I feel as though I could return to work with enthusiasm." This would seem to confirm the interpretation we made of his cablegram.

Governor Warren is returning to the United States on the S.S. Stockholm, leaving Europe on the 18th, and arriving in New York on the 27th.

For the moment I see no way of communicating with him, but I think that if it is convenient for you, some contact should be made with him immediately after he lands so as to firm up any future plans.

This presidential memorandum—revealing Warren's response to Eisenhower's inquiries upon the death of Chief Justice Vinson—suggest that Governor Warren was eager to take the post were it offered. Indeed it was, and Warren would go on to oversee dramatic shifts in Supreme Court doctrine in the areas of criminal procedure, individual liberties, and civil rights. It was soon apparent that Eisenhower held a dim view of Warren's judicial decisions. Later, Richard Nixon would make what he perceived to be the liberal excesses of the Warren Court the central focus of his presidential campaign. Nixon and Warren had become political adversaries of the first order. Indeed, as Warren was dying, President Nixon refused to grant the chief justice access to Bethesda Naval Hospital. And from his deathbed at Georgetown Medical Center, Warren urged his colleagues on the Court to reject Nixon's claims of executive privilege in the case regarding the Watergate tapes.

Source: "Eisenhower, Dwight D., Personal and Confidential to Herbert Brownell Jr., 5 August 1953," in *The Papers of Dwight David Eisenhower,* Vol. 14, edited by L. Galambos and D. van Ee, Part II, Chapter 5, Document #373, p. 461 (Baltimore: Johns Hopkins University Press, 1996). © 1996 The Johns Hopkins University Press, used by permission.

Nixon's "Checkers" Speech

**Television Address
by Richard Nixon**

September 23, 1952

INTRODUCTION

In 1952 Richard Nixon, the junior senator from California, was selected by Dwight D. Eisenhower to be his vice presidential running mate. Nixon had developed a reputation as a true conservative and an aggressive warrior against communism. He was young, a die-hard Republican, and from an important swing state. He seemed the right person for the ticket.

By early September, however, reports began to surface of a secret campaign fund established on Nixon's behalf following his Senate race in 1950. The fund was created by Nixon supporters, and on occasion Nixon had used these monies for mailings and travel. While it was not illegal, many observers wondered if the fund was simply a way for supporters to channel bribes to the young senator. Nixon had campaigned for office against corruption, so was he a hypocrite?

Nixon's spot on the presidential ticket was threatened. Eisenhower and many in the Republican Party began to wonder if the scandal would ruin their chances in November. Many openly suggested that Nixon be dropped.

Nixon cut short several campaign events to give this live televised speech. It was a last-ditch effort to save his political career.

My Fellow Americans:

I come before you tonight as a candidate for the Vice Presidency and as a man whose honesty and integrity have been questioned.

The usual political thing to do when charges are made against you is to either ignore them or to deny them without giving details.

I believe we've had enough of that in the United States, particularly with the present Administration in Washington, D.C. To me the office of the Vice Presidency of the United States is a great office and I feel that the people have got to have confidence in the integrity of the men who run for that office and who might obtain it.

I have a theory, too, that the best and only answer to a smear or to an honest misunderstanding of the facts is to tell the truth. And that's why I'm here tonight. I want to tell you my side of the case.

I am sure that you have read the charge and you've heard that I, Senator Nixon, took $18,000 from a group of my supporters.

Now, was that wrong? And let me say that it was wrong—I'm saying, incidentally, that it was wrong and not just illegal. Because it isn't a question of whether it was legal or illegal, that isn't enough. The question is, was it morally wrong?

I say that it was morally wrong if any of that $18,000 went to Senator Nixon for my personal use. I say that it was morally wrong if it was secretly given and secretly handled. And I say that it was morally wrong if any of the contributors got special favors for the contributions that they made.

And now to answer those questions let me say this:

Not one cent of the $18,000 or any other money of that type ever went to me for my personal use. Every penny of it was used to pay for political expenses that I did not think should be charged to the taxpayers of the United States. . . .

Everyone understood that campaign accounts could be created and used for political events. But personal use was akin to bribery, so Nixon pushed hard to make that distinction clear.

Do you think that when I or any other Senator makes a political speech, has it printed, should charge the printing of that speech and the mailing of that speech to the taxpayers? Do you think, for example, when I or any other Senator makes a trip to his home state to make a purely political speech that the cost of that trip should be charged to the taxpayers? Do you think when a Senator makes political broadcasts or political television broadcasts, radio or television, that the expense of those broadcasts should be charged to the taxpayers? . . .

Franking—using government money for mailings—was common practice, as was the use of public money for legislative trips. What Nixon was saying here in essence was that the fund was saving taxpayers money and was thus even more ethical than what other legislators had grown accustomed to. The fund was saving the U.S. Treasury money!

My wife's sitting over here. She's a wonderful stenographer. She used to teach stenography and she used to teach shorthand in high school. That was when I met her. And I can tell you folks that she's worked many hours at night and many hours on Saturdays and Sundays in my office and she's done a fine job. And I'm proud to say

In several passages Nixon makes reference to his wife, Pat, and their modest lifestyle. Then as now, it was important for politicians to come across as average middle-class folks.

tonight that in the six years I've been in the House and the Senate of the United States, Pat Nixon has never been on the Government payroll. . . .

I was born in 1913. Our family was one of modest circumstances and most of my early life was spent in a store out in East Whittier. It was a grocery store—one of those family enterprises. The only reason we were able to make it go was because my mother and dad had five boys and we all worked in the store.

I worked my way through college and to a great extent through law school. And then, in 1940, probably the best thing that ever happened to me happened; I married Pat—who is sitting over here. We had a rather difficult time after we were married, like so many of the young couples who may be listening to us. I practiced law; she continued to teach school. Then in 1942 I went into the service. . . .

Again, Nixon worked hard to make those middle-class connections.

When we came out of the war, Pat and I—Pat during the war had worked as a stenographer and in a bank and as an economist for a Government agency—and when we came out the total of our saving from both my law practice, her teaching and all the time that I was in the war— the total for that entire period was just a little less than $10,000. Every cent of that, incidentally, was in Government bonds.

. . . We lived rather modestly. For four years we lived in an apartment in Park Fairfax, in Alexandria, Va. The rent was $80 a month. And we saved for the time that we could buy a house. . . .

One other thing I probably should tell you because if we don't they'll probably be saying this about me too, we did get something—a gift—after the election. A man down in Texas heard Pat on the radio mention the fact that our two youngsters would like to have a dog. And, believe it or not, the day before we left on this campaign trip we got a message from Union Station in Baltimore saying they had a package for us. We went down to get it. You know what it was.

It was a little cocker spaniel dog in a crate that he'd sent all the way from Texas. Black and white spotted. And our little girl—Tricia, the 6-year old—named it Checkers. And you know, the kids, like all kids, love the dog and I just want to say this right now, that regardless of what they say about it, we're gonna keep it. . . .

These passages, as it turns out, were brilliant. While never known for excellent speech making, Nixon hit a home run. By linking the family dog and his children to the scandal, Nixon vaporized the charge of corruption. In fact, he made the allegations seem ridiculous.

But just let me say this last word. Regardless of what happens I'm going to continue this fight. I'm going to campaign up and down America until we drive the crooks and the Communists and those that defend them out of Washington. And remember, folks, Eisenhower is a great man. Believe me. He's a great man. And a vote for Eisenhower is a vote for what's good for America.

Nixon's speech was heard by 60-million Americans—the largest television audience of that time. It worked, as there was an outpouring of support for the young senator. Nixon also came across as a fighter. Eisenhower kept Nixon on the ticket, and in November he became vice president of the United States. Nixon's "Checkers" speech saved his career.

Source: Richard Nixon, "Checkers Speech." Miller Center, http://millercenter.org/president/speeches/detail/4638.

Election of 1956

Eisenhower and Desegregation

The President's News Conference
August 8, 1956

INTRODUCTION

When the U.S. Supreme Court ruled unanimously in *Brown v. Board of Education* (1954) that racially segregated public schools were unconstitutional, the Court overturned the separate-but-equal doctrine established in *Plessy v. Ferguson* (1896). But the result of the Court's decision was not the immediate desegregation of public schools. In fact, by the 1956 election season, only 0.14% of all African American schoolchildren were in integrated schools in the South. And it would not be until the late 1960s and early 1970s that the majority of schools were integrated. The explanation for the slow process of desegregation is multilayered. Segregationist southern governors surely played a role; local school boards, southern state legislatures, and U.S. House and Senate delegations from southern states were similarly opposed. The reluctance of the Eisenhower administration to engage the issue slowed the process as well.

With the Democratic Party split on the issue (southern Democrats opposed integration), there was little incentive for Eisenhower and the Republic Party to throw its weight behind the desegregation effort. In fact, by not engaging the issue, Eisenhower's reelection campaign was able to pull support away from Democrats.

THE PRESIDENT. Sit down, please.

Good morning. We will go right to questions.

The Republican Party had been soundly defeated by the New Deal Coalition that arose during Franklin D. Roosevelt's presidency. For example, in 1936 the Republican Party controlled only 16 seats in the Senate, compared to 75 seats for the Democrats. Eisenhower's presidency was an opportunity to reshape the Republican Party.

Q. Marvin L. Arrowsmith, Associated Press: Mr. President, you spoke last week of your interest in rebuilding the Republican Party. You have discussed that subject before, but I wonder whether you could tell us at this point shortly before the conventions, something of the changes you would like to see in the party.

THE PRESIDENT. Well, Mr. Arrowsmith, you have opened up such a vast subject that I think it would take the rest of the period to talk about it in detail. I really believe it is something that we have to wait and let it come out in the Republican platform. I am certain the Republican platform will reflect what I believe to be those principles, policies, and programs which will represent some reorientation, and what I would call looking toward a rebuilding of its strength and vigor.

Q. Chalmers M. Roberts, Washington Post and Times Herald: Mr. President, do you believe, sir, that the Republican Party plank on civil rights should contain a specific endorsement of the Supreme Court decision voiding segregation in the public schools?

THE PRESIDENT. I don't know, Mr. Roberts, how the Republican plank on this particular point is going to be stated, and I haven't given any thought of my own as to whether it should just state it in that way.

The only thing I can say is, I am sworn to uphold the Constitution of the United States; but what we are talking about, probably, is procedures rather than principles. Everybody knows I am sworn to uphold the Constitution of the United States. That is my job.

Q. Thomas N. Schroth, Congressional Quarterly: Mr. President, as the school year approaches, it becomes apparent that some States are not proceeding with deliberate speed to carry out the Supreme Court decision to desegregate schools. Does your administration have any plans to enforce that decision this fall?

THE PRESIDENT. I believe the Supreme Court decision stated that the cases must come before the local Federal district judges, isn't that correct? That is where there must be first jurisdiction; their whole plan was that local conditions would be taken into consideration, because some States can unquestionably begin to make this change earlier, more efficiently, than others. Let's never forget this—I have said this before, I know: from 1896 to 1954 the school pattern of the South was built up in what they thought was absolute accordance with the law, with the Constitution of the United States, because that's what the decision was, that equal but separate ruling.

As I have always believed, we have got to make certain reforms by education. No matter how much law we have, we have a job in education, in getting people to understand what

The 1956 Republican platform included the following plank regarding *Brown v. Board of Education*:
"The Republican Party accepts the decision of the U.S. Supreme Court that racial discrimination in publicly supported schools must be progressively eliminated. We concur in the conclusion of the Supreme Court that its decision directing school desegregation should be accomplished with 'all deliberate speed' locally through Federal District Courts. The implementation order of the Supreme Court recognizes the complex and acutely emotional problems created by its decision in certain sections of our country where racial patterns have been developed in accordance with prior and long-standing decisions of the same tribunal."

President Eisenhower was immensely popular, yet he refused to lend his authority and popularity to the cause of desegregation. At no point did he offer the support of his office to ensure compliance with *Brown* other than to note the important role that federal district courts were to play in implementing *Brown II* (the May 31, 1955, companion decision to *Brown v. Board of Education* that required schools to integrate "with all deliberate speed"). Many southern states interpreted the decision in *Brown II* as justifying more deliberation and less speed in their integration efforts. The silence of the Eisenhower administration permitted that interpretation. In fact, Eisenhower had refused to take action in 1956 when Texas officials forcibly removed African American students from schools that had complied with *Brown* and integrated.

are the issues here involved. I think that is the reason for the Supreme Court's reluctance just to issue an order for compliance, but instead created this term of "deliberate speed" and put the jurisdiction before the district courts.

Now, I think that these district courts will have to take some cognizance, if there is no action taken at all in their areas.

Source: "Dwight D. Eisenhower: The President's News Conference, August 8, 1956." The American Presidency Project, http://www.presidency.ucsb.edu/ws/ ?pid=10562.

As the 1956 presidential campaign unfolded, the Democratic Party faced a dramatic division regarding the issue of desegregation. The entire congressional delegations of the states of Alabama, Arkansas, Georgia, Louisiana, Mississippi, South Carolina, and Virginia—Democrats all—had signed on to the "Southern Manifesto" declaring opposition to the Supreme Court's decisions on integration. Democrats from outside the South, however, were largely committed to ensuring compliance with the Court's decisions.

As a consequence, Republicans were able to make inroads among African American voters in the North, especially by supporting the Civil Rights Act that eventually passed in 1957. On that too Eisenhower was silent until the last minute, when the campaign to pull African American votes away from Adlai Stevenson (the Democratic candidate) required a statement of support.

Eisenhower and the Suez Crisis

The President's News Conference
August 8, 1956

INTRODUCTION

On the eve of the U.S. presidential election of 1956, Cold War tensions were running high. Egyptian president Gamal Abdel Nasser nationalized the Suez Canal, an action that was precipitated by the United States and Great Britain withdrawing their financial support for the construction of the Aswan Dam in Egypt due to a series of weapons purchases that Egypt had made from Soviet-controlled Czechoslovakia and diplomatic overtures that Egypt had made with China. Once the canal was nationalized, Britain, France, and Israel responded with military force. The Eisenhower administration was insistent that Britain, France, and Israel pull out of the region. This policy placed the U.S. government at odds with its long-standing allies and risked alienating a critically important group whose support Eisenhower would need to win reelection: supporters of the State of Israel.

The U.S. approach to the Suez Crisis also created an interesting dynamic between the United States and the Soviet Union. Nasser was engaged in a strategic ploy to not associate too closely with either the United States or the Soviet Union; rather, he hoped to increase his own bargaining power with each superpower by playing them against one another.

THE PRESIDENT. Sit down, please.

Good morning. We will go right to questions.

Q. Louis Cassels, United Press: Mr. President, would you tell us, sir, how you feel about the use or threat of military force in the Suez dispute?

THE PRESIDENT. Well, I can't answer that question quite as abruptly and directly as you have asked it.

The United States has every hope that this very serious difficulty will be settled by peaceful means. We have stood for the conference method not only as a solution to this problem but in all similar ones.

It is well to remember that we are dealing with a waterway here that is not only important to all the economies of the

24

world, but by treaty was made an international waterway in 1888, and is exactly that.

It is completely unlike the Panama Canal, for example, which was a national undertaking carried out under bilateral treaty.

I can't conceive of military force being a good solution certainly under conditions as we know them now and in view of our hopes that things are going to be settled peacefully.

[. . .]

Q. Charles von Fremd, CBS News: Mr. President, do you think, sir, on the basis of what you know and the reports you have received from Secretary Dulles, that there is a danger that the two sides have committed themselves so deeply that a peaceful solution would be very difficult or virtually impossible?

Eventually Britain and France did pull out, giving the Eisenhower administration a victory in nuanced diplomatic negotiations. The larger story of the demise of colonialism in the Middle East was at least in part attributable to the efforts of the U.S. government on behalf of Egypt. But little good it did the United States, as Nasser was pulled ever closer to the Soviet orbit.

THE PRESIDENT. Not yet. I think there is good reason to hope that good sense will prevail. Here is something that is so important to the whole world that I think a little sober second thinking is going to prevail in a good many quarters. It is one of those things that just has to be settled, and I would like to point out that damage and destruction are no settlement when you are trying to build and to construct.

[. . .]

Q. William McGaffin, Chicago Daily News: Mr. President, in the event that a war does develop over the Suez Canal, do you think the United States will be in it?

Here, the press conference takes a turn toward Eisenhower's cross-partisan appeal. He was a war hero and was generally perceived as nonideological and supremely capable. In his response to Montgomery's question, note the sense of obligation toward the public good that Eisenhower seemed to feel. Due to this sense of responsibility that he felt, many scholars have described him as a "reluctant candidate." This descriptor, by the way, did not extend to Eisenhower's vice president.

THE PRESIDENT. I am not going to speculate that far ahead. That is piling an if on top of an if, and I think I will not try to comment.

Q. Ruth S. Montgomery, International News Service: Mr. President, it is well known that at one time you could also have had the nomination on the Democratic ticket. Was this a question of sort of marrying a man to reform him, or why did you choose the Republican Party then? [Laughter]

THE PRESIDENT. Well, I thought I had gone into that in the past in great detail.

Frankly, I very definitely thought that after one party had been in Washington 20 years, that there invariably would grow up some abuses that that party was really incapable of straightening out, because there were too many things going on that were the particular pets of the people in power. I thought that change was needed if we were going to get the clean-cut type of cleaning out that seemed necessary to me. That is one of the reasons, and I think a very powerful one.

Q. John Scali, Associated Press: Mr. President, if I may return to Suez for a moment, sir, there have been reports that Egypt may refer the Suez problem to the United Nations. Would you regard United Nations consideration of the Suez matter as an acceptable substitute or supplementary action to the scheduled London meeting?

THE PRESIDENT. Well, of course you always have the veto in the United Nations. Here was a matter that seemed to demand not a hurried solution but a prompt one; and I think to get the nations who, by their maritime activities and by the character of their economies, were most interested, to get them together was a better method at the moment.

The trouble with the other one would be, I think, its slowness.

Q. Paul Scott Rankine, Reuters: Mr. President, your earlier remarks on the Suez Canal might be interpreted as meaning that you were opposed to the use of military force under any circumstances—

THE PRESIDENT. I didn't say that. I was very careful not to say that. I said every important question in the world in which more than one nation is interested should be settled by negotiation. We have tried to substitute the conference table for the battlefield.

I don't mean to say that anyone has to surrender rights without using everything they can to preserve their rights.

Source: "Dwight D. Eisenhower: The President's News Conference, August 8, 1956." The American Presidency Project, http://www.presidency.ucsb.edu/ws/?pid=10562.

After the European pullout and the end of the Suez Crisis, the event seemed to buttress the perception of Eisenhower as patient, thoughtful, and successful in important foreign policy contexts. While the event did little to resolve Cold War tensions, it did presage a shift toward a consolidation of U.S. power, away from Western Europe. The effect on the election, then, was to reinforce the perception of competence in foreign affairs—a boon to the reelection hopes of the Eisenhower campaign.

Election of 1960

Eisenhower, Nixon, and the U2 Spy Plane Incident

**Telegram from the Embassy
in the Soviet Union to the
Department of State, Moscow, 7:00 p.m.**

May 9, 1960

INTRODUCTION

The Central Intelligence Agency's Operation GRAND SLAM was scheduled to begin in early May 1960 and coincided with the last year of the Dwight D. Eisenhower administration and the general election campaign of the incumbent vice president, Richard M. Nixon. It was to be the largest intelligence gathering overflight of the Soviet Union yet by U.S. spy planes. CIA pilot Francis Gary Powers flew at 66,000 feet into Soviet airspace on May Day to take pictures of key military sites within the Soviet Union. But because it was a holiday, almost all flights were grounded, so it was quite a simple task for Soviet antiaircraft batteries to track the invading U.S. overflight. It was shot down soon after its penetration into Soviet airspace. The U2 spy plane and its cameras and images survived the crash, as did Powers, who was captured by farmers and turned over to the Soviet military.

U.S. officials all believed that the plane would simply disintegrate if it was shot down at such a high altitude; certainly there could be no hope for its pilot either. As a consequence of this assumption, the U.S. government released a statement identifying the plane as a NASA weather research flight. The government claimed that the plane was conducting routine operations in Turkey and that faulty oxygen equipment caused the flight to veer off course. As a cover for the story, the U.S. government grounded all weather flights for oxygen checks. The Eisenhower administration did not realize that the Soviet Union had the reconnaissance plane, its array of espionage equipment and photos, and its pilot.

Nikita Khrushchev played the situation perfectly. He released information about what the Soviet Union had in its possession only incrementally, forcing the U.S. government deeper and deeper into its fabricated story. That story was ultimately revealed to be untrue once the Soviet Union let the world know that Powers had survived the crash and had admitted to spying for the CIA.

2771. At beginning of Czech reception today Khrushchev greeted me warmly, took me aside, and before I could make any remark said he was sure not only that I knew nothing about this overflight but that I was opposed to such operations. He said they could not help but suspect that someone had launched this operation with deliberate intent of spoiling summit meeting. He explained they had not protested overflights because on an occasion when they did do so we had blandly denied any knowledge of them. He expressed resentment at Department statement about incident, particularly suggestion that because they had closed areas and secrets this was justification for overflights. He said they had known of these activities for very long time and said to me and later repeated publicly that day after General Twining left Moscow where he had been courteously received as guest, one of these planes had been sent far into Soviet Union. He referred to Senator Mansfield's remarks[1] and said that in due course they would probably let us see pilot. He indicated they would produce their evidence at press conference including [garbled] Ambassadors tomorrow or next day. In this connection I referred to Litvinov agreement.[2] He said this incident showed bombers were useless and they had no plans to send bombers to US and should occasion arise would only use rockets. He also said, if I understood him correctly, that they were no longer producing medium-range rockets, apparently because they had already sufficient stock. I said I had no instructions in matter but hoped they did not in fact intend to take this case to Security Council since this would certainly worsen atmosphere as we would be obliged to defend ourselves. He said nevertheless they had decided to do so and added that if situation were reversed he was sure we would do same thing.

Khrushchev remarked that the one thing that bothered him, and he was telling me this only personally, was that Soviet public opinion was concerned and it could be that during President's visit some people might show their resentment. He said of course they did not want any such thing to happen and when President came here as guest they wanted him received as such. Throughout conversation Khrushchev was very affable, said he sympathized with my position but "what could he do about it?" . . .

Although it could be simply a desire to get in best negotiating position against US I cannot help but interpret his public remarks and appeal to Security Council as a determination to go through with separate treaty unless he gets some satisfaction on Berlin at summit meeting. He obviously intends to exploit this incident to hilt with our allies, particularly Norway, Pakistan and Turkey. Although he denied wanting

"Although he denied wanting to add fuel to the flames during his public speech, he seemed to be doing exactly that."

to add fuel to flames during his public speech, he seemed to be doing exactly that. Nevertheless press and other treatment has been restrained.

In reply to my question Khrushchev said as far as they were concerned Vershinin would proceed with his visit.

Notes

1. Reference may be to Senator Mansfield's remarks on May 5 and 8 in which he said he believed Eisenhower had not been told of the U-2 flight. For text, see *The New York Times*, May 6 and 9, 1960.

The fallout from the revelation that the U.S. government had a long-standing program of intelligence-gathering high-altitude overflights of the Soviet Union was substantial. Eisenhower was scheduled to meet in an important summit with Khrushchev, but the U2 incident scuttled those talks, further inflaming the Cold War. The incident limited the ability of the U.S. government to use foreign bases, such as Pakistan, to support military operations and generally placed the U.S. government in the position of having lied to the world, impairing its prestige and ability to project legal and moral authority.

Nixon, Eisenhower's vice president and candidate for president in 1960, was forced to confront the difficult situation created by the Eisenhower administration. Peace talks had stalled, hope for a thawing of relations were stymied, and Eisenhower's administration was responsible. Gary Powers would not be released into U.S. custody until after the 1960 election.

Later, Khrushchev noted in his memoir that "by waiting to release U-2 pilot Gary Powers until after the election, we kept Nixon from being able to claim that he could deal with the Russians; our ploy made a difference of at least a half a million votes, which gave Kennedy the edge he needed."

2. In the exchange of letters between President Roosevelt and Soviet Commissar Maxim Litvinov, which established diplomatic relations between the two nations in November 1933, the Soviet Union agreed, among other things, that requests by U.S. consular representatives in the Soviet Union to visit U.S. nationals detained in Soviet jails would be granted without delay.

Source: U.S. Department of State, *Foreign Relations of the United States, Vol. X, Part 1, 1958–60: E. Europe Region; Soviet Union; Cyprus* (Washington, DC: U.S. Government Printing Office, 1958–1960), 519.

Nixon's Fifty–State Pledge

Richard Nixon's Acceptance Speech at the Republican National Convention

July 28, 1960

INTRODUCTION

It had been a long uphill battle to the Republican nomination for Richard Nixon. It was true that as a two-term vice president under Dwight D. Eisenhower, Nixon's tenure was not marked by any significant accomplishment. In fact, early on he was caught up in a minor financial scandal and was never well liked by the media. On top of all this, his boss, Eisenhower, seemed able to give Nixon only a tepid endorsement.

Mr. Chairman, Delegates to this Convention, my fellow Americans:

I have made many speeches in my life, and never have I found it more difficult to find the words adequate to express what I feel, as I find them tonight.

To stand here before this great Convention, to hear your expression of affection for me, for Pat, for our daughters, for my mother, for all of us who are representing our Party, is, of course, the greatest moment of my life. . . .

And may I say also that—may I say also that I have been wanting to come to this convention, but because of the protocol that makes it necessary for a candidate not to attend the convention until the nominations are over I've had to look at it on television; but I want all of you to know that I have never been so proud of my Party as I have been in these last three days, and, as I have compared this convention, the conduct of our delegates and our speakers, with what went on in my native State of California just two weeks ago. And I congratulate Chairman Halleck and Chairman Morton and all of those who have helped to make this convention one that will stand in the annals of our Party forever as one of the finest we have ever held.

The protocol that Nixon refers to has been loosened in recent years. It is increasingly common for presumptive nominees to make a quick appearance at the convention prior to their formal acceptance of the nomination.

Have you ever stopped to think of the memories you will take away from this convention?

The things that run through my mind are these:

That first day with the magnificent speeches; Mr. Hoover with his great lesson for the American people; Walter Judd with one of the most outstanding keynote addresses in either Party in history; and last night our beloved, fighting President making the greatest speech that I have ever heard him make before this convention; your platform and its magnificent presentation by Chuck Percy, the Chairman.

References to the two-party system were common in those years. During the presidential debate that Nixon would soon have with John F. Kennedy, both candidates would make mention of their party's platform dozens of times. Today, direct references to partisanship and to party platforms are rare. One should keep in mind, however, that there were very few independent voters in the late 1950s.

For these and for so many other things, I want to congratulate you tonight and to thank you from the bottom of my heart and on behalf of Americans—not just Republicans—Americans everywhere, for making us proud of our country and of our two-party system, for what you have done.

And tonight, too, I particularly want to thank this convention for nominating as my running mate a world statesman of the first rank, my friend and colleague, Henry Cabot Lodge of Massachusetts.

Lodge came from a long line of prominent New England statesmen. It is also worth noting that the choice of Lodge seemed to be an effort to create greater geographic balance on the ticket, given that Nixon was from California. By contrast, John F. Kennedy selected Lyndon Johnson as his running mate early that summer. Kennedy was a northeastern liberal, and Johnson was thought to be a southern conservative, or what in those days they called a "Boll Weevil" (meaning a southern conservative Democrat).

In refreshing contrast to what happened in Los Angeles, you nominated a man who shares my views on the great issues and who will work with me and not against me in carrying out our magnificent platform.

Rockefeller, the governor of New York, was Nixon's principal opponent for the Republican nomination that year.

And may I say that during this week we Republicans, who feel our convictions strongly about our Party and about our country, have had our differences, but as the speech by Senator Goldwater indicated yesterday, and the eloquent and gracious remarks of my friend, Nelson Rockefeller, indicated tonight, we Republicans know that the differences that divide us are infinitesimal compared to the gulf between us and what the Democrats would put upon us from what they did at Los Angeles at their convention two weeks ago.

Eisenhower was still popular, so Nixon linking his candidacy to the previous eight years was more than merely paying homage to his former boss.

It was only eight years ago that I stood in this very place after you had nominated as our candidate for the President one of the great men of our century. And I say to you

tonight that for generations to come, Americans, regardless of party, will gratefully remember Dwight Eisenhower as the man who brought peace to America as the man—as the man under whose leadership America enjoyed the greatest progress and prosperity in history. But above all, they will remember him as the man who restored honesty, integrity, and dignity to the conduct of government in the highest office of this land.

And my fellow Americans, I know now that you will understand what I next say, because the next President of the United States will have his great example to follow, because the next President will have new and challenging problems in the world of utmost gravity. This truly is a time for greatness in America's leadership. . . .

I have been asked by the newsmen sitting on my right and my left all week long: "When is this campaign going to begin, Mr. Vice President? On the day after Labor Day or one of the other traditional starting dates?"

And this is my answer: This campaign begins tonight—here and now—and it goes on—and this campaign will continue from now until November 8th without any letup.

And I've also been asked by my friends in the press on either side here—they say, "Mr. Vice President, where are you going to concentrate? What states are you going to visit?" And this is my answer: In this campaign we are going to take no states for granted, and we aren't going to concede any states to the opposition.

And I announce to you tonight, and I pledge to you, that I, personally, will carry this campaign into every one of the 50 states of this nation between now and November the 8th.

A hundred years ago, Abraham Lincoln was asked, during the dark days of the tragic war between the States, whether he thought God was on his side. His answer was, "My concern is not whether God is on our side, but whether we are on God's side."

This remark proved to be the most important of the speech—but not in the way Nixon had imagined. As the race progressed, polling data showed that the outcome would be very close and that in all likelihood it would come down to a few states. As the finish line drew near and as Kennedy concentrated on those neck-and-neck states, Nixon was reminded of the pledge and was forced to spend critical time visiting the states he had not yet been to—all of which were not considered swing states. So why would a candidate visit states where the outcome was set? Because of the pledge, Nixon had little choice.

In the end, the race did come down to a handful of votes in several states. In Hawaii, Illinois, Missouri, California, New Mexico, and New Jersey, the outcome was decided by less than 1 percent of the vote. Other than California, Nixon lost each. We will never know for sure, but it is likely that Nixon might have won if he had not had to spend days at the end of the campaign fulfilling his pledge.

No candidate since Nixon has made a similar pledge, for obvious reasons.

Nixon lost the general election, of course, and two years later he would lose a bid for governor of California. It had seemed that his political career was over. At a press conference on the evening of his California defeat, Nixon himself commented that "You won't have Nixon to kick around anymore because, gentlemen, this is my last press conference."

Nixon reemerged in 1968, however, and was elected president that year and again in 1972.

And my fellow Americans, may that ever be our prayer for our country, and in that spirit, with faith in America, with faith in her ideals and in her people, I accept your nomination for President of the United States.

Source: "Richard Nixon: Address Accepting the Presidential Nomination at the Republican National Convention in Chicago, July 28, 1960." The American Presidency Project, http://www.presidency.ucsb.edu/ws/?pid=25974.

Kennedy's Religion Speech

**John F. Kennedy's Speech
on Religious Bigotry to the Greater
Houston Ministerial Association**

September 12, 1960

INTRODUCTION

We take it for granted that Catholic candidates do not confront religious bigotry in America. Yet until 1960, no Catholic candidate had ever been elected president. This did not mean that all of the former presidents were devout Protestants. Indeed, some were Unitarians, others were Deists, and others—such as Thomas Jefferson and Abraham Lincoln—did not have a religious affiliation. But electing a Catholic president was thought to be something a bit different—at least in 1960. This is because official church doctrine requires Catholics throughout the world to be loyal to the church and to demonstrate an allegiance to the pope. Would a Catholic president feel an ultimate devotion to the U.S. Constitution or to the Vatican? What would happen when the country's national interests were pitted against the interests of the Vatican? Al Smith, a Catholic, ran as the Democratic nominee in 1928, and his defeat cast a shadow over the prospects of another Catholic candidate's success.

Democrat John F. Kennedy confronted the issue of his Catholicism in an address at the Greater Houston Ministerial Association in the autumn of that year. Everyone knew that it would be an important speech; press coverage was intense. Could the young senator put the issue to rest, or would the speech simply draw greater attention to his religion?

Reverend Meza, Reverend Reck, I'm grateful for your generous invitation to state my views.

While the so-called religious issue is necessarily and properly the chief topic here tonight, I want to emphasize from the outset that I believe that we have far more critical issues in the 1960 campaign. . . . But because I am a Catholic, and no Catholic has ever been elected President, the real issues in this campaign have been obscured—perhaps deliberately, in some quarters less responsible than this. So it is apparently necessary for me to state once again—not what kind of church I believe in, for that should be important only to me—but what kind of America I believe in.

I believe in an America where the separation of church and state is absolute; where no Catholic prelate would tell

Kennedy surprised many with victories in several key primary elections in the spring of 1960, particularly in West Virginia and Wisconsin. He won the nomination, but could a Democrat win a general election without significant support from the South, where a vast majority of voters were Protestants (mostly conservative Baptists)? Would religious bigotry rear its ugly head in the privacy of the voting booth?

tell the President—should he be Catholic—how to act, and no Protestant minister would tell his parishioners for whom to vote; where no church or church school is granted any public funds or political preference, and where no man is denied public office merely because his religion differs from the President who might appoint him, or the people who might elect him.

I believe in an America that is officially neither Catholic, Protestant nor Jewish; where no public official either requests or accepts instructions on public policy from the Pope, the National Council of Churches or any other ecclesiastical source; where no religious body seeks to impose its will directly or indirectly upon the general populace or the public acts of its officials, and where religious liberty is so indivisible that an act against one church is treated as an act against all. . . .

By 2012, this warning would seem particularly prophetic. In that election, for the first time in our nation's history, a Mormon (Mitt Romney) received the presidential nomination of a major party. Polling data on this issue shifted throughout the course of the campaign, but roughly speaking one-third of Americans expressed some level of discomfort with the prospects of electing a Mormon president.

For while this year it may be a Catholic against whom the finger of suspicion is pointed, in other years it has been—and may someday be again—a Jew, or a Quaker, or a Unitarian, or a Baptist. It was Virginia's harassment of Baptist preachers, for example, that led to Jefferson's statute of religious freedom. Today, I may be the victim, but tomorrow it may be you—until the whole fabric of our harmonious society is ripped apart at a time of great national peril.

Finally, I believe in an America where religious intolerance will someday end, where all men and all churches are treated as equals, where every man has the same right to attend or not to attend the church of his choice, where there is no Catholic vote, no anti-Catholic vote, no bloc voting of any kind, and where Catholics, Protestants, and Jews, at both the lay and the pastoral levels, will refrain from those attitudes of disdain and division which have so often marred their works in the past, and promote instead the American ideal of brotherhood.

That is the kind of America in which I believe. And it represents the kind of Presidency in which I believe, a great office that must be neither humbled by making it the instrument of any religious group nor tarnished by arbitrarily withholding it—its occupancy from the members of any one religious group. I believe in a President whose views on religion are his own private affair, neither imposed upon him by the nation, nor imposed by the nation upon him as a condition to holding that office. . . .

This is the kind of America I believe in—and this is the kind of America I fought for in the South Pacific, and the kind my brother died for in Europe. No one suggested then that we might have a divided loyalty, that we did not believe in liberty, or that we belonged to a disloyal group that threatened—I quote—"the freedoms for which our forefathers died." . . .

For contrary to common newspaper usage, I am not the Catholic candidate for President. I am the Democratic Party's candidate for President who happens also to be a Catholic.

I do not speak for my church on public matters; and the church does not speak for me. Whatever issue may come before me as President, if I should be elected, on birth control, divorce, censorship, gambling or any other subject, I will make my decision in accordance with these views—in accordance with what my conscience tells me to be in the national interest, and without regard to outside religious pressure or dictates. And no power or threat of punishment could cause me to decide otherwise. . . .

By contemporary standards, Kennedy's list of potential Catholic hot-button issues—birth control, divorce, censorship, and gambling—seems rather odd. One should bear in mind, however, that abortion did not jump to the fore until the 1970s, and gay marriage was not an issue until the late 1990s.

But if this election is decided on the basis that 40 million Americans lost their chance of being President on the day they were baptized, then it is the whole nation that will be the loser, in the eyes of Catholics and non-Catholics around the world, in the eyes of history, and in the eyes of our own people.

But if, on the other hand, I should win this election, then I shall devote every effort of mind and spirit to fulfilling the oath of the Presidency—practically identical, I might add, with the oath I have taken for 14 years in the

Kennedy's poignant, powerful speech was well received by those in the hall as well as by members of the media and the millions of voters who read about it in the newspaper. Kennedy said that "I believe in an America where religious intolerance will someday end; where all men and all churches are treated as equal;

where every man has the same right to attend or not attend the church of his choice." The issue was dead. Perhaps more important, Kennedy appeared thoughtful, articulate, and serious. Given that he was a young candidate, the speech suggested that he was indeed up for the job.

In the spring of 2012, Republican presidential nomination candidate Rick Santorum, also a Catholic, suggested that Kennedy's speech was ill-conceived and that it made Santorum "want to throw up." Many were surprised that a fellow Catholic, but this time a true conservative, would balk at the ideas expressed in Kennedy's speech.

Congress. For without reservation, I can, solemnly swear that I will faithfully execute the office of President of the United States, and will to the best of my ability preserve, protect, and defend the Constitution—so help me God.

Source: "John F. Kennedy: Speech of Senator John F. Kennedy, Greater Houston Ministerial Association, Rice Hotel, Houston, TX, September 12, 1960." The American Presidency Project, http://www.presidency.ucsb.edu/ws/?pid=25773.

Kennedy, Nixon, and the First Televised Presidential Debate

Stills from the Nixon-Kennedy Debate

September 26, 1960

INTRODUCTION

During the debate, Nixon repeatedly asserted that Kennedy was "too immature" for the presidency. The candidates were roughly the same age. Nixon was born in 1913, and Kennedy was born in 1917. Nixon's assertion, though, was that Kennedy lacked the kind of experience that matters—leadership on an international stage. Nixon, after all, had been Eisenhower's vice president and had successfully debated Khrushchev in the famous Kitchen Debate in 1959. Here's Kennedy's response in full and Nixon's terse reaction.

▲ AP Photo

The election of 1960 between Richard M. Nixon and John F. Kennedy was historically important for a number of reasons, not the least of which was the key role that television would play in the campaign coverage. On September 26, the two candidates met in Chicago for the first of four policy debates. This debate focused on domestic issues; later debates would cover foreign policy. More than 70 million viewers watched this first televised presidential debate. Millions more tuned in on their radios.

Perhaps not surprisingly for the first televised presidential debate, subsequent news coverage included many observations about the candidates' personal appearance. An article in *The New York Times* noted that Kennedy, "using no television makeup, rarely smiled during the hour and maintained an expression of gravity suitable for a candidate for the highest office in the land," while Nixon, "wearing pancake makeup to cover his dark beard, smiled more frequently as he made his points and dabbed frequently at the perspiration that beaded out on his chin."

Nixon's discomfort was understandable. He had been ill for weeks prior to the television event. He came to the station wan, weak, and wearing an ill-fitting suit. His sweating in the heat of the staging lights and what appeared to be his unshaven face all contributed to the sense that he was uncomfortable in the debate. The image that he projected stood in stark contrast to Kennedy's sharp energy across the dais. Many later accounts of the debate picked up on the claims made the following day by a polling organization: that voters who watched the debate on television overwhelmingly thought that Kennedy had won the debate, while those who listened to the debate on the radio were more inclined to think that Nixon had prevailed. Those claims have to be considered in light of who you might imagine to have televisions and radios. By 1960, the vast majority of U.S. homeowners had a television. But those who did not were likely to live in regions of the country (i.e., the South) where Nixon was sure to have more appeal than Kennedy.

▲ AP Photo

MR. KENNEDY: Well, the vice president and I came to the Congress together [in] 1946; we both served in the Labor Committee. I've been there now for 14 years, the same period of time that he has, so that our experience in, uh, government is comparable. Secondly, I think the question is, uh, what are the programs that we advocate, what is the party record that we lead? I come out of the Democratic Party, which in this century has produced Woodrow Wilson and Franklin Roosevelt and Harry Truman, and which supported and sustained these programs which I've discussed tonight. Mr. Nixon comes out of the Republican Party. He was nominated by it. And it is a fact that through most of these last 25 years the Republican leadership has opposed federal aid for education, medical care for the aged, development of the Tennessee Valley, development of our natural resources. I think Mr. Nixon is an effective leader of his party. I hope he would grant me the same. The question before us is: Which point of view and which party do we want to lead the United States?

MR. SMITH: Mr. Nixon, would you like to comment on that statement?

MR. NIXON: I have no comment.

The election would be one of the closest in history. Kennedy won by 0.1% of the popular vote. The first televised debate was an important development for the Kennedy campaign. Relative to his adversary, Kennedy was able to project confidence and gravity. As many scholars have found, televised debates may be important ways for citizens to become more familiar with issues and candidates. However, televised debates also tend to reinforce preexisting biases that voters have for candidates. The conventional view of this first televised debate was that image mattered. It may have, but probably only marginally—and for Kennedy.

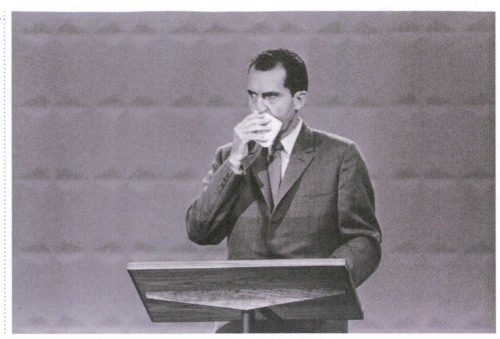

▲ AP Photo/File

Source (for text in margin comments): "Presidential Debate in Chicago, September 26, 1960." The American Presidency Project, http://www.presidency.ucsb.edu/ws/?pid=29400.

"Nixon's Experience?" Ad

Anti–Richard Nixon Campaign Ad
1960

INTRODUCTION

Throughout most of American history, the vice presidency was considered an insignificant office. Benjamin Franklin once quipped that the vice president should be addressed as "your Superfluous Excellency." Thomas Marshall, the vice president under Woodrow Wilson, once told a story of two brothers: "One ran away to sea; the other was elected vice president. And nothing was heard of either of them again." In 1848, Senator Daniel Webster—who as one of his party's most influential figures had long hoped to gain the presidency—declined the vice presidential place on the Whig Party ticket. "I do not propose to be buried until I am dead," he snorted. John Nance Garner, Franklin D. Roosevelt's first vice president and a former Speaker of the House, is quoted as saying that the vice presidency is "not worth a pitcher of warm spit."

Also, a surprisingly scant number of vice presidents are later elected president. In fact, when Richard Nixon put his hat in the ring for the presidency in 1960, only three other vice presidents had ever won that election: John Adams in 1796, Thomas Jefferson in 1800, and Martin Van Buren in 1836. (Later, in 1988, George H. W. Bush would do the same.) Precisely why this is true has puzzled many political scientists, given that many vice presidents have been smart, skilled politicians. And they were certainly qualified to fill the post. Perhaps it has been because the public simply views the position as inconsequential, as suggested by the quotes, and views its inhabitants as second-string players.

This was precisely the obstacle that Nixon confronted in 1960. He had served in the House and the Senate and then had served two terms as vice president. He had grown particularly adept at foreign policy matters. But many voters wondered if he was up for the job.

To compound matters, Nixon's boss, Dwight D. Eisenhower, was asked at a press conference about Nixon's work at the White House. The response was quickly turned into a television ad by John F. Kennedy's team. The transcript of that ad is presented here.

MALE NARRATOR: Every Republican politician wants you to believe that Richard Nixon is "experienced." They even want you to believe that he has actually been making decisions in the White House. But listen to the man who should know best, the president of the United States. A reporter recently asked President Eisenhower this question about Mr. Nixon's experience:

THE SCENE: A PRESS CONFERENCE, EISENHOWER AT A PODIUM

MALE REPORTER: I just wondered if you could give us an example of a major idea of his that you had adopted in that role as the, as the decider and, and final—

EISENHOWER: If you give me a week I might think of one. I don't remember.

[Crowd and Eisenhower laughter]

MALE NARRATOR: At the same press conference, President Eisenhower said:

EISENHOWER: No one can make a decision except me.

MALE NARRATOR: And as for any major ideas from Mr. Nixon:

EISENHOWER: If you give me a week, I might think of one. I don't remember.

MALE NARRATOR: President Eisenhower could not remember, but the voters will remember. For real leadership in the '60s, help elect Senator John F. Kennedy president.

Source: "Nixon's Experience? Kennedy (1960)." Museum of the Moving Image: The Living Room Candidate, http://www.livingroomcandidate.org/commercials/1960/nixons-experience.

Needless to say, this was a devastating commercial. It was true and certainly well known that Eisenhower and Nixon did not get along. It was a rocky eight-year relationship. But surely Nixon played a role in many policy initiatives, so why Eisenhower would respond this way remains a mystery.

Eisenhower would later make reference to numerous initiatives by Nixon, but this did not seem to matter. The ad was played over and over throughout the campaign. Given the narrowness of the final outcome, it is certainly reasonable to suspect that this ad changed the course of history.

Election of 1964

Rockefeller on Goldwater's Extremism

Nelson Rockefeller's Remarks to the Republican National Convention

July 14, 1964

INTRODUCTION

The 1964 Republican National Convention at the Cow Palace in San Francisco was a critical moment in the history of the Republican Party. The convention featured the tension between two very divergent views of what the Party stood for. Nelson Rockefeller, governor of New York and former official of both the Harry S. Truman and Dwight D. Eisenhower administrations, reflected the liberal to moderate wing of the Republican Party. Senator Barry Goldwater of Arizona was the darling of the far right wing of the party. The moderates were limping into the convention due to the difficulties presented by Rockefeller's divorce and his recent second marriage. Those events made the nomination of Goldwater all but secure. Nonetheless, Rockefeller took to the stage at the convention to warn of the dangers presented by extremism within the Republican Party. This was not well received by the conservatives in the audience. In fact, in their exuberance for the nomination of Goldwater, they jeered at Rockefeller, showering him with boos for his plea for moderation.

TEXT OF REMARKS BY GOVERNOR NELSON A. ROCKEFELLER PREPARED FOR DELIVERY BEFORE THE THIRD SESSION OF THE 1964 REPUBLICAN NATIONAL CONVENTION IN MOVING ADOPTION OF THE AMENDMENT TO THE REPORT OF THE COMMITTEE ON RESOLUTIONS ON THE SUBJECT OF EXTREMISM, COW PALACE, SAN FRANCISCO, CALIFORNIA JULY 14, 1964

Mr. Chairman, fellow delegates, I move that the following language be inserted in the proposed 1964 Republican Platform as a new full paragraph between the present sixth and seventh paragraphs under the section headed "For a Free People."

In something of a preview of the so-called Southern Strategy, the Ku Klux Klan threw its support behind the Goldwater campaign largely due to his position on civil rights and his opposition to the Civil Rights Act of 1964. Goldwater would go on to win only his home state of Arizona and five states in the Deep South.

"The Republican Party fully respects the contribution of responsible criticism, and defends the right of dissent in the democratic process. But we repudiate the efforts of irresponsible, extremist groups, such as the Communists, the Ku Klux Klan, the John Birch Society and others, to discredit our Party by their efforts to infiltrate positions of responsibility in the Party, or to attach themselves to its candidates."

The time has come for the Republican party to face this issue realistically and take decisive action. It is essential that this Convention repudiate here and now any doctrinaire, militant minority, whether Communist, Ku Klux Klan or Bircher which would subvert this party to purposes alien to the very basic tenets which gave this party birth.

Precisely one year ago today on July 14, 1963, I issued a statement wherein I warned that:

"The Republican party is in real danger of subversion by a radical, well-financed and highly disciplined minority."

At that time I pointed out that the purpose of this minority were "wholly alien to the sound and honest conservatism that has firmly based the Republican party in the best of a century's traditions, wholly alien to the sound and honest Republican liberalism that has kept the party abreast of human needs in a changing world, wholly alien to the broad middle course that accommodates the mainstream of Republican principles."

It is worth noting that Rockefeller is speaking to a convention dominated by conservatives who had just voted down a proposal to include support for the recently passed 1964 Civil Rights Act in the party's platform. There was a national consensus developing around support for civil rights, but more than 70 percent of the delegates to the convention voted against adoption of the plank. That position was a reflection of the deep division that was emerging between the moderates, who were generally supportive of civil rights, and the conservatives, who were not. Rockefeller saw this as an ominous sign for the party. The heckling that he received as he delivered this address confirmed his suspicions about the extremist elements.

Our sole concern must be the future well-being of America, and of freedom and respect for human dignity—the preservation and enhancement of these principles upon which this nation has achieved its greatness.

During this year, I have criss-crossed this nation fighting for those principles, fighting to keep the Republican party of all the people—and warning of the extremist threat, its danger to the party and its danger to the nation.

The methods of these extremist elements I have experienced at first hand.

Their tactics have ranged from cancellation by coercion of a speaking engagement before a college audience to outright threats of personal violence.

These things have no place in America, but I can personally testify to their existence. And so can countless others who have also experienced:

Anonymous midnight and early-morning telephone calls.

Unsigned threatening letters.

Smear and hate literature.

Strong arm and "goon" tactics.

Bomb threats and bombing.

Infiltration and take-over of established political organizations by Communist and Nazi methods.

Influential Republic Party activist Phyllis Schlafly had written (and distributed to convention delegates) a book titled *A Choice, Not an Echo* that was a defense of and rallying cry for the more conservative elements in the Republican Party. In the book, she assailed Rockefeller Republicans and was particularly critical of their view of America's role in the world.

These extremists feed on fear, hate and terror. They have no program for America—no program for the Republican party. They have no solution for our problems of chronic unemployment, of education of agriculture, or racial injustice or strife.

These extremists have no plan and no program to keep the peace and bring freedom to the world.

On the contrary—they spread distrust. They engender suspicion. They encourage disunity. And they operate from the dark shadows of secrecy.

They have called President Eisenhower "a dedicated, conscious agent of the Communist conspiracy."

They have labeled a great Republican Secretary of State, the late John Foster Dulles, "a Communist agent."

They have demanded that the United States get out of the United Nations and that the United Nations get out of the United States.

There is no place in this Republican party for such hawkers of hate, such purveyors of prejudice, such fabricators of fear, whether Communist, Ku Klux Klan or Bircher.

There is no place in this Republican party for those who would infiltrate its ranks, distort its aims, and convert it into a cloak of apparent respectability for a dangerous extremism.

And make no mistake about it—the hidden members of the John Birch Society and others like them are out to do just that!

These people have nothing in common with Republicanism.

These people have nothing in common with Americans.

The Republican party must repudiate these people.

I move the adoption of this resolution.

Source: "Remarks on Extremism at the 1964 Republican National Convention." Rockefeller Archive Center, http://www.rockarch.org/inownwords/nar1964text .php. Used by permission of the Republican National Committee.

The divisive convention rejected Rockefeller's warning and admonition and selected Goldwater. In doing so, the Republican conventioneers inadvertently handed Lyndon Johnson his strongest campaign issue—Goldwater's extremism.

When Goldwater secured the nomination, he approached the delegates in triumph, heralding a new force within the Republican Party that would come to be a dominant dimension of the party for years to come.

Goldwater's Rejoinder to Rockefeller

**Barry Goldwater's Acceptance Speech
at the Republican National Convention**

July 14, 1964

INTRODUCTION

As seen in Nelson Rockefeller's speech, the 1964 Republican National Convention was marred by a divisive fight for the heart of the Republican Party. Rockefeller admonished the party to reject the extremely conservative elements such as the John Birch Society and the Ku Klux Klan that had played an important role in the surge of support for Barry Goldwater. The Goldwater delegates at the convention roundly criticized Rockefeller and even booed him off the stage at one point. An impassioned call for moderation from a center-right politician within the Republican ranks was not a popular position in the nominating convention. Just days after Rockefeller's speech, Goldwater accepted the nomination.

With relish in response to Rockefeller's plea for moderation, Goldwater delivers a line that would live on as an oft-cited defense of extreme positions.

. . . Today, as then, but more urgently and more broadly than then, the task of preserving and enlarging freedom at home and safeguarding it from the forces of tyranny abroad is great enough to challenge all our resources and to require all our strength. Anyone who joins us in all sincerity, we welcome. Those who do not care for our cause, we don't expect to enter our ranks in any case. And let our Republicanism, so focused and so dedicated, not be made fuzzy and futile by unthinking and stupid labels.

Goldwater's message also contributed significantly to Lyndon B. Johnson's success in November, as many moderate Republicans either crossed party lines to vote for Johnson or stayed home on election day.

I would remind you that extremism in the defense of liberty is no vice. And let me remind you also that moderation in the pursuit of justice is no virtue.

The beauty of the very system we Republicans are pledged to restore and revitalize, the beauty of this Federal system of ours is in its reconciliation of diversity with unity. We must not see malice in honest differences of opinion, and no matter how great, so long as they are not inconsistent with the pledges we have given to each other in and through our Constitution. Our Republican cause is not to level out the world or make its people conform in computer regimented sameness. Our Republican cause is to free our people and light the way for liberty throughout the world.

Ours is a very human cause for very humane goals.

This Party, its good people, and its unquestionable devotion to freedom, will not fulfill the purposes of this campaign which we launch here now until our cause has won the day, inspired the world, and shown the way to a tomorrow worthy of all our yesteryears. . . .

Source: "Goldwater's 1964 Acceptance Speech." *Washington Post,* http://www.washingtonpost.com/wp-srv/politics/daily/may98/goldwaterspeech.htm/. Used by permission of the Republican National Committee.

Many observers credit Democrat Lyndon Johnson's victory in the 1964 general election to Goldwater's success in the Republican National Convention and the movement of the Republican Party to the far right. The party had nominated someone so fundamentally opposed to moderation that the vast majority of the voting public was turned off. It wasn't until Ronald Reagan's election in 1980 that the views that Goldwater espoused would come to be mainstream among the voting public. Nonetheless, the tensions between Rockefeller Republicans and Goldwater Republicans that were on display at the Cow Palace in 1964 remain an important issue within the Republican Party and are often reflected in presidential primaries.

"Peace Little Girl" ("Daisy Girl") Ad

Campaign Ad for Lyndon B. Johnson by the Democratic National Committee

September 7, 1964

INTRODUCTION

Lyndon B. Johnson was sworn in as president within hours of John F. Kennedy's assassination in November 1963. As the 1964 election approached, most observers assumed that Johnson would win. He was very popular, having moved quickly with several important pieces of legislation. But elections are never a sure thing until the voters have spoken, so Johnson's team mounted an aggressive effort against the opponent, Republican senator Barry Goldwater from Arizona. The "Peace Little Girl" ad for Johnson (also known as "Daisy Girl")—the most well-known attack ad in American history—was one of many that the Johnson team ran that year.

It is a black-and-white ad. The commercial opens with a little girl, perhaps four or five years old, standing in a field of flowers. She is by herself, happy and content. Birds are chirping in the background, and it seems to be a bright, sunny spring day. The little girls is slowly picking the petals off a flower—a daisy.

Clearly, with this opening shot the Johnson team was seeking to draw the viewer to a peaceful time. In fact, it is common for candidates and other advertisers to make reference to tranquil rural scenes when they wish to convey notions of stability and harmony. For example, when Ronald Reagan was running for reelection in 1984, his team ran an ad called "Morning in America" (discussed later in this volume). Much of the imagery in that ad, as with this one, was of tranquil scenes in rural America.

The use of a child in the ad is significant. Our nation was in the middle of the Cold War, and the threat of nuclear holocaust seemed all too real. Americans worried about the Soviet Union, and of course they fretted about their children's and grandchildren's futures. This was the era of aboveground nuclear bombs testing. Americans had grown accustomed to these massive explosions and the terrifying prospects of nuclear war. A mushroom cloud, perhaps more than anything else, was a cognitive cue of how precarious things seemed in the 1960s.

In the ad, the little girl's face freezes, and the camera slowly zooms into the pupil of her eye.

CHILD'S VOICE: One, two, three, four, five, seven, six, six, eight, nine, nine.

In the ad, the girl's eye turns into a dark frame, and then quickly there is the vision and sound of a nuclear explosion. A massive mushroom cloud is seen, with darkness at the edges.

MALE VOICE: Ten, nine, eight, seven, six, five, four, three, two, one, zero.

JOHNSON'S VOICE [voiceover]: These are the stakes: To make a world in which all of God's children can live, or to go into the darkness. We must either love each other, or we must die.

MALE NARRATOR: Vote for President Johnson on November 3. The stakes are too high for you to stay home.

Source: "Peace Little Girl (Daisy) (Johnson, 1964)." Museum of the Living Image: The Living Room Candidate, http://www.livingroomcandidate.org/commercials/1964/peace-little-girl-daisy.

It is telling that Barry Goldwater is never mentioned in the ad. Yet the ad was seen as a powerful attack on the Republican. The narrative pushed by the Johnson team was that Goldwater was erratic, irresponsible, and even scary. They sought to remind voters about Goldwater's comment that "tactical nuclear weapons" might be used in Vietnam, that he had voted against the International Nuclear Test Ban Treaty, and that he had suggested that nuclear bombs were "merely another weapon." To many Americans, Goldwater seemed to be an extremist, out of the mainstream. The ad sought to reinforce this idea without ever mentioning his name.

Because Johnson was way ahead in the polls, his team worried that many supporters would stay at home. This ad and many others pushed voters to turn out on election day.

As a paid advertisement, "Peace Little Girl" only ran once—during an NBC evening movie. Yet because it was so controversial, most major news outlets discussed and reran the ad for more than a week. For the Johnson team, this was the ultimate success: they paid to run the ad just once, but the entire nation was talking about it.

Goldwater's Sanity

"1,189 Psychiatrists Say Goldwater Is Psychologically Unfit to be President!"
FACT Magazine
September 1964

INTRODUCTION

The 1964 presidential campaign between Johnson and Goldwater was without question one of the most divisive and bitter campaigns in the modern era. Just two months prior to the election, FACT magazine published an issue titled "The Unconscious of a Conservative: A Special Issue on the Mind of Barry Goldwater." The main argument of the issue was that Goldwater was simply unfit for public office; he was unstable and was too paranoid to be president. The magazine reported the results of a very nonscientific poll that it had conducted by contacting psychiatrists around the country and inviting them to diagnose a patient they had never examined. Soon after publication of the results by Ralph Ginzburg and Warren Boroson, Goldwater brought a libel suit against the magazine. The following is an excerpt of the FACT article.

The American Medical Association (AMA) was quick to distance itself from Ginzburg and Boroson. The AMA was severely critical of the piece and argued that the names of the 12,356 psychiatrists were acquired by the magazine through a third party.

On July 24, one week after Barry Goldwater received the Republican nomination, FACT sent a questionnaire to all of the nation's 12,356 psychiatrists asking, "Do you believe Barry Goldwater is psychologically fit to serve as President of the United States?" (The names were supplied by the American Medical Association.)

In all, 2,417 psychiatrists responded. Of these, 571 said they did not know enough about Goldwater to answer the question; 657 said they thought Goldwater was psychologically fit; and 1,189 said that he was not. (It might be pointed out that the majority of those who thought Goldwater was psychologically fit nevertheless said they were not voting for him.)

The article went on to display the many comments that the magazine received regarding Goldwater's psyche. On the back cover of the issue, the editor had placed several select comments submitted by psychiatrists.

FACT's questionnaire left room for "Comments" and over a quarter of a million words of professional opinion were received. On the next page we present a sampling of these comments, which, all together, constitute the most intensive character analysis ever made of a living human being.

B.G. is in my opinion emotionally unstable, immature, volatile, unpredictable, hostile, and mentally unbalance. He is totally unfit for public office and a menace to society.

My clinical impression is that he is a paranoid personality with dominance of subjective views over objective.

His theme is 'freedom'—but from what? Unconsciously, it seems to be from his mother's domination.

B.G.'s proneness to aggressive behavior and destructiveness indicates an attempt to prove his manliness.

He consciously wants to destroy the world with atomic bombs. He is a mass-murderer at heart and a suicide. He is amoral and immoral. A dangerous lunatic!

As a human being he is to be pitied. As President of the United States he would be a disaster.

Source: R. Ginzburg, ed., "1,189 Psychiatrists Say Goldwater Is Psychologically Unfit to Be President!" *FACT*, Special Issue, "The Unconscious of a Conservative: A Special Issue on the Mind of Barry Goldwater," September–October 1964, 24–64.

Unfortunately for Goldwater, the libel suit was brought after the election. Although he prevailed in his suit, he was able to win only six states: his home state of Arizona and five states of the conservative Deep South. The magazine article, though certainly not the cause of his campaign's difficulty in November, fed into a very popular sense cultivated by the Johnson campaign that Goldwater was an ideological extremist. The huge majority garnered by Johnson revealed a deep suspicion among many voters for Goldwater's campaign, a suspicion that grew as the campaign unfolded. In some sense, the article was the culmination of that narrative. But the narrative had its own force, largely from the difficult divide that was growing between moderate Republicans and Goldwater's supporters on the far right. The resurgence today of the so-called "movement conservatives" can be traced back to the Goldwater campaign of 1964.

Election of 1968

Wallace's Third-Party Run

Stand Up for America: George Wallace
Campaign Brochure
1968

INTRODUCTION

George Wallace was a well-known former Democratic governor of Alabama with strong segregationist views. In fact, during his gubernatorial inaugural address in 1963, he proclaimed "segregation now, segregation tomorrow, segregation forever." His positions on race and on law and order became the centerpiece of a campaign strategy reminiscent of Strom Thurmond's segregationist appeal as a Dixiecrat in 1948. When Wallace entered the 1968 presidential race, he did so not as a Democrat (as he had in other presidential nomination campaigns that he entered) but instead as the nominee from the American Independent Party. The following is a campaign brochure from Wallace's third-party run.

The Man . . .

QUALIFICATIONS 1945–1967

Outstanding attorney

Assistant Alabama Attorney General

Member of State Legislature

Circuit Judge

Governor

FISCAL RESPONSIBILITY

Put Alabama on a firm financial basis

Eliminated state limousines, yachts, and other costly luxuries

Put purchases on strict competitive bid

Developed a surplus in the state treasury

ACCOMPLISHMENTS

EDUCATION . . .   stablished a new university, 14 junior colleges, 15 trade schools and raised teachers' salaries.

INDUSTRY . . . 100,000 new jobs. Highest total employment and lowest unemployment in state's history. Obtained $2 billion worth of new and expanded industry.

ROADBUILDING . . . invested over $549 million in the greatest 4 year roadbuilding performance in Alabama's history— without any hint of graft corruption or swindles.

WELFARE . . . record high help to the aged, the handicapped, mentally and physically ill. Old age pensions at highest level in Alabama history.

AGRICULTURE . . . greatly increased agricultural research, land fertilization, crop yield, and farm income.

His Views . . .

AS EXPRESSED IN HIS OWN PUBLIC STATEMENTS

ON LABOR

Issued executive order incorporating minimum union wage rates in all state contracts. Increased Workmen's and Unemployment Compensation benefits 37%. Promoted and passed legislation that reduced firemen's work week from 72 to 56 hours and substantially increased retirement pensions.

ON STATES RIGHTS

. . . recommend that the states of the Union continue to determine the policies of their domestic institutions themselves and that the bureaucrats and theoreticians in Washington let people in Ohio and New York and California decide themselves . . . what type of school system they are going to have. I recommend states rights and local government, and territorial democracy . . .

This is the core of the segregationist argument. Those who objected to the Civil Rights Act of 1964 or the Voting Rights Act of 1965 generally did so on states' rights grounds. In their view—and in Wallace's—it was not within the proper power of the central government to compel states to desegregate public accommodations or to run elections in a particular and/or nondiscriminatory way.

On Crime

The first thing I would do as President is to make an announcement that I'd give my Moral Support as President to the policemen of this country and to the firemen of the country. I'd say, "We stand behind you because you are the thin line between complete anarchy in the streets and the physical safety of our person."

On Vietnam

Recall that Lyndon B. Johnson had decided not to run for reelection in 1968, largely due to the war in Vietnam.

... think the first thing we ought to do in this country is to impress upon Hanoi and Peking and Moscow the resolve of the American people. Those few people today who are out advocating sedition and raising money and clothes and supplies for the Viet Cong—these college professors who are making speeches advocating victory for the Viet Cong Communists—I would deal with these people as they ought to be dealt with, as traitors.

Constitutional Government

George C. Wallace is the undisputed leader in the fight for personal and property rights, and against excessive taxation and the takeover of personal rights by the "great society."

He believes in victory over Communism and Socialism at home and abroad.

George Wallace can win Presidency with only a Plurality of Votes

Can former Alabama Governor George C. Wallace be elected President of the United States, in the Nov. 5 election?

The answer is a simple "Yes."

He not only CAN be elected, but WILL be elected president.

All that needs to happen for George Wallace to become president is for history to repeat itself.

This argument—that he could win with a plurality of votes—is interesting in that his campaign recognized the limit to his draw outside of the Deep South. Indeed, part of the campaign's strategy was to pull enough votes away from the Democratic and Republican candidates (whom he considered to have "not a dime's worth of difference between them") to either claim a plurality victory or take the election to the U.S. House of Representatives.

All Governor Wallace needs to do to win is to get a plurality of the vote. A plurality, not a majority.

Mathematically speaking the recognized Wallace strength in southern and border states adds up to some 150 electoral vote, . . . a giant stepping stone toward the 270 electoral votes needed to put George Wallace in the White House.

And strong grassroots Wallace support in states outside the south—coupled with the simple fact that only slightly more than one-third of the popular vote is needed in a three-way race to give a candidate a state's electoral votes—dramatically projects Governor Wallace to the forefront of the 1968 presidential race. With working organizations and already demonstrated vote, appeal in states such as Wisconsin, California, Ohio, Pennsylvania, Indiana and Maryland, the number of electoral votes needed to elect George C. Wallace President in 1968 is clearly within reach.

Repeating, all George Wallace needs to be elected president is a plurality of the votes, not a majority.

If he gets 34 percent of the votes in a state and the other two candidates get 33 percent apiece, he wins the electoral vote, of the state and the election.

And this has happened several times in the past. Abraham Lincoln did it. Thomas Jefferson did it. John Quincy Adams did it. John F. Kennedy did it.

Abraham Lincoln, for example, got only 40 percent of the popular vote. The late John F. Kennedy got only 49.7 percent, Yet they were elected president.

Source: Box SG034467, Folder 15, Wallace Family Papers collection, Alabama Department of Archives and History. ADAH Digital Collections, http://digital.archives.alabama.gov/cdm/singleitem/collection/voices/id/5360/rec/5. Used by permission of the Alabama Department of Archives and History, Montgomery, Alabama.

Both major candidates, Hubert H. Humphrey and Richard Nixon, had reason to be concerned about Wallace's entry into the race. Both of the candidates stood to lose votes to Wallace. Nixon's campaign was also a law and order campaign, marked by implicit appeals to disaffected white voters in the South through the Southern Strategy. Wallace's right-wing platform might cut into the support for Nixon among anti-integration voters. For his part, Humphrey had reason to be concerned that Wallace's anti–Vietnam War rhetoric and everyman populist campaign appeal might pull Democrats away.

As it turns out, Wallace's third-party bid cut into Nixon's support far more than Humphrey's, although Nixon ultimately won the election. Wallace did exceptionally well for a third-party candidate, winning five Southern states and coming extremely close to taking several other states outside of the Deep South. In retrospect, Wallace's 1968 campaign seems to have been something of a high-water mark for modern third-party presidential bids.

RFK Announces His Candidacy

Robert F. Kennedy's Announcement of Candidacy for President

March 16, 1968

INTRODUCTION

Democrat Robert F. Kennedy's announcement was not an ordinary presidential campaign announcement speech. Kennedy was saying that the sitting president, Lyndon Johnson, also a Democrat, should be replaced. It has been very rare in American history that a prominent member of a political party would challenge a sitting president of the same party. One of the most popular Democrats in the nation was saying that another very popular Democrat, the president, was unfit to lead.

This line about opposing any man is illustrative. It was well known that Robert Kennedy and Lyndon Johnson did not get along. The feud went back to the Democratic National Convention in 1960. Kennedy's brother, John, would be nominated as the party's presidential candidate. But who would run on the ticket as the vice presidential candidate? Many of the leaders in the party wanted Johnson, the Senate majority leader and a Texan (a state with a large number of electoral votes). John Kennedy also thought that this would be a good choice, but Robert, his brother and key adviser, balked at the idea. Eventually Johnson was asked to join the ticket, but all knew that Robert had lobbied against the choice. Moreover, Robert worked hard to keep Johnson, as vice president, out of important decision-making meetings. Johnson was not a key player in the Kennedy White House because Robert wanted it that way.

Johnson became president after John Kennedy's assassination in November 1963. At the time, Robert Kennedy was the attorney general. He stayed in that position until 1964 (surely an awkward year), when he left the cabinet and was elected to the U.S. Senate from New York. Many had pushed Kennedy to run for the presidency in 1968 as an antiwar candidate.

Our nation's involvement in Vietnam began during the Dwight D. Eisenhower administration but accelerated dramatically under Lyndon Johnson. By 1968, America was deeply engulfed in a war in Southeast Asia. Johnson had become the so-called war president, and as the antiwar movement grew, their ire was directed at him.

I am today announcing my candidacy for the presidency of the United States.

I do not run for the presidency merely to oppose any man but to propose new policies. I run because I am convinced that this country is on a perilous course and because I have such strong feelings about what must be done, and I feel that I'm obliged to do all that I can.

I run to seek new policies—policies to end the bloodshed in Vietnam and in our cities, policies to close the gaps that now exist between black and white, between rich and poor, between young and old, in this country and around the rest of the world.

I run for the presidency because I want the Democratic Party and the United States of America to stand for hope instead of despair, for reconciliation of men instead of the growing risk of world war.

I run because it is now unmistakably clear that we can change these disastrous, divisive policies only by changing the men who are now making them. For the reality of recent events in Vietnam has been glossed over with illusions.

The Report of the Riot Commission has been largely ignored.

The crisis in gold, the crisis in our cities, the crisis in our farms and in our ghettos have all been met with too little and too late.

No one [who] knows what I know about the extraordinary demands of the presidency can be certain that any mortal can adequately fill that position.

But my service in the National Security Council during the Cuban Missile Crisis, the Berlin crisis of 1961 and 1962, and later the negotiations on Laos and on the Nuclear Test Ban Treaty have taught me something about both the uses and limitations of military power, about the opportunities and the dangers which await our nation in many corners of the globe in which I have traveled.

All understood that the core issues in 1968 were foreign affairs and the war in Vietnam. Kennedy was a first-term senator and the former attorney general, and thus his foreign policy could be viewed as light. This section of the speech was designed to bolster his credentials in this area.

As a member of the cabinet and member of the Senate I have seen the inexcusable and ugly deprivation which causes children to starve in Mississippi, black citizens to riot in Watts; young Indians to commit suicide on their reservations because they've lacked all hope and they feel they have no future, and proud and able-bodied families to wait out their lives in empty idleness in eastern Kentucky.

I have traveled and I have listened to the young people of our nation and felt their anger about the war that they are sent to fight and about the world they are about to inherit.

The extent to which Kennedy attempted to persuade Johnson to alter his policies in Vietnam is unknown. While Kennedy's candidacy was clearly centered on the antiwar movement, many scholars suggest that his opposition was somewhat muted until the spring of 1968.

In private talks and in public, I have tried in vain to alter our course in Vietnam before it further saps our spirit and our manpower, further raises the risks of wider war, and further destroys the country and the people it was meant to save.

I cannot stand aside from the contest that will decide our nation's future and our children's future.

The remarkable New Hampshire campaign of Senator Eugene McCarthy has proven how deep are the present divisions within our party and within our country. Until that was publicly clear, my presence in the race would have been seen as a clash of personalities rather than issues.

Eugene McCarthy, a lesser-known and poorly funded Democratic senator from Minnesota, had thrown his hat into the ring for the nomination several months earlier. Few gave McCarthy a chance, but he pushed forward in the first primary election (New Hampshire) with a legion of young volunteers. To everyone's surprise, McCarthy netted 42 percent of the vote. This signaled that Johnson was vulnerable. But it was not until after McCarthy's strong showing that Kennedy jumped into the race. Several liberal journalists and party activists criticized Kennedy for waiting to enter the race until McCarthy had demonstrated Johnson's weakness. In their view, Kennedy was an opportunist. Many other Democrats, however, were simply glad that a strong antiwar candidate had finally decided to challenge Johnson. Either way, it was imperative that Kennedy recognize the role of McCarthy in drawing attention to the divisions in the party.

But now that the fight is on and over policies which I have long been challenging, I must enter the race. The fight is just beginning and I believe that I can win.

While it was well known that Kennedy and Johnson did not get along, it was also recognized that they put aside animosity after the assassination of John Kennedy. In fact, there is a good bit of evidence to suggest that Johnson extended an olive branch to Robert Kennedy and that Kennedy refrained from criticizing Johnson because of this gracious gesture to his family.

Finally, my decision reflects no personal animosity or disrespect toward President Johnson. He served President Kennedy with the utmost loyalty and was extremely kind to me and members of my family in the difficult months which followed the events of November of 1963.

I have often commended his efforts in health, in education, and in many other areas, and I have the deepest sympathy for the burden that he carries today.

But the issue is not personal. It is our profound differences over where we are heading and what we want to accomplish.

I do not lightly dismiss the dangers and the difficulties of challenging an incumbent President. But these are not ordinary times and this is not an ordinary election.

Because of McCarthy's strong showing in New Hampshire and because of Kennedy's announcement, Johnson stunned the nation by announcing on March 31, 1968, that he would not seek or accept the Democratic nomination for the presidency.

At stake is not simply the leadership of our party and even our country. It is our right to moral leadership of this planet.

Source: Papers of Robert F. Kennedy, Presidential Campaign Papers. John F. Kennedy Presidential Library.

LBJ Not Seeking Reelection

President Lyndon B. Johnson's Remarks on Decision Not to Seek Reelection

March 31, 1968

INTRODUCTION

Lyndon Johnson became president of the United States upon the assassination of John F. Kennedy in November 1963. Having spent decades in Congress and having been the Senate majority leader prior to becoming vice president, Johnson was a skilled politician. He knew how the legislative process worked and understood how to move public policy proposals forward. His broad domestic policy initiatives, dubbed the Great Society, fundamentally transformed many aspects of our world. Passage of the Civil Rights Act in 1964 marked the high point of his presidency.

Nevertheless, the Vietnam War plagued Johnson's presidency. It is true that U.S. efforts to aid South Vietnam in its struggle against communist North Vietnam had begun under Dwight Eisenhower and were continued under John Kennedy. But it is also true that the massive escalation of U.S. involvement lay at Johnson's door. By the time he gave this speech, some half million Americans were deployed in the region.

Night after night, Americans watched the evening news and saw horrific battles and the mounting casualties. By 1968, the antiwar movement was in full force. Johnson, the hero of progressive Democrats a few years before, had become a war president and was the target of their rage.

Good evening, my fellow Americans:

Tonight I want to speak to you of peace in Vietnam and Southeast Asia.

No other question so preoccupies our people. No other dream so absorbs the 250 million human beings who live in that part of the world. No other goal motivates American policy in Southeast Asia. . . .

A vast majority of this speech—some 3,000 words that are omitted here— outlines recent military efforts in Vietnam. Johnson lays out moves to secure peace in South Vietnam. He also spends a good bit of time outlining the cost of the war and how he believes partisan wrangling in Congress has prevented the adoption of a tax measure to pay for these costs.

. . . One day, my fellow citizens, there will be peace in Southeast Asia.

It will come because the people of Southeast Asia want it— those whose armies are at war tonight, and those who, though threatened, have thus far been spared.

Peace will come because Asians were willing to work for it—and to sacrifice for it—and to die by the thousands for it.

But let it never be forgotten: Peace will come also because America sent her sons to help secure it.

It has not been easy—far from it. During the past 4 years, it has been my fate and my responsibility to be Commander in Chief. I have lived—daily and nightly—with the cost of this war. I know the pain that it has inflicted. I know, perhaps better than anyone, the misgivings that it has aroused.

Bear in mind that this was during the Cold War, and the fall of any nation to communism was perceived by some observers to be a threat to the United States.

Throughout this entire, long period, I have been sustained by a single principle: that what we are doing now, in Vietnam, is vital not only to the security of Southeast Asia, but it is vital to the security of every American.

Surely we have treaties which we must respect. Surely we have commitments that we are going to keep. Resolutions of the Congress testify to the need to resist aggression in the world and in Southeast Asia.

But the heart of our involvement in South Vietnam—under three different presidents, three separate administrations—has always been America's own security.

And the larger purpose of our involvement has always been to help the nations of Southeast Asia become independent and stand alone, self-sustaining, as members of a great world community—at peace with themselves, and at peace with all others.

With such an Asia, our country—and the world—will be far more secure than it is tonight.

I believe that a peaceful Asia is far nearer to reality because of what America has done in Vietnam. I believe that the men who endure the dangers of battle—fighting there for us tonight—are helping the entire world avoid far greater conflicts, far wider wars, far more destruction, than this one.

While Johnson seemed to offer hope that the war would end quickly—that a peace treaty would soon be reached—hopes had been dashed on many occasions before. It is likely that few observers accepted his premise that the war was nearing an end. In fact, our involvement in Vietnam continued for another four years. In the end, some 55,000 Americans lost their lives in the war.

The peace that will bring them home someday will come. Tonight I have offered the first in what I hope will be a series of mutual moves toward peace.

I pray that it will not be rejected by the leaders of North Vietnam. I pray that they will accept it as a means by which the sacrifices of their own people may be ended. And I ask your help and your support, my fellow citizens, for this effort to reach across the battlefield toward an early peace.

Finally, my fellow Americans, let me say this:

Of those to whom much is given, much is asked. I cannot say and no man could say that no more will be asked of us.

Yet, I believe that now, no less than when the decade began, this generation of Americans is willing to "pay any price, bear any burden, meet any hardship, support any friend, oppose any foe to assure the survival and the success of liberty."

Since those words were spoken by John F. Kennedy, the people of America have kept that compact with mankind's noblest cause.

And we shall continue to keep it.

Yet, I believe that we must always be mindful of this one thing, whatever the trials and the tests ahead. The ultimate strength of our country and our cause will lie not in powerful weapons or infinite resources or boundless wealth, but will lie in the unity of our people.

This I believe very deeply.

Throughout my entire public career I have followed the personal philosophy that I am a free man, an American, a public servant, and a member of my party, in that order always and only.

For 37 years in the service of our Nation, first as a Congressman, as a Senator, and as Vice President, and now as your President, I have put the unity of the people first. I have put it ahead of any divisive partisanship.

And in these times as in times before, it is true that a house divided against itself by the spirit of faction, of party, of region, of religion, of race, is a house that cannot stand.

There is division in the American house now. There is divisiveness among us all tonight. And holding the trust that is mine, as President of all the people, I cannot disregard the peril to the progress of the American people and the hope and the prospect of peace for all peoples.

Even though Johnson lays the blame of the division on partisan difference, the root of the discord was clearly war policies in Southeast Asia.

So, I would ask all Americans, whatever their personal interests or concern, to guard against divisiveness and all its ugly consequences.

Fifty-two months and 10 days ago, in a moment of tragedy and trauma, the duties of this office fell upon me. I asked then for your help and God's, that we might continue America on its course, binding up our wounds, healing our history, moving forward in new unity, to clear the American agenda and to keep the American commitment for all of our people.

United we have kept that commitment. United we have enlarged that commitment.

Through all time to come, I think America will be a stronger nation, a more just society, and a land of greater opportunity and fulfillment because of what we have all done together in these years of unparalleled achievement.

Our reward will come in the life of freedom, peace, and hope that our children will enjoy through ages ahead.

What we won when all of our people united just must not now be lost in suspicion, distrust, selfishness, and politics among any of our people.

Believing this as I do, I have concluded that I should not permit the Presidency to become involved in the partisan divisions that are developing in this political year.

With America's sons in the fields far away, with America's future under challenge right here at home, with our hopes and the world's hopes for peace in the balance every day, I do not believe that I should devote an hour or a day of my time to any personal partisan causes or to any duties other than the awesome duties of this office—the Presidency of your country.

This comment stunned the nation. Nearly all presidents, particularly in the 20th century, sought reelection. By not seeking another term, Johnson was in essence admitting his defeat—that he would not win reelection. He was a beaten man.

Accordingly, I shall not seek, and I will not accept, the nomination of my party for another term as your President.

But let men everywhere know, however, that a strong, a confident, and a vigilant America stands ready tonight to seek an honorable peace—and stands ready tonight to defend an honored cause—whatever the price, whatever the burden, whatever the sacrifice that duty may require.

Thank you for listening. Good night and God bless all of you.

Source: Lyndon B. Johnson, *Public Papers of the Presidents of the United States: Lyndon B. Johnson, 1968–1969,* Book 1, entry 170, pp. 475–476 (Washington, DC: U.S. Government Printing Office, 1970).

It should also be noted that Johnson's withdrawal from the presidential race was precipitated by Minnesota senator Eugene McCarthy's strong showing in the New Hampshire Democratic primary a few weeks earlier. McCarthy, little known outside his state and with scant resources, was able to garner 42 percent of the vote against a sitting president. This said to many, including Johnson, that his chances for reelection had evaporated. Polling data also seemed to confirm this.

Johnson's withdrawal set up a very heated battle for the party nomination—a battle that pitted party bosses against antiwar Democrats.

RFK and MLK

Robert F. Kennedy Relaying News of the Assassination of Martin Luther King Jr.

April, 4, 1968

INTRODUCTION

Martin Luther King Jr. was assassinated at 6:01 p.m. on April 4, 1968. At that time, Robert F. Kennedy, Democratic candidate for president, was in Muncie, Indiana, delivering a campaign address as part of his effort to win the Indiana Democratic primary. His next stop was a poor inner-city neighborhood in Indianapolis to address a crowd of more than 2,500 supporters, the vast majority of whom were African American. They had been awaiting Kennedy's arrival through a cool, wet night and had not yet heard the news of King's death.

Kennedy's security detail requested that he skip the event in light of King's assassination by a white man. But Kennedy was determined to address the crowd and convey the tragic news. He spoke without notes from the back of a flatbed truck, drew from his own family's experience of loss and anger, and implored the audience to work for that which King had dedicated his life's work: decency, compassion, and love.

Ladies and Gentlemen,

I'm only going to talk to you just for a minute or so this evening, because I have some—some very sad news for all of you—Could you lower those signs, please?—I have some very sad news for all of you, and, I think, sad news for all of our fellow citizens, and people who love peace all over the world; and that is that Martin Luther King was shot and was killed tonight in Memphis, Tennessee.

Martin Luther King dedicated his life to love and to justice between fellow human beings. He died in the cause of that effort. In this difficult day, in this difficult time for the United States, it's perhaps well to ask what kind of a nation we are and what direction we want to move in. For those of you who are black—considering the evidence evidently is that there were white people who were responsible—you can be filled with bitterness, and with hatred, and a desire for revenge.

We can move in that direction as a country, in greater polarization—black people amongst blacks, and white amongst whites, filled with hatred toward one another. Or we can make an effort, as Martin Luther King did, to understand, and to comprehend, and replace that violence, that

71

stain of bloodshed that has spread across our land, with an effort to understand, compassion, and love.

For those of you who are black and are tempted to fill with—be filled with—hatred and mistrust of the injustice of such an act, against all white people, I would only say that I can also feel in my own heart the same kind of feeling. I had a member of my family killed, but he was killed by a white man.

But we have to make an effort in the United States. We have to make an effort to understand, to get beyond, or go beyond these rather difficult times.

My favorite poem, my—my favorite poet—was Aeschylus. And he once wrote:

Even in our sleep, pain which cannot forget

falls drop by drop upon the heart,

until, in our own despair,

against our will,

comes wisdom

through the awful grace of God.

What we need in the United States is not division; what we need in the United States is not hatred; what we need in the United States is not violence and lawlessness, but is love, and wisdom, and compassion toward one another, and a feeling of justice toward those who still suffer within our country, whether they be white or whether they be black.

So I ask you tonight to return home, to say a prayer for the family of Martin Luther King—yeah, it's true—but more importantly to say a prayer for our own country, which all of us love—a prayer for understanding and that compassion of which I spoke.

Riots engulfed hundreds of American cities that night, but Indianapolis was quiet. Kennedy's words of sorrow and hope, pain and compassion, implored the crowd to work for justice, not to seek vengeance.

We can do well in this country. We will have difficult times. We've had difficult times in the past, but we—and we will have difficult times in the future. It is not the end of violence; it is not the end of lawlessness; and it's not the end of disorder.

But the vast majority of white people and the vast majority of black people in this country want to live together, want to improve the quality of our life, and want justice for all human beings that abide in our land.

And let's dedicate ourselves to what the Greeks wrote so many years ago: to tame the savageness of man and make gentle the life of this world. Let us dedicate ourselves to that, and say a prayer for our country and for our people.

Thank you very much.

Source: "Robert F. Kennedy: On the Death of Martin Luther King (1968)," The History Place: Great Speeches Collection, http://www.historyplace.com/speeches/rfk-mlk.htm.

To many observers, Kennedy's impromptu address revealed a genuine sensitivity to African American anger and frustration and solidified his support among African American voters in the Democratic primary. Two months later, Kennedy was brought down by an assassin's bullet.

Ted Kennedy on Robert's Death

Ted Kennedy's Address at the Public Memorial Service for Robert F. Kennedy

June 8, 1968

INTRODUCTION

When John F. Kennedy was elected president in 1960, he tapped his brother, Robert F. Kennedy, to be attorney general. To some critics, hiring one's brother for such an important position was flagrant nepotism, but most other Americans understood that Robert was the president's closest adviser—his right-hand man, so to speak. They were exceedingly tight, and by most accounts the president relied on his brother's advice for every significant decision.

After John Kennedy's assassination on November 22, 1963, Robert Kennedy continued to serve as attorney general under Lyndon Johnson for nine more months, even though the two were never close. Kennedy left the administration in September 1964 and was elected to the U.S. Senate from New York two months later.

By 1968 as the antiwar movement began to build steam, many voters began to urge Kennedy to run for the presidency. At first he balked at the idea. Yet he and others watched Senator Eugene McCarthy of Minnesota mount a strong challenge to Lyndon in early Democratic primaries. Kennedy eventually jumped into the race, and two weeks later at the end of March, Johnson stunned the nation and withdrew his bid for reelection.

Your Eminences, Your Excellencies, Mr. President:

On behalf of Mrs. Kennedy, her children, the parents and sisters of Robert Kennedy, I want to express what we feel to those who mourn with us today in this Cathedral and around the world.

We loved him as a brother, and as a father, and as a son. From his parents, and from his older brothers and sisters—Joe and Kathleen and Jack—he received an inspiration which he passed on to all of us. He gave us strength in time of trouble, wisdom in time of uncertainty, and sharing in time of happiness. He will always be by our side.

Love is not an easy feeling to put into words. Nor is loyalty, or trust, or joy. But he was all of these. He loved life completely and he lived it intensely.

Robert Kennedy was late in entering the presidential nomination race, but he was able to secure several early primary victories. In fact, he stunned the Establishment by winning the California primary on June 4, 1968. After giving a rousing speech to his supporters just after midnight on June 5, he turned from the podium and walked through the hotel kitchen en route to his motorcade. There in the kitchen, he was shot three times by Sirhan Sirhan, a 24-year-old Palestinian-born Jordanian. Kennedy died just at 1:44 a.m. on June 6.

A few years back, Robert Kennedy wrote some words about his own father which expresses the way we in his family felt about him. He said of what his father meant to him, and I quote:

"What it really all adds up to is love—not love as it is described with such facility in popular magazines, but the kind of love that is affection and respect, order and encouragement, and support. Our awareness of this was an incalculable source of strength, and because real love is something unselfish and involves sacrifice and giving, we could not help but profit from it."

And he continued,

This notion of a social conscience would become a guidepost for Edward Kennedy as well. Indeed, it would seem a bit ironic that a politician from one of the most affluent political families in American politics would become the champion of the poor and working classes. Kennedy would make frequent reference to a biblical passage from Luke 12:48. "For everyone to whom much is given, of him shall much be required."

"Beneath it all, he has tried to engender a social conscience. There were wrongs which needed attention. There were people who were poor and needed help. And we have a responsibility to them and to this country. Through no virtues and accomplishments of our own, we have been fortunate enough to be born in the United States under the most comfortable conditions. We, therefore, have a responsibility to others who are less well off."

That is what Robert Kennedy was given. What he leaves to us is what he said, what he did, and what he stood for. A speech he made to the young people of South Africa on their Day of Affirmation in 1966 sums it up the best, and I would like to read it now:

"There is discrimination in this world and slavery and slaughter and starvation. Governments repress their people; millions are trapped in poverty while the nation grows rich and wealth is lavished on armaments everywhere. These are differing evils, but they are the common works of man. They reflect the imperfection of human justice, the inadequacy of human compassion, our lack of sensibility towards the suffering of our fellows. But we can perhaps remember— even if only for a time—that those who live with us are our brothers; that they share with us the same short moment of life; that they seek—as we do—nothing but the chance to live out their lives in purpose and happiness, winning what satisfaction and fulfillment they can.

Surely, this bond of common faith, this bond of common goal, can begin to teach us something. Surely, we can learn, at least, to look at those around us as fellow men. And surely we can begin to work a little harder to bind up the wounds among us and to become in our own hearts brothers and countrymen once again. The answer is to rely on youth—not a time of life but a state of mind, a temper of the will, a quality of imagination, a predominance of courage over timidity, of the appetite for adventure over the love of ease. The cruelties and obstacles of this swiftly changing planet will not yield to the obsolete dogmas and outworn slogans. They cannot be moved by those who cling to a present that is already dying, who prefer the illusion of security to the excitement and danger that come with even the most peaceful progress. . . .

Few are willing to brave the disapproval of their fellows, the censure of their colleagues, the wrath of their society. Moral courage is a rarer commodity than bravery in battle or great intelligence. Yet it is the one essential, vital quality for those who seek to change a world that yields most painfully to change. And I believe that in this generation those with the courage to enter the moral conflict will find themselves with companions in every corner of the globe.

For the fortunate among us, there is the temptation to follow the easy and familiar paths of personal ambition and financial success so grandly spread before those who enjoy the privilege of education. But that is not the road history has marked out for us. Like it or not, we live in times of danger and uncertainty. But they are also more open to the creative energy of men than any other time in history. All of us will ultimately be judged, and as the years pass we will surely judge ourselves on the effort we have contributed to building a new world society and the extent to which our ideals and goals have shaped that event.

Our future may lie beyond our vision, but it is not completely beyond our control. It is the shaping impulse of America that neither fate nor nature nor the irresistible tides of history, but the work of our own hands, matched to reason and principle, that will determine our destiny. There is pride in that, even arrogance, but there is also experience and truth. In any event, it is the only way we can live."

That is the way he lived. That is what he leaves us.

There are many passages from this speech that would be repeated in the days, months, and years to follow. This was probably the most frequently used line.

My brother need not be idealized, or enlarged in death beyond what he was in life; to be remembered simply as a good and decent man, who saw wrong and tried to right it, saw suffering and tried to heal it, saw war and tried to stop it.

Those of us who loved him and who take him to his rest today, pray that what he was to us and what he wished for others will some day come to pass for all the world.

As he said many times, in many parts of this nation, to those he touched and who sought to touch him:

"Some men see things as they are and say why. I dream things that never were and say why not."

Source: Edward M. Kennedy, "Tribute to Robert F. Kennedy," TedKennedy.org, http://tedkennedy.org/ownwords/event/eulogy.

This was a line from Robert Kennedy's campaign stump speech. As his brother Edward read it one last time, the din of weeping in the church was palpable. And of course, all of America was watching through their televisions. It was, to be sure, a very sad day in our nation's history.

We will never know if Robert Kennedy would have secured the Democratic nomination in 1968 and if he had done so whether he would have defeated Republican Richard Nixon in November. We do know that once again the nation was crippled by grief and that the Democratic Party was left deeply divided by the war in Vietnam. This issue would plague the party at its national convention in Chicago and contribute to the party's defeat in November.

Nixon's Campaign against the Warren Court

**Richard Nixon's Acceptance Speech
at the 1968 Republican National
Convention**

August 8, 1968

INTRODUCTION

Having campaigned for Barry Goldwater in 1964, Richard Nixon was able to demonstrate his commitment to conservative principles that prepared him well for attracting Republican support for his own 1968 campaign. The 1968 campaign's Southern Strategy included an appeal to disaffected whites in the newly desegregated South that was characterized by a call to rein in judicial power. For years the U.S. Supreme Court, under Chief Justice Earl Warren (a longtime rival of Nixon since their days as Republican politicians in California), had been upholding civil rights laws and ruling in support of desegregation, busing, and criminal defendants' rights. To Nixon and many white Southerners, a campaign against the Warren Court—and by extension against desegregration and lawlessness—would serve the party well in 1968.

Mr. Chairman, delegates to this convention, my fellow Americans.

Eight years ago, I had the highest honor of accepting your nomination for President of the United States. Tonight, I again proudly accept that nomination for President of the United States.

But I have news for you. This time there is a difference.

This time we are going to win.

The choice we make in 1968 will determine not only the future of America but the future of peace and freedom in the world for the last third of the Twentieth Century.

And the question that we answer tonight: can America meet this great challenge?

As we look at America, we see cities enveloped in smoke and flame.

We hear sirens in the night.

The Nixon campaign occurred in a deeply unsettled social context. Protests against the war in Vietnam, large-scale political unrest in the United States, the 1968 assassinations of Martin Luther King Jr. and Democratic candidate Robert F. Kennedy, and rioting in major American cities all contributed to the tumult. A resonant theme emerged for Nixon: the lack of law and order.

We see Americans dying on distant battlefields abroad.

We see Americans hating each other; fighting each other; killing each other at home.

And as we see and hear these things, millions of Americans cry out in anguish.

Did we come all this way for this?

Did American boys die in Normandy, and Korea, and in Valley Forge for this?

Here, Nixon tries to distinguish between peaceful acts of civil disobedience and the actions of mobs that more closely resemble riots. The obligation to avoid riots, he seems to suggest, is borne by those who advocate peaceful civil disobedience.

Listen to the answer to those questions.

It is another voice. It is the quiet voice in the tumult and the shouting.

It is the voice of the great majority of Americans, the forgotten Americans—the non-shouters; the non-demonstrators.

They give steel to the backbone of America. They are good people, they are decent people; they work, and they save, and they pay their taxes, and they care.

Like Theodore Roosevelt, they know that this country will not be a good place for any of us to live in unless it is a good place for all of us to live in.

When the strongest nation in the world can be tied down for four years in a war in Vietnam with no end in sight;

When the richest nation in the world can't manage its own economy;

When the nation with the greatest tradition of the rule of law is plagued by unprecedented lawlessness;

When a nation that has been known for a century for equality of opportunity is torn by unprecedented racial violence;

And when the President of the United States cannot travel abroad or to any major city at home without fear of a hostile demonstration—then it's time for new leadership for the United States of America.

My fellow Americans, tonight I accept the challenge and the commitment to provide that new leadership for America.

For five years hardly a day has gone by when we haven't read or heard a report of the American flag being spit on; an embassy being stoned; a library being burned; or an ambassador being insulted some place in the world. And each incident reduced respect for the United States until the ultimate insult inevitably occurred.

Today, too often, America is an example to be avoided and not followed.

A nation that can't keep the peace at home won't be trusted to keep the peace abroad.

A President who isn't treated with respect at home will not be treated with respect abroad.

Let those who have the responsibility to enforce our laws and our judges who have the responsibility to interpret them be dedicated to the great principles of civil rights.

But let them also recognize that the first civil right of every American is to be free from domestic violence, and that right must be guaranteed in this country.

And to those who say that law and order is the code word for racism, there and here is a reply:

Our goal is justice for every American. If we are to have respect for law in America, we must have laws that deserve respect.

Government can pass laws. But respect for law can come only from people who take the law into their hearts and their minds—and not into their hands.

Government can provide opportunity. But opportunity means nothing unless people are prepared to seize it.

A President can ask for reconciliation in the racial conflict that divides Americans. But reconciliation comes only from the hearts of people.

The responsibility for "ours becoming a lawless society," as Nixon had earlier claimed, was U.S. Supreme Court chief justice Earl Warren's to bear. Law and order as well as the Court's liberalism became the single most dominant theme of the Nixon campaign. Changing the composition of the Court, then, was an important dimension of the Southern Strategy. The strategy was not an overt appeal to racism but instead was a more subtle attempt to deal with unlawful behavior and urban disorder by rolling back Court decisions that extended civil rights. In that respect, Nixon could separate himself from the segregationist candidacy of George Wallace, for example, but still level a compelling critique of the soft-on-crime decisions of the Warren Court.

The next President of the United States will face challenges which in some ways will be greater than those of Washington or Lincoln. Because for the first time in our nation's history, an American President will face not only the problem of restoring peace abroad but of restoring peace at home.

My fellow Americans, the long dark night for America is about to end.

Source: "Richard Nixon: Address Accepting the Presidential Nomination at the Republican National Convention in Miami Beach, Florida, August 8, 1968." The American Presidency Project, http://www.presidency.ucsb.edu/ws/?pid=25968.

Ribicoff: "Gestapo Tactics in the Streets of Chicago!"

Abraham Ribicoff's Speech Nominating George McGovern for the U.S. Presidency

August 28, 1968

INTRODUCTION

By 1968, Senator Abe Ribicoff of Connecticut had been in public life for a hearty three decades. He was a well-respected Democrat and a longtime friend of the Kennedy family. In fact, John F. Kennedy had asked Ribicoff to serve in his cabinet in 1960. After the withdrawal of Lyndon Johnson from the presidential race and in the wake of the assassination of Robert Kennedy, Ribicoff aligned himself with several antiwar presidential candidates, eventually backing the liberal Senator George McGovern of South Dakota. McGovern stood little chance of winning the nomination in 1968, but Ribicoff's nomination speech turned into a verbal assault on Establishment elements of the party who had seemed to turn a deaf ear to the growing antiwar movement.

George McGovern is a man full of goodness. He is a man without guile. He is a whole man. And because he is a whole man, he can bring a sense of wholeness to a divided nation that so desperately needs its parts put together.

George McGovern is a man who has peace in his soul. And because George McGovern has peace in his soul, he can translate that peace to our cities, our states, the nation, and this world.

The basic problem that we face here tonight is an indivisible peace—peace abroad and peace at home—and here was a man, long before it was a cause that was popular to espouse, George McGovern in 1963 called attention to the great problems of Vietnam, and its significance and meaning to the United States of America—at home, abroad—in its relationship with all the people of the entire world.

George McGovern understood from the very depths of his being that napalm, and gas, and 500,000 Americans in the swamps of Vietnam was not the answer to the people of Vietnam or the people of the United States.

McGovern was the darling of the Left, due in large measure to the credentials that he carried from the Kennedy administration.

George McGovern, ladies and gentlemen, had another solution for Vietnam. I served with him in the Kennedy Administration. And there, George was in charge for President Kennedy of the Food for Peace program. And George's concept for underdeveloped countries is food; his concept is shelter, education, health, opportunity, and to bring a sense of brotherhood to submerged billions of people, wherever they may be.

I'll tell you why I'm for George McGovern. George McGovern is one of the few men in public life today any place in the world who has passion in his heart and a commitment to the very depths of his soul. And what this nation lacks, lady [*sic*] and gentlemen, is a sense of commitment and a sense of passion for all the people of this entire nation and the entire world.

George McGovern is not satisfied that 10 million Americans go to bed hungry every night. George McGovern is not satisfied that four and a half million Americans—families—live in rat infested and roach encrusted houses. George McGovern is not satisfied that in this nation of ours—in this great nation of ours—our infant mortality is so high that we rank 21st in all the nations of the world.

George McGovern brings out of the prairies of South Dakota a new wind, a wind that will be able to lift the smog of uncertainty from throughout our great land of ours. We need unity; and we can only have unity with a new face and new ideas and new ideals. The youth of America rallied to the standards of men like George McGovern like they did to the standards of John F. Kennedy and Robert Kennedy.

This was clearly the most powerful and most memorable part of the speech. Ribicoff, rather explicitly, was accusing Richard Daley, mayor of Chicago and head of the Cook County Democratic Committee, of using violent, brutal tactics. Ribicoff was referring to the massive numbers of Chicago police officers who moved in to the streets surrounding the International Amphitheatre (where Ribicoff was giving his speech) to break up the antiwar protests. Rather than simply dispelling the crowd, the police used tear gas and wooden clubs. They showed little restraint, and the result was a violent, awful spectacle. All of it was shown on live television. Democrats, many of them young, were speaking out against the war in Vietnam, and the Chicago police were pounding them into submission. Many protesters were hauled away in handcuffs with blood streaming down their faces.

And with George McGovern as President of the United States we wouldn't have to have Gestapo tactics in the streets of Chicago!

With George McGovern we wouldn't have a National Guard. You bet. You bet.

[Prolonged cheers and boos from various quarters of the audience, including shouts of "You faker!" from Mayor Richard Daley, among others around him.]

How hard it is—How hard it is—How hard it is to accept the truth.

How hard it is to accept the truth, when we know the problems facing our nation.

350 years ago, some 350 years ago, a handful of Englishmen came to the rock-bound New England coast, and millions more followed them. And they crossed the Connecticut River, and they crossed the Hudson River, and they crossed the Ohio River, and they crossed the Mississippi and the Missouri and the Rocky Mountains, and they went to the Pacific Coast. And at no time, as they built a nation of 200 million people, did they think they had crossed the River Jordan into the Promised Land. And we built that kind of a nation; and this nation now is beset at [*sic*] problems and there are those, because of our affluence, who think we have crossed the River Jordan and the Promised Land.

But George McGovern is the kind of a man that knows there are obligations and duties that come, and there are burdens that must be carried on the shoulders of all mankind.

And George McGovern in his peaceful soul and his wholeness as a man—George McGovern is a candidate that I am proud of. And I come here, lonely from my own state, without support in my own state, to espouse the cause of one of the greatest of all Americans, and it is a great honor to nominate for the presidency of the United States: George McGovern!

The Democratic Party was coming undone. The division over the war in Vietnam and the presidential nomination race of 1968 had left the party in shambles. Vice President Hubert Humphrey received the nomination, but of course he lost to Richard Nixon in November. This year, and in a very real sense this speech, marked a change in the way the party would conduct presidential nominations.

The current process relies on binding primaries and caucuses to nominate candidates and essentially leaves party bosses, such as Richard Daley, on the sidelines. But does it really make sense to leave party leaders out of the process? Many scholars suggest that there are downsides to relying on average party followers to select the party nominees, not the least of which is the possibility of internal strife—as was the case in 1968.

Source: Abraham Ribicoff, "Speech Nominating George McGovern for the U.S. Presidency: Delivered 28 August 1968, Democratic National Convention, Chicago, Illinois." American Rhetoric Online Speech Bank, http://www.americanrhetoric.com/speeches/abrahamribicoff1968dnc.htm.

Election of 1972

McGovern-Fraser Commission Report

Report for the Democratic National Committee by the McGovern-Fraser Commission

1971

INTRODUCTION

In two very concrete ways, the Democratic National Committee suffered humiliating defeats in 1968. First, the presidential nominating process seemed to tear the party apart. On one side of an epic battle was the party Establishment: the national, state, and local party leaders. These party bosses supported President Lyndon Johnson for the nomination until he decided not to run and then backed Vice President Hubert Humphrey. On the other side of the dispute was the anti–Vietnam War activist, who did not back either Johnson or Humphrey because they were thought to be the pro–war candidates. The clash between these wings of the party became vivid at the 1968 Democratic National Convention in Chicago that summer. Second, the party lost the general election to Richard Nixon.

In response to these two events, the Democratic Party set up a commission to explore the failings of the presidential nominating process. The commission was headed by South Dakota Senator George McGovern and Minnesota House member Donald Fraser. Presented here is an excerpt from that report.

For more than a century, party leaders were at the center of the presidential nominating process. A small percentage of states selected their delegates to the nomination conventions by primary elections, but most simply allowed local party leaders to handpick delegates. Thus, the system was very much driven by elites.

The outcome of the report and the subsequent new rules by the Democratic National Committee has been the adoption of binding primaries and caucuses. This means that average party followers are allowed to express their preferences at either elections (primaries) or meetings (caucuses) and that these preferences will be used to select delegates who are bound to support particular candidates. In other words, the role of local party leaders was greatly reduced.

B-2   Clarity of Purpose

An opportunity for full participation in the delegate selection process is not meaningful unless each Party member can clearly express his preference for candidates for delegates to the National Convention, or for those who will select such delegates. In many States, a Party member who wishes to affect the selection of the delegation must do so by voting for delegates or Party officials who will engage in many activities unrelated to the delegate selection process.

Whenever other Party business is mixed, without differentiation, with the delegate selection process, the Commission requires State Parties to make it clear to voters how they are participating in a process that will nominate their Party's candidate of President. Furthermore, in States which employ a convention or committee system, the Commission requires State Parties to clearly designate the delegate selection procedures as distinct from other Party business. . . .

B-5   Unit Rule

In 1968, many States used the unit rule at various stages in the processes by which delegates were selected to the National Convention. The 1968 Convention defined unit rule, did not enforce the unit rule on any delegation in 1968, and added language to the 1972 Call requiring that "the unit rule not be used in any stage of the delegate selection process." In light of the Convention action, the Commission requires State Parties to add to their explicit written rules provision which forbid the use of the unit rule or the practice of instructing delegates to votes against their stated preferences at any state of the delegate selection process.

The unit rule was deemed unfair because it would allot delegates based on a proportional system. This means that if candidate A netted 40 percent and candidates B and C each got 30 percent of the vote share, only candidate A would win delegates. The new system would rely on a proportional system.

B-6   Adequate Representation of Minority Views on Presidential Candidates at Each Stage in the Delegate Selection Process

The Commission believes that a full and meaningful opportunity to participate in the delegate selection process is precluded unless the presidential preference of each Democrat is fairly represented at all levels of the process. Therefore, the Commission urges each State Party to adopt procedures which will provide fair representation of minority views on presidential candidates and recommends that the 1972 Convention adopt a rule requiring State Parties to provide for the representation of minority views to the highest level of the nominating process.

The Commission believes that there are at least two different methods by which a State Party can provide for such representation. First, in at-large elections it can divide delegate votes among presidential candidates in proportion to their demonstrated strength. Second, it can choose delegates from fairly apportioned districts no larger than congressional districts. . . .

C-2   Automatic (ex-officio) Delegates

In some States, certain public or Party officeholders are delegates to county, State and National Conventions by virtue of their official position. The Commission believes that State laws, Party rules and Party resolutions which so provide are inconsistent with the Call to the 1972 Convention for three reasons:

1. The Call requires all delegates to be chosen by primary, convention or committee procedures. Achieving delegate status by virtue of public or Party office is not one of the methods sanctioned by the 1968 Convention.

2. The Call requires all delegates to be chosen by a process which begins within the calendar year of the Convention. Ex-officio delegates usually were elected (or appointed) to their positions before the calendar year of the Convention.

3. The Call requires all delegates to be chosen by a process in which all Democrats have a full and meaningful opportunity to participate. Delegate selection by a process in which certain places on the delegation are not open to competition among Democrats is inconsistent with a full and meaningful opportunity to participate.

With this provision and many others, local party bosses are stripped of their power to control the nominating process.

Accordingly, the Commission requires State Parties to repeal Party rules or resolution which provide for ex-officio delegates. When State law controls, the Commission requires State Parties to make all feasible efforts to repeal, amend or otherwise modify such laws to accomplish the stated purpose. . . .

C-4   Premature Delegate Selection (timeliness)

The 1968 Convention adopted language adding to the Call to the 1972 Convention the requirement that the delegate selection process must begin within the calendar year of the Convention. In many States, Governors, State Chairmen, State, district and county committees who are chosen before the calendar year of the Convention, select—or choose agents to select—the delegates. These practices are inconsistent with the Call.

The Commission believes that the 1968 Convention intended to prohibit any untimely procedures which have any direct bearing on the processes by which National Convention delegates are selected. The process by which delegates are nominated is such a procedure. Therefore, the Commission requires State Parties to prohibit any practices by which officials elected or appointed before the calendar year choose nominating committees or propose or endorse a slate of delegates—even when the possibility for a challenge to such slate or committee is provided.

When State law controls, the Commission requires State Parties to make all feasible efforts to repeal, amend, or modify such laws to accomplish the stated purposes. . . .

Source: *Mandate for Reform: A Report of the Commission on Party Structure and Delegate Selection to the Democratic National Committee* (Washington, DC: Democratic National Committee, 1970). Appears in the Congressional Record, September 22, 1971, p. 32908.

Not long after the Democrats changed their nominating process rules, the Republicans did more or less the same. There are some differences between the processes used by the two parties, but for the most part each relies on a vastly more open, timely, and representative process than the method used prior to 1972. Indeed, today's numerous and important presidential primaries and caucuses spring from the work of the McGovern-Fraser Commission Report.

Muskie and the *Manchester Union Leader*

**Don Nicoll's Interview
with Tony Podesta**

February 1972

INTRODUCTION

In February 1972 in the days leading up to the New Hampshire primary, Democratic candidate Senator Edmund Muskie from Maine was ahead in the polls against his closest rival, George McGovern. A deeply respected and towering figure in the U.S. Senate, Muskie enjoyed favorite-son status among New Hampshire voters and was widely expected to prevail by a large margin.

But as accounts later revealed, the Richard Nixon campaign reached deep into its bag of dirty tricks to spoil what it saw as its most formidable general election adversary. The goal of the Nixon campaign was to destabilize the Democratic primaries and smooth the way for its preferred candidate, McGovern. As part of that strategy, the right-wing newspaper publisher William Loeb published two editorials. One alleged that Muskie had made a discriminatory remark about French Canadians (an important New Hampshire constituency), and the other was a nasty attack on the senator's wife.

Muskie felt compelled to respond. On a snowy Saturday, he spoke to a gathering of reporters in Manchester, New Hampshire. There seemed to be tears on his face, but it could also have been melting snow. Contemporary reports revealed different accounts.

In this interview, Tony Podesta, one of Muskie's chief aides, reflects on the event and the consequences of the coverage for the senator's primary campaign. Podesta's interviewer, Donald Nicoll, was also a confidant and staffer for Muskie.

DN: Can you recall the circumstances of that event when he made the speech at Manchester Union Leader?

TP: Sure, he came in the night before, and it was I think the day before that Loeb had written this really nasty editorial about Jane Muskie which had gotten under the senator's skin. And he came in with a, you know, said, "I want to get a, I want a flatbed truck, I want a sound system, I want to go stand out in front of that newspaper and I want to tell that guy what I think of him."

He was, you know, he was, he had a, his, I'm probably not the first person to say he had a bit of a temper. And he was sort of pounding on the table and raising his voice and was really furious with Loeb, and furious with what he had said about Jane, and furious with the fact that he had attacked, you know, brought his family into it and it was sort of really a low blow.

And so we all, you know, he got in at like, I don't know, it was ten o'clock at night and we were all scurrying around to do an open air speech at nine o'clock the next morning, which was not the easiest advance assignment we had but we managed to sort of get it all together. And I don't think he, you know, I think he just planned to speak his mind and ended up, his voice cracked and he stopped for a moment, and he, you know, he finished what he was doing, he got back in the car, we went on to the next stop.

I was actually in the car with him and he said to me, when we got in the car, he said, "I wish," he said, "I shouldn't have broken down like that." And I said, "Oh, you know, it's a human, you're a human being, it's a human situation. People want to, you know, it's not, I don't think people will. . . ." Shows you how smart I was. You know, I kind of tried to say, you know, that it all seemed authentic and real, this was not a canned political speech, this was not something your speech writer wrote for you, you know, you're speaking from the gut, that's what people want to hear from you. You know, what is it, what do you have in your gut that says you should be the next president. So I said, "Don't worry about it, it's a good thing."

So we went on to the next stop, another one, and then he flew off to another state. And I got a call from Bob Squier I remember, saying, Bob called and we had this conver—, he probably had the same conversation that I had with Senator Muskie, you know, was it a good thing or a bad thing, was it a terrible thing and so forth and so on. And Bob said, "Oh no, it's a great thing. It humanizes him; it's fabulous." But it turned out that, it turned out I guess a little bit otherwise.

In contemporary politics, demonstrations of emotion from contemporary politicians are not typically perceived as weakness. Rather, such displays can be positive portrayals of sensitivity and compassion that serve to soften a candidate's image. But in 1972, the public's perception of candidate emotion was quite different.

Saturday, it was a Saturday morning when this happened. Saturday night, the evening news ran, didn't mention it. Sunday the New Hampshire papers didn't mention it,

Washington Post reporter David Broder was among those present to document the event. His account came to be the dominant view of what happened in Manchester. Broder wrote:

"With tears streaming down his face and his voice choked with emotion, Senator Edmund S. Muskie (D-Maine) stood in the snow outside the Manchester Union Leader this morning and accused its publisher of making vicious attacks on him and his wife, Jane. . . .

In defending his wife, Muskie broke down three times in as many minutes—uttering a few words and then standing silent in the near blizzard, rubbing at his face, his shoulders heaving, while he attempted to regain his composure sufficiently to speak."

Boston Globe **didn't mention it. On Sunday morning the** *Washington Post,* **though, David Broder, did a story in which he almost suggested that for someone to break down and, you know, someone to cry in public was evidence of mental instability and therefore how could you be president if you were so, if you were, if you couldn't control your emotions like that, which was on the front page of the** *Washington Post.* **And the** *Washington Post* **news service then circulated and it was, on Monday morning it was on the front page of the** *Boston Globe* **and front page of the** *Chicago Sun Times,* **and the front page of the** *Milwaukee Journal.* **And the next several primaries they had this Broder story which kind of made it all into a very different thing. And it was, you know, and the networks all by Monday night all had, you know, sort of big stories on, you know, is Muskie out of it. Saturday night it was sort of like it was fine, but you know.**

So one of my, you know, one of the things about the whole experience was if David Broder had not been there, no one would ever have remembered this. It was only because of David Broder that this, that Ed Muskie crying became a kind of, you know, history changing political event.

Muskie won the New Hampshire primary, but the margin of his victory was far short of expectations. His campaign ground to a halt as McGovern went on to win the nomination. The Manchester episode was not the only contributor to Muskie's failed campaign, but it certainly contributed to the perception that Muskie was too sensitive and not fit to lead, and his political opponents jumped on that theme. For his part, Broder later came to regret the role that he played by unwittingly being a part of the Nixon campaign's dirty tricks.

The rest of the journalists, you know, Jim Naughton who was covering the campaign for *The New York Times,* **had a story in the Sunday** *New York Times* **on page A27, and it was in the sixteenth paragraph that Muskie's voice cracked with emotion when he attacked Bill Loeb. So it was clearly, you know,** *New York Times* **thought it was nothing, the networks all thought it was nothing. But Broder just drove the story, and then we sort of reeled for a while after that.**

Source: "Interview with Anthony 'Tony' Podesta by Don Nicoll," September 16 and 18, 2002, MOH 374. Used by permission of the Edmund S. Muskie Archives and Special Collections Library, Bates College. Bates College Digital Library, http://digilib.bates.edu/collect/muskieor/index/assoc/HASHacdd.dir/doc.pdf.

Attempted Assassination of Wallace

"Wallace Shooting: A Campaign Altered by Violence" *Congressional Quarterly Weekly Report* **(May 20, 1972)**

May 15, 1972

INTRODUCTION

In 1972, Alabama governor George Wallace decided to run yet again for president. This time, however, he did not expect to prevail. He drew upon his appeal from inside and outside the Deep South to send a message to Washington that echoed his beleaguered everyman brand of populism.

On May 15, 1972, as Wallace was shaking hands with supporters after a campaign rally in Laurel, Maryland, he was shot by someone in the crowd. The shooting left him paralyzed below the waist and forced him out of the campaign. At the time he had been polling well nationally, and he even went on to win the Democratic primary in Maryland.

The Democratic presidential campaign of Gov. George C. Wallace of Alabama was halted, at least temporarily, by an assassination attempt at a May 15 campaign in Laurel, Md.

Wallace, 52, was partially paralyzed by one of four .38-caliber bullets that struck his body and caused internal injuries. Doctors at the Silver Spring, Md., hospital where he was taken expressed hope that later removal of a bullet lodged in the lower spine would prevent total permanent paralysis of both legs.

Doctors treating the governor were quoted as saying they were doubtful that Wallace, the 1968 presidential candidate of the American Independent Party, ever would walk again. But Wallace's aides said they were determined to continue the campaign.

Three other persons—a woman campaign worker, an Alabama state trooper and a Secret Service man—were injured in the spray of gunfire at the suburban Washington, D.C., shopping center on the eve of the May 16 Maryland primary. A suspect in the shooting was arrested immediately and held in Baltimore county jail in Towson, Md., on state and federal charges. He was identified as Arthur H. Bremer, 21, of

Milwaukee. Bremer was held in lieu of $200,000 bail. Federal officials said he was believed to have acted alone and not as part of a conspiracy.

Wallace was shot after a speech in a shopping center, one of several scheduled stops that day. Wallace won the primary with 39.1 percent of the votes and also won the Michigan presidential primary the same day. . . .

Peak Effort. The shooting occurred as Wallace's 1972 primary effort was reaching its peak. He had won four state primaries—in Florida, Alabama, Tennessee and North Carolina—and had collected 210 national convention delegate votes. Wallace said he would not repeat his 1968 third-party campaign in the general election if his views were accommodated at the Democratic national convention. . . .

Reaction. The two chief rivals for the Democratic nomination, Senators Hubert H. Humphrey (Minn.) and George McGovern (S.D.), temporarily ceased active campaigning immediately after the shooting. Humphrey, who went to the hospital where Wallace was taken said, "All I can say is that it is a sad business. It's getting so you don't know what's going to happen in our country any more in politics."

McGovern, in Kalamazoo, Mich., said, "I'm totally shocked by this savage act. If we've gotten to the point in this country where public figures can't speak out on the issues of the day and seek the presidency without being shot, then I tremble for the future of our nation."

President Nixon, who dispatched a White House physician to Wallace's aid, called the incident "senseless and tragic" and added, "Our nation has suffered more than enough already from the intrusion of violence into its political processes. We must all stand together to not permit the shadow of violence to fall over our country again." Nixon extended Secret Service protection to Sen. Edward M. Kennedy (D Mass.), Rep. Shirley Chisholm (D N.Y.) and Rep. Wilbur D. Mills (D Ark.).

Continuation Promised. Billie Joe Camp, Wallace's press secretary, said May 16, "The campaign is going to continue."

Wallace had repudiated his segregationist views of the past, including his infamous gubernatorial inaugural speech (January 14, 1963) but retained his opposition to busing and championed his familiar law and order appeal throughout his 1972 campaign.

Wallace's articulation of a law and order platform was a reflection of a policy that would seem to favor the Democrat. Nixon had run on a similar theme in 1968, but by 1972 violent crime rates had actually increased. In addition, the war in Vietnam was now Nixon's (rather than Johnson's), unemployment was on the rise, inflation had increased substantially, the first whiffs of scandal appeared in the Nixon administration, and growing deficits and dissatisfaction looked to give Democrats an advantage in the 1972 race.

He said the governor's wife and other prominent persons would speak on Wallace's behalf. He said a television campaign would be mounted and suggested that, "the governor could do some campaigning in a wheel chair."

Some observers pointed out that no other figure in American politics could immediately capture Wallace's constituency. His name was to be on only three remaining primary ballots, in Oregon and Rhode Island May 23 and in New Mexico June 6. . . .

He campaigned more openly as a racial segregationist in 1968 than in 1972. His message in the 1972 Democratic primaries had been directed toward the "little man." He spoke about what he defined as the two central grievances of working-class whites: busing of schoolchildren away from neighborhood schools and burdensome federal taxes. He urged his supporters to "send a message" to Washington by voting for him. At campaign rallies, his speeches seldom varied—he deplored efforts by the Department of Justice and Health, Education and Welfare to interfere with local control of schools and he criticized corporations and foundations that did not pay a fair share of taxes. Wallace attracted large crowds to his rallies and stump appearances and hundreds of thousands of dollars in small campaign contributions. . . .

Wallace's populist approach was tinged with racial overtones. On his inauguration to his first term as governor in 1963, he announced a policy of "segregation now—segregation tomorrow—and segregation forever." He admitted that he was a segregationist but insisted that he was not a racist. "A racist is a man who dislikes another man because he is black—he despises the handiwork of God," said Wallace. "A segregationist is a man who likes people and knows that when God made some men black and some men white, He separated us Himself in the beginning."

Wallace would continue to be active in politics as governor of Alabama again and would attempt his fourth and final presidential bid in 1975.

Even though registered Democrats outnumbered Republicans two to one, Nixon went on to win the presidency with 61 percent of the popular vote.

Source: "Wallace Shooting: A Campaign Altered by Violence," *Congressional Quarterly Weekly Report* 30 (May 20, 1972): 1123–1125. Used by permission.

Nixon and the Watergate Scandal

Final Report of the Senate Select Committee on Presidential Campaign Activities (June 1974)

June 17, 1972

INTRODUCTION

Senator Sam J. Ervin Jr. (D-NC) once described the Watergate Scandal as the most severe constitutional crisis since the Civil War. The Watergate Scandal consisted of two separate events: the conspiracy to disrupt and destabilize the 1972 Democratic presidential primaries and the cover-up of that conspiracy.

Nixon's campaign to destabilize the Democratic primaries was part of a larger offensive that included manipulating the news media, neutralizing Congress, destroying the antiwar movement, and dividing the Democratic Party through the use of wedge issues, such as abortion and race.

The political strategy of the Committee to Re-Elect the President in early 1971 and 1972 was unambiguous: undercut Senator Muskie in the Democratic primaries, divide the Democratic Party so that it could not unite after the convention, and assist where possible in getting the weakest Democratic candidate nominated. The absence of a serious fight for re-nomination gave the CRP and the White House the luxury of focusing their political efforts during this period on potential Democratic opponents rather than serious primary contenders within their own party. In the meantime, the various Democratic contenders had to concentrate their own political efforts on obtaining their party's nomination.

Ed Muskie, the popular statesman-like Democratic senator from Maine, soon became the primary target of the dirty tricks campaign of Nixon.

The Nixon strategy was best embodied in a series of political memorandums written by speechwriter Patrick Buchanan and his assistant, Ken Khachigian. The early concern with Senator Muskie resulted from a series of public opinion polls in April, May, and June of 1971, which showed Senator Muskie leading both President Nixon and Governor Wallace in a three-way race.

Buchanan outlined a "Muskie" strategy in a lengthy memorandum to President Nixon on March 24, 1971. Buchanan proposed creating a "Muskie Watch," "an operation working perhaps within the Republican National Committee, which may even be a publicized operation, doing constant research on Ed [Muskie] and putting out materials to interest groups, and to the press."

A few months later, Buchanan wrote:

> **Thus, Senator Muskie is target A as of midsummer for our operation. Our specific goals are (a) to produce political problems for him, right now, (b) to hopefully help defeat him in one or more of the primaries (Florida looks now to be the best early bet, California, the best later bet), and (c) finally, to visit upon him some political wounds that will not only reduce his chances for nomination—but damage him as a candidate, should he be nominated.**

The strategy Buchanan advocated was to force Muskie to take more stands on controversial issues and to have President Nixon attack Muskie "on issues that divide Democrats." The anti-Muskie plan involved much "negative campaigning" against the Senator rather than positive campaigning on behalf of President Nixon. In addition, such a strategy would subject Muskie to the "pressures and harassments that go with being a front runner, pressures and harassments he is not getting today."

In addition, Buchanan advocated concentrating on dividing the Democrats so that they would be unable to unite for the general election. In a July 2, 1971 memo, Buchanan advised:

[We] maintain as guiding political principle that our great hope for 1972 lies in maintaining or exacerbating the deep Democratic rift between the elite, chic, New Left, intellectual avant garde, isolationist, bell-bottomed environmentalist, new priorities types on the one hand—and the hard hat, Dick Daley, Holy Name Society, ethnic, blue collar, Knights of Columbus, NYPD, Queens Democrats on the other.

The liberal Democrats should be pinioned to their hippie supporters. The Humphrey Democrats should be reminded of how they were the fellows who escalated and cheered the war from its inception.

The stated intent of the Nixon offensive was to use the government to ruin his enemies. This included destroying all Democratic candidates' primary campaigns (other than George McGovern's), using so-called plumbers to fix leaks by placing wiretaps on journalists' phones, maintaining an enemies list to target particular individuals who opposed Nixon's policies, and illegally using campaign funds to support these and similar efforts of the Committee to Re-Elect the President.

This "attack strategy" of dividing the opposition was a main tenet of political faith both at the White House and the CRP throughout the 1972 campaign.

McGovern was clearly perceived to be the weaker candidate among the likely Democratic presidential nominees. Given the margin of Nixon's victory in the 1972 general election, that judgment was rather on target.

> By April 12, 1972, Buchanan observed, "Our primary objective, to prevent Senator Muskie from sweeping the early primaries, locking up the convention in April, and uniting the Democratic Party behind him for the fall has been achieved." Further on in the same memorandum, Buchanan rhetorically raised the question of "whom we want to run against." Buchanan's clear choice was Senator George McGovern. Later in April, Buchanan noted, "we must do as little as possible at this time to impede McGovern's rise."

The above strategy, while not improper in itself, was ultimately converted by others into the dirty tricks outlined below. The various operatives and agents of the White House and the CRP also had three major objectives in the 1972 campaign: to weaken Senator Muskie, to divide the Democrats, and to nominate the weakest Democratic candidate.

The conspiracy was uncovered when the plumbers were discovered to have broken into among other places the Democratic National Committee's headquarters in the Watergate Hotel in Washington, D.C. Once the conspiracy was uncovered, another conspiracy began—that of the cover-up. The cover-up was maintained long enough to allow Nixon's landslide victory over McGovern in the 1972 presidential election, but the Senate voted to appoint a special prosecutor to investigate the White House's involvement. Ultimately the evidence did reveal a White House conspiracy and cover-up, and the House Judiciary Committee approved three articles of impeachment against Nixon.

> The absence of primary opponents for President Nixon allowed his political strategists to target their efforts on the Democrats. The abundance of money in the CRP allowed the political operatives to set up a concerted effort to infiltrate and interfere with the Democratic primaries. The result was a campaign to reelect President Nixon that [was] filled with illegal, improper, and unethical activity. . . .

Source: *Final Report of the Senate Select Committee on Presidential Campaign Activities* (Washington, DC: U.S. Government Printing Office, 1974), 158–160.

McGovern and the Eagleton Affair

Excerpts from Thomas Eagleton's Press Conference, Custer, South Dakota

July 25, 1972

INTRODUCTION

Senator George McGovern of South Dakota secured the Democratic nomination for the 1972 presidential campaign on July 12 at the convention in Miami, Florida. That victory only came after last-minute changes in rules that had cost him many delegates in California. His next hurdle, however, would turn out to be more difficult. McGovern now had to identify a vice presidential running mate. After Senators Edward Kennedy (D-MA) and Abraham Ribicoff (D-CT) declined to be considered, McGovern and his staff came up with a long list of options. But time was running out. They now had less than half an hour to file. In the waning minutes, McGovern offered the job to Senator Gaylord Nelson (D-WI), who also declined. With fifteen minutes remaining before the filing deadline, McGovern got on the phone to offer the vice presidency to a man he barely knew and who would not remain on the ticket for long, Senator Thomas Eagleton (D-MO).

Eagleton was quick to accept the proffered opportunity. But in his rather quick conversation with McGovern staffers, including Gary Hart (who would later run for president himself), Eagleton declined to mention health problems he had experienced in recent years, including treatment for depression. He had, in fact, been hospitalized three times in the past decade for depression (he was later diagnosed with bipolar II disorder) and had undergone electroshock therapy as part of his treatment. None of this was disclosed to the McGovern campaign until word leaked to the press.

McGovern: I am very proud of my running mate. The more I come to know Sen. Eagleton, the more confident I am that he is the best possible man I could find in this country. We watched him with great admiration in the U.S. Senate for the past four years. . . .

Now there is one matter that Sen. Eagleton and Mrs. Eagleton and my wife and I discussed here this morning on which I prefer that Sen. Eagleton address you. I am very proud to present him here in my own state and give him an opportunity to say what is on his mind.

Eagleton: In political campaigning it is part and parcel of that campaigning that there will be rumors about candidates.

Rumors have followed me during my political career, dating back when I first ran for office in 1956. . . . There have been some rumors circulating as to my health. Thus today I wish to give you as complete a picture as I possibly can as a layman about my own personal health.

I charge no one here with malice as far as spreading these rumors, but I think it is a legitimate question the press has to ask me about whether my health is such that I can hold the high office of the Vice President of the United States.

On three occasions in my life I have voluntarily gone into hospitals as a result of nervous exhaustion and fatigue. A few in this room know me well . . . and they know me to be an intense and hard fighting person.

I sometimes push myself too far. In 1960, John F. Kennedy was running for President and I was a Democratic nominee for attorney general [for Missouri]. . . . I was in many instances my own car driver. The day of Secret Service escorts wasn't my cup of tea in 1960, and I pushed myself, terribly hard, long hours day and night.

After that campaign was over I did experience exhaustion and fatigue. I was, on my own volition, hospitalized in Barnes Hospital in St. Louis, Mo. . . . The period of that hospitalization, as best I can recall it, was probably four weeks. It started around Dec. 1 and culminated perhaps the first day of January or soon afterwards in 1961.

The Second experience was perhaps four days in length. I went to Mayo Clinic in Rochester, Minn., between Christmas, Dec. 25, 1964, and New Year's Day, Jan. 1 1965. During that week, the holiday week, I was in Mayo's for four days for physical examination. Part of the manifestation of my fatigue and exhaustion relates to the stomach. I am like the fellow in the Alka Seltzer ad who says I can't believe I ate the whole thing.

But I do get, when I do overwork and tire myself, kind of nervous stomach situation. It's one of the physical manifestations of what I have experienced.

Eagleton and McGovern were visiting together in South Dakota to discuss Eagleton's health issue when McGovern confronted Eagleton with a leaked report of his treatments in a hospital in St. Louis. Eagleton called this press conference immediately and disclosed the details of his past hospitalizations to the public. During the press conference, McGovern expressed his faith in his running mate and supported him "one thousand percent."

The third and final time, ladies and gentleman, was in perhaps middle or late September of 1966 when I once again went back to Mayo Clinic, once again for exhaustion and fatigue. The length of that stay, I think, was approximately three weeks.

One could ask and should ask well, in light of that history, have you learned anything. All of us live our lives, I guess, in the attempt to learn more about ourselves. . . . In many respects we are our own worst enemies and took these experiences, these tough experiences, for me to learn a little bit about myself.

I am still an intense person, I still push very hard. But I pace myself a great deal better than I did in earlier years. The past six years, from 1966 to date, I've experienced good, solid, sound health. I make it a regular practice to be as idle as I can on Sundays. . . . In the winter months that's my day to lie on the couch and watch the Redskins and the St. Louis football Cardinals and the Kansas City Chiefs, the last two being my favorite teams.

So I believe and I have every confidence that at age 42 I've learned how to pace myself and learned how to measure my own energies and know the limits of my own endurance. Insofar as this campaign is concerned I intend to give it all I have but on a measured basis, and not to repeat the experiences that I have experienced as heretofore mentioned. So as far as the initial exposition is concerned I've about said all I can and now I'll take questions from the press on any matter that they feel pertinent to what I have just said.

Q: Was Senator McGovern aware of these things . . . before he decided on you as a candidate?

Eagleton: No, he was not. He was made aware of it on the weekend or the Monday after the convention.

Q: How did Senator McGovern react to it?

McGovern: Well let me say, Mr. Schumacher, that when I talked to Sen. Eagleton about my decision to ask him to go as my running mate I asked if he had any problems in his

"I am like the fellow in the Alka Seltzer ad who says I can't believe I ate the whole thing."

"As far as I am concerned, there is no member of that Senate who is any sounder of mind, body, and spirit than Tom Eagleton."

past that were significant or worth discussing with me. He said no and I agree with that.

I am fully satisfied on the basis of everything I've learned about these brief hospital visits that what is manifested in Sen. Eagleton's part was the good judgment to seek out medical care when he was exhausted. I have watched him in the U.S. Senate for the past four years. As far as I am concerned, there is no member of that Senate who is any sounder of mind, body and spirit than Tom Eagleton. I am fully satisfied and if I had known every detail that he discussed this morning . . . he still would have been my choice for Vice President.

Q: At risk of being indelicate did you find during these periods of exhaustion that it affected your ability to make rational judgments?

Eagleton: No, I was in a position to make rational judgments and decisions. I was depressed. My spirits were depressed. This was one of the manifestations, along with the stomach upset, of the exhaustion and fatigue I heretofore described.

Q: Was alcohol at all involved?

Eagleton: Alcohol was not involved in any iota, in any way, shape or form whatsoever, I can assure you—categorically and without hesitation—there's been no trace, no hint, not one iota of alcoholism as part of these rumors—as part of the actual facts.

Q: During these periods did you receive any kind of psychiatric help?

Eagleton: Yes, I did.

Q: What kind of treatment?

Eagleton: When I entered the hospitals, voluntarily as I have described, my physician was an internist, Dr. William Perry of St. Louis. He's still practicing in St. Louis and he's no longer my physician since I moved to Washington. I used the services of the Senate, which is Dr. Pearson and his staff. Parenthetically, not to avoid your questions, I have received a Senate exam and another one at Bethesda Naval Hospital and all the doctors have found so far is that I'm two pounds overweight and have half a hemorrhoid. . . . I was treated by a psychiatrist, Dr. Frank Shobe.

Q: Can you tell us what type of psychiatric treatment you received?

Eagleton: Counseling from a psychiatrist, including electric shock.

Q: Any drugs?

Eagleton: Sleeping pills.

Q: Was the electric shock treatment in all three hospitals?

Eagleton: No. Barnes in 1960 and Mayo's in 1966, not at Mayo's in 1964.

Q: What were the purposes of the electric shock treatment?

Eagleton: At the time it was part of the prescribed treatment for one who is suffering from nervous exhaustion and fatigue and manifestations of depression.

Source: "One's Life Becomes More and More an Open Book," *St. Petersburg Times*, July 26, 1972, 19A, http://news.google.com/newspapers?nid=888&dat=1 9720726&id=u5sMAAAAIBAJ&sjid=4GADAAAAIBAJ&pg=7244.

On July 31, just two weeks after naming Eagleton as his running mate, McGovern dropped the Missouri senator from the ticket. The pressure to do so was intense. The *Washington Post* and *The New York Times* both ran editorials admonishing McGovern to reconsider Eagleton. The Nixon campaign chimed in as well, reminding voters of the order of presidential succession, seeming to say that it would be Eagleton's finger that might be on the nuclear button. Keeping Eagleton was quickly becoming untenable for McGovern, even if he thought him to be a capable, decent person; McGovern's hand was forced. Sargent Shriver agreed to replace Eagleton as the Democratic candidate for the vice presidency. Nixon went on to win in a landslide with 97 percent of the electoral vote. As difficult a situation as the Eagleton affair was for McGovern, it was probably not the only reason that Nixon ultimately prevailed in the general election. No matter who McGovern selected, the campaign was fighting an uphill battle. But surely there must be something to the proper vetting of a vice president; 15 minutes might not suffice.

Ford Pardons Nixon

**President Gerald Ford's Announcement
of Nixon's Pardon**

September 8, 1974

INTRODUCTION

On September 8, 1974, President Gerald Ford announced his decision to pardon former president Richard Nixon. As you might imagine, Ford's pardon of Nixon played an important role in the 1976 general election. The Democratic candidate, Jimmy Carter, did not refer to the pardon directly but repeatedly reminded voters of the Nixon-Ford White House and the scandals that undercut the authority of the office. Ford was simply unable to step outside of the shadow of the Watergate Scandal and lost the election.

Ladies and gentlemen:

[. . .]

I have asked your help and your prayers, not only when I became President but many times since. The Constitution is the supreme law of our land and it governs our actions as citizens. Only the laws of God, which govern our consciences, are superior to it.

As we are a nation under God, so I am sworn to uphold our laws with the help of God. And I have sought such guidance and searched my own conscience with special diligence to determine the right thing for me to do with respect to my predecessor in this place, Richard Nixon, and his loyal wife and family.

Not coincidentally, a protracted legal inquiry and prosecution of the former president would certainly overshadow his vice president's election campaign. Thus, Ford had an interest in putting an end to the litigation.

Theirs is an American tragedy in which we all have played a part. It could go on and on and on, or someone must write the end to it. I have concluded that only I can do that, and if I can, I must.

There are no historic or legal precedents to which I can turn in this matter, none that precisely fit the circumstances of

105

a private citizen who has resigned the Presidency of the United States. But it is common knowledge that serious allegations and accusations hang like a sword over our former President's head, threatening his health as he tries to reshape his life, a great part of which was spent in the service of this country and by the mandate of its people.

After years of bitter controversy and divisive national debate, I have been advised, and I am compelled to conclude that many months and perhaps more years will have to pass before Richard Nixon could obtain a fair trial by jury in any jurisdiction of the United States under governing decisions of the Supreme Court.

[. . .]

The facts, as I see them, are that a former President of the United States, instead of enjoying equal treatment with any other citizen accused of violating the law, would be cruelly and excessively penalized either in preserving the presumption of his innocence or in obtaining a speedy determination of his guilt in order to repay a legal debt to society.

During this long period of delay and potential litigation, ugly passions would again be aroused. And our people would again be polarized in their opinions. And the credibility of our free institutions of government would again be challenged at home and abroad.

In the end, the courts might well hold that Richard Nixon had been denied due process, and the verdict of history would even more be inconclusive with respect to those charges arising out of the period of his Presidency, of which I am presently aware.

But it is not the ultimate fate of Richard Nixon that most concerns me, though surely it deeply troubles every decent and every compassionate person. My concern is the immediate future of this great country.

[. . .]

As President, my primary concern must always be the greatest good of all the people of the United States whose servant

"[S]erious allegations and accusations hang like a sword over our former President's head, threatening his health as he tries to reshape his life..."

I am. As a man, my first consideration is to be true to my own convictions and my own conscience.

My conscience tells me clearly and certainly that I cannot prolong the bad dreams that continue to reopen a chapter that is closed. My conscience tells me that only I, as President, have the constitutional power to firmly shut and seal this book. My conscience tells me it is my duty, not merely to proclaim domestic tranquility but to use every means that I have to insure it.

[. . .]

I feel that Richard Nixon and his loved ones have suffered enough and will continue to suffer, no matter what I do, no matter what we, as a great and good nation, can do together to make his goal of peace come true.

[At this point, the President began reading from the proclamation granting the pardon.]

"Now, therefore, I, Gerald R. Ford, President of the United States, pursuant to the pardon power conferred upon me by Article II, Section 2, of the Constitution, have granted and by these presents do grant a full, free, and absolute pardon unto Richard Nixon for all offenses against the United States which he, Richard Nixon, has committed or may have committed or taken part in during the period from July [January] 20, 1969 through August 9, 1974."

[The President signed the proclamation and then resumed reading.]

"In witness whereof, I have hereunto set my hand this eighth day of September, in the year of our Lord nineteen hundred and seventy-four, and of the Independence of the United States of America the one hundred and ninety-ninth."

Source: Gerald R. Ford, "Remarks on Signing a Proclamation Granting Pardon to Richard Nixon, September 8, 1974," in *Gerald R. Ford, 1974: Containing the Public Messages, Speeches, and Statements of the President, August 9 to December 31, 1974* (Washington, DC: Office of the Federal Register, National Archives and Records Service, General Services Administration, 1975), 103.

As a consequence of the pardon, Nixon would not face criminal charges stemming from the Watergate Scandal that had forced his resignation as president. To many contemporary observers, the pardon would mean that the nation would never see justice done in the scandal. Ford had not placed conditions on the pardon either, which meant that further evidence of Nixon's complicity and responsibility for the scandal would not see the light of day. Some critics even suggested that the pardon was part of a deal brokered between Nixon and Ford. In fact, John Dean, Nixon's White House counsel, suggested that as vice president, Ford was instrumental in obstructing the inquiry into the Watergate Scandal.

Ford had tremendous difficulty communicating his rationale for pardoning Nixon. Skepticism as to Ford's motives for the pardon and a deep cynicism that linked his campaign to the previous occupant of the White House doomed his candidacy. Surely the reaction from Congress and the public could have been anticipated by Ford, yet he chose to pardon Nixon anyway.

Ford steadfastly maintained that he had pardoned Nixon to help the nation heal: to put the ill effects of Watergate behind us and once again return to a time of trust in government. As a few recent scholars have noted, Ford's action was perhaps good medicine, even if many citizens felt that it was deeply problematic at the time. Indeed, the action was perceived at the time to have undercut Ford's credibility and opened the door to a challenge within the party primary from California governor Ronald Reagan.

Election of 1976

"To Restore America"

Ronald Reagan's Speech at the Republican National Convention

March 31, 1976

INTRODUCTION

Not long after the 1972 election, Vice President Spiro Agnew became embroiled in a tax evasion scandal. He resigned from office in October 1973, and President Richard Nixon selected House Majority leader Gerald Ford of Michigan to become vice president. Consistent with the provisions of the Twenty-fifth Amendment, Ford's nomination had to be confirmed by a majority vote in both houses of Congress. This happened rather quickly, as Ford was well known and well respected. It also seemed of modest consequence, because vice presidents, after all, had few real responsibilities.

But the Watergate Scandal forced Nixon from office, and on August 9, 1974, Ford was sworn in as president. One month later, he made the controversial decision to pardon Nixon. Ford did it, he said, to save the nation from a prolonged, painful "national tragedy."

Most sitting presidents are not seriously challenged by prominent members of their own party. But many prominent Republicans considered Ford to be damaged goods after his pardoning of Nixon. The most serious challenge for the Republican nomination in 1976 came from Ronald Reagan, who had served as governor of California from 1967 to 1975. Reagan, a former actor, was popular and charismatic. His campaign picked up steam, and soon the Ford nomination seemed to be hanging by a thread. This speech, delivered rather early in the nomination process, was a clear statement of Reagan's rationale for running for the presidency and of the assault against Ford.

Good evening to all of you from California.

Today, many conservatives cherish the memory of Ronald Reagan. Certainly his legacy as president springs from a broad range of conservative policies. But he had some credibility in reaching out to Democrats and Independents in 1976 given that he had governed California from the middle, and earlier in his career he had actually been a Democrat.

Tonight, I'd like to talk to you about issues. Issues which I think are involved—or should be involved in this primary election season. I'm a candidate for the Republican nomination for president. But I hope that you who are Independents and Democrats will let me talk to you also tonight because the problems facing our country are problems that just don't bear any party label.

In this election season the White House is telling us a solid economic recovery is taking place. It claims a slight drop in unemployment. It says that prices aren't going up as fast, but they are still going up, and that the stock market has shown some gains. But, in fact, things seem just about as they were back in the 1972 election year. Remember, we were also coming out of a recession then. Inflation had been running at round 6 percent. Unemployment about 7 [percent]. Remember, too, the upsurge and the optimism lasted through the election year and into 1973. And then the roof fell in. Once again we had unemployment. Only this time not 7 percent, more than 10 [percent]. And inflation wasn't 6 percent, it was 12 percent. Now, in this election year 1976, we're told we're coming out of this recession just because inflation and unemployment rates have fallen, to what they were at the worst of the previous recession. If history repeats itself, will we be talking recovery four years from now merely because we've reduced inflation from 25 percent to 12 percent?

The fact is, we'll never build a lasting economic recovery by going deeper into debt at a faster rate than we ever have before. It took this nation 166 years until the middle of World War II to finally accumulate a debt of $95 billion. It took this administration just the last 12 months to add $95 billion to the debt. And this administration has run up almost one-fourth of the total national debt in just these short 19 months. . . .

Soon after he took office, Mr. Ford promised he would end inflation. Indeed, he declared war on inflation. And, we all donned those WIN buttons to "Whip Inflation Now." Unfortunately the war—if it ever really started—was soon over. Mr. Ford without WIN button, appeared on TV, and promised he absolutely would not allow the Federal deficit to exceed $60 billion (which incidentally was $5 billion more than the biggest previous deficit we'd ever had). Later he told us it might be as much as $70 billion. Now we learn it's 80 billion or more.

Then came a White House proposal for a $28 billion tax cut, to be matched by a $28 billion cut in the proposed spending—not in present spending, but in the proposed spending in the new budget. Well, my question then and my question now is, if there was $28 billion in the new budget that could be cut, what was it doing there in the first place?

Lines of this sort—about fiscal restraint and about cutting the size of government—resonated with a growing pool of Republican voters and activists.

This was a not-so-subtle swipe at Ford. As governor, Reagan could claim that he was not part of the so-called Washington Establishment. Ford, having served in the House for two decades, was thus certainly considered to be part of the problem.

Unfortunately, Washington doesn't feel the same pain from inflation that you and I do. As a matter of fact, government makes a profit on inflation. For instance, last July Congress vaccinated itself against that pain. It very quietly passed legislation (which the president signed into law) which automatically now gives a pay increase to every Congressman every time the cost of living goes up. . . . .

Now isn't it time that Congress looked after your welfare as well as its own? Those whose spending policies cause inflation to begin with should be made to feel the painful effect just as you and I do. . . .

No one who lived through the Great Depression can ever look upon an unemployed person with anything but compassion. To me, there is no greater tragedy than a breadwinner willing to work, with a job skill but unable to find a market for that job skill. Back in those dark depression days I saw my father on a Christmas eve open what he thought was a Christmas greeting from his boss. Instead, it was the blue slip telling him he no longer had a job. The memory of him sitting there holding that slip of paper and then saying in a half whisper, "That's quite a Christmas present"; it will stay with me as long as I live. . . .

An effort has been made in this campaign to suggest that there aren't any real differences between Mr. Ford and myself. Well, I believe there are, and these differences are fundamental. One of them has to do with our approach to government. Before Richard Nixon appointed him Vice President, Mr. Ford was a Congressman for 25 years. His concern, of necessity, was the welfare of his congressional district. For most of his adult life he has been a part of the Washington Establishment. Most of my adult life has been spent outside of government. My experience in government was the eight years I served as governor of California. If it were a nation, California would be the 7th-ranking economic power in the world today. . . .

The extent of state and local government prerogative has been an important issue during all of our nation's history. In the 1960s and 1970s, the federal government moved on an

The truth is, Washington has taken over functions that don't truly belong to it. In almost every case it has been

a failure. Now, understand, I'm speaking of those programs which logically should be administered at state and local levels. Welfare is a classic example. Voices that are raised now and then urging a federalization of welfare don't realize that the failure of welfare is due to federal interference. Washington doesn't even know how many people are on welfare—how many cheaters are getting more than one check. It only knows how many checks it's sending out. Its own rules keep it from finding out how many are getting more than one check. . . .

array of Great Society programs. Many conservatives saw this as a usurpation, a violation of states' rights. Reagan echoes these concerns here.

Recently on one of my campaign trips I was doing a question-and-answer session, and suddenly I received a question from a little girl—couldn't have been over six or seven years old—standing in the very front row. I'd heard the question before but somehow in her asking it, she threw me a little bit. She said, why do you want to be president? Well, I tried to tell her about giving government back to the people; I tried to tell her about turning authority back to the states and local communities, and so forth; winding down the bureaucracy. [It] might have been an answer for adults, but I knew that it wasn't what that little girl wanted, and I left very frustrated. It was on the way to the next stop that I turned to Nancy and I said I wish I had it to do over again because I—I'd like to answer her question.

Well, maybe I can answer it now. I would like to go to Washington. I would like to be president, because I would like to see this country become once again a country where a little six-year old girl can grow up knowing the same freedom that I knew when I was six years old, growing up in America. If this is the America you want for yourself and your children; if you want to restore government not only of and for but by the people; to see the American spirit unleashed once again; to make this land a shining, golden hope God intended it to be, I'd like to hear from you. Write, or send a wire. I'd be proud to hear your thoughts and your ideas.

Thank you, and good night.

Reagan eventually lost the nomination race to Ford—but only by a whisker. With Ford's defeat to Jimmy Carter in the general election, most Republicans realized that Reagan would be a formidable candidate four years later. Indeed, Reagan locked up the Republican nomination in 1980 rather quickly and defeated Carter by a landslide in the general election.

Source: Ronald Reagan, "To Restore America: March 31, 1976." Reagan 2020, http://reagan2020.us/speeches/To_Restore_America.asp.

"Bio" Ad: The Man from Plains

Campaign Ad for Jimmy Carter
1976

INTRODUCTION

The 1976 primaries were the second set of primaries and caucuses under the new rules instituted by the McGovern-Fraser Commission. The commission's report gave rise to a primary and caucus system that limited the role of local party leaders and radically altered the structure of the presidential nominating process.

How a little-known peanut farmer and former governor of a state from the Deep South came to capture the 1976 Democratic nomination for president is no small puzzle. It is clear that for this early postreform primary, Carter provided subsequent long-shot candidates a playbook for making a run at grabbing the nomination in a multicandidate primary. He did so with a national campaign strategy built on gaining momentum through early primary and caucus victories. Those early wins in Iowa, New Hampshire, and Florida generated positive media coverage and increased contributions, endorsements, and campaign volunteers, all of which amounted to critically important momentum for the Carter campaign. The early momentum turned Carter from a long-shot candidate to a competitive candidate as he headed into the delegate-rich primary contests.

Every long-shot candidate wants early momentum. How Carter was able to generate that early momentum had its source in a long period of very effective grassroots work and on-the-ground mobilization in states such as Iowa and New Hampshire. When it came time for the early contests, his was the only campaign that had an effective organizational capacity already in place. He was still a long shot but was no longer unknown where it mattered most—those momentum-generating early contests.

Delegate strategy aside, Carter's message resonated with the Democratic primary voters. Although he was from Georgia, he ceded the very conservative southern vote to Wallace, preferring to appeal to moderates in the South and elsewhere. As you can see in the ad transcribed here, Carter's emphasis is on integrity in government, religious values, and a kind of folksy humility that appealed to many primary voters, even outside the South, given the recent events surrounding the Watergate Scandal and the pardon of Richard Nixon by President Gerald Ford.

[Upbeat background music]

This emphasis on Carter's everyman biography—hard work, thrift, independence, and seriousness—was meant to distinguish him from career politicians, upon whom many voters laid blame for recent events and crises that undermined public authority.

MALE NARRATOR: 1976. Across our land a new beginning is under way, led by a man whose roots are founded in the American tradition.

[Acoustic folk music]

[TEXT: OCTOBER 1924]

[TEXT: U.S. NAVAL ACADEMY]

JIMMY CARTER: My folks have been farmers in Georgia for more than 200 years and we've been living around here for, oh, 150 years.

LILLIAN CARTER: We had to work every afternoon. He didn't, couldn't, didn't have a chance to run around. We didn't have a car phone, and he had to come home every afternoon and work, work real hard out in the field.

JIMMY CARTER: Everybody in the family loved each other. We had to work together. We didn't recognize hardships. We thought we were having a great life, and I think we probably were, and it was a tight-knit family life bound together with love.

LILLIAN CARTER: I never did, I never did spank him. He was—Jim, I never did spank. I might have given you a little licking in passing, but, I mean, a real whipping, I never gave him one. That was, I left that with his father.

JIMMY CARTER: Although I've had a good chance to get an education as an engineer and a scientist, nobody in my family before my generation ever had a chance to finish high school. We've always worked for a living. We know what it means to work.

MALE NARRATOR: And it was the working people, not the special interests, that Jimmy Carter represented as governor of the largest state east of the Mississippi. He gave them an administration responsive to their needs and proved that an efficient and well-managed government can be achieved.

[Fireworks]

MALE NARRATOR: Jimmy Carter's candidacy is truly of the people and for the people. He spent the last twenty-two months listening, discussing, sharing his concern.

In preparation for the Democratic primary campaign, Carter had engaged in a hugely successful strategy of retail politics, meeting early primary voters and introducing himself to them in their homes, stores, and restaurants. He invested heavily in those early contests to gain momentum that would propel him through the later primaries.

ROSALYNN CARTER: People ask me every day, "How can you stand for your husband to be in politics, and everybody know everything you do?" And I just tell them that we were born and raised and still live in Plains, Georgia. It has a population of 683, and everybody has always known everything I did.

[Group laughter]

And Jimmy has never had any hint of scandal in his personal or his public life. I really believe he can restore that honesty, integrity, openness, confidence in government that we so sorely need in our country today. I think he'll be a great President.

JIMMY CARTER: I have a vision of America, a vision that has grown and ripened as I've traveled and talked and listened and learned and gotten to know the people of this country.

[Background music]

I see an America poised, not only at the beginning of a new century, but at the brink of a long, new era of more effective, and efficient, and sensitive and competent government. I see an America that has turned away from scandals and corruption. I see an American President who governs with vigor and with vision, and affirmative leadership, a President who is not isolated from our people, but a President who feels your pain and who shares your dreams. I see an America on the move again, united, its wounds healed, an America entering its third century, with confidence and competence and compassion, an America that lives up to the majesty of its Constitution and the simple decency of its people. This is my vision of America. I hope you share it, and I hope you will help me fight for it.

MALE NARRATOR: On November 2nd vote for Jimmy Carter.

Source: Courtesy of the Jimmy Carter Presidential Library.

The 1976 race followed on the heels of the Watergate Scandal. Carter's appeal regarding integrity in public officials is a thinly veiled reminder to voters of what was at stake in this election.

As you consider Carter's 1976 strategy—to do the intensive early groundwork required to lay a foundation for early primary success—consider the more recent changes that have occurred in presidential primaries. More and more states are front-loading their primaries. That is, they are holding the primaries earlier and earlier in the nominating season. Many scholars argue that long-shot candidates are disadvantaged by this front-loading, as it may have an effect on candidate strategy for generating momentum. If long shots are indeed disadvantaged in presidential nominating contests, our choices for president become much more limited.

The Gaffe Heard around the World

The Second Carter-Ford Presidential Debate

October 6, 1976

INTRODUCTION

Budding students of the American electoral process often assume that televised presidential debates have taken place ever since the historical clash between John Kennedy and Richard Nixon in 1960. In truth, however, general election presidential debates were not held after 1960 until 1976. Republican candidate Gerald Ford and Democratic candidate Jimmy Carter agreed to three events, and they established the precedent of a single vice presidential debate. The material presented here is an excerpt from the second debate, which focused on foreign policy.

Ms. FREDERICK: Good evening. I'm Pauline Frederick of NPR, moderator of this second of the historic debates of the 1976 campaign between Gerald R. Ford of Michigan, Republican candidate for president, and Jimmy Carter of Georgia, Democratic candidate for president. Thank you, President Ford and thank you, Governor Carter, for being with us tonight. . . .

MR. FRANKEL: Governor, since the Democrats last ran our foreign policy, including many of the men who are advising you, our country has been relieved of the Vietnam agony and the military draft, we've started arms control negotiations with the Russians, we've opened relations with China, we've arranged the disengagement in the Middle East, we've regained influence with the Arabs without deserting Israel, now, maybe we've even begun a process of peaceful change in Africa. Now you've objected in this campaign to the style with which much of this was done, and you've mentioned some other things that—that you think ought to have been done. But do you really have a quarrel with this Republican record? Would you not have done any of those things?

Carter would have to fight against the perception that Democrats were less adept at foreign policy and less stalwart in confronting Soviet aggression. In fact, the idea that the Democrats are better on domestic policy and that the Republicans are more skillful at foreign policy lasted for decades. This helps explain why Republican presidential candidates were more successful during the Cold War, even though Democrats continued to maintain control of Congress.

MR. CARTER: Well I think this Republican administration has been almost all style, and spectacular, and not substance.

118

We've uh—got a chance tonight to talk about, first of all, leadership, the character of our country, and a vision of the future. In every one of these instances, the Ford administration has failed, and I hope tonight that I and Mr. Ford will have a chance to discuss the reasons for those failures. Our country is not strong anymore; we're not respected anymore. We can only be strong overseas if we're strong at home; and when I became president we'll not only be strong in those areas but also in defense—a defense capability second to none. We've lost in our foreign policy, the character of the American people. . . .

Ms. FREDERICK: President Ford, would you like to respond?

MR. FORD: Governor Carter again is talking in broad generalities. Let me take just one question that he raises—the military strength and capability of the United States. Governor Carter in November of 1975 indicated that he wanted to cut the defense budget by $15 billion. A few months later, he said he wanted to cut the defense budget by eight or nine billion dollars. And more recently, he talks about cutting the defense budget by five to seven billion dollars. There is no way you can be strong militarily and have those kind of reductions in our military uh—appropriation. . . .

Ms. FREDERICK: Mr. Frankel, a question for President Ford.

MR. FRANKEL: Mr. President, I'd like to explore a little more deeply our relationship with the Russians. They used to brag back in Khrushchev's day that because of their greater patience and because of our greed for—for business deals that they would sooner or later get the better of us. Is it possible that despite some setbacks in the Middle East, they've proved their point? Our allies in France and Italy are now flirting with Communism. We've recognized the permanent Communist regime in East Germany. We've virtually signed, in Helsinki, an agreement that the Russians have dominance in Eastern Europe. We've bailed out Soviet agriculture with our huge grain sales. We've given them large loans, access to our best technology and if the Senate hadn't interfered with the Jackson Amendment, maybe we—you would've given them even larger loans. Is that what you call a two-way street of traffic in Europe?

MR. FORD: I believe that we have uh—negotiated with the Soviet Union since I've been president from a position of strength. And let me cite several examples. Shortly after I became president in uh—December of 1974, I met with uh—General Secretary Brezhnev in Vladivostok and we agreed to a mutual cap on the ballistic missile launchers at a ceiling of twenty-four hundred—which means that the Soviet Union, if that becomes a permanent agreement, will have to make a reduction in their launchers that they now have or plan to have. I've negotiated at Vladivostok with uh—Mr. Brezhnev a limitation on the MIRVing of their ballistic missiles at a figure of thirteen-twenty, which is the first time that any president has achieved a cap either on launchers or on MIRVs. It seems to me that we can go from there to uh—the uh—grain sales. The grain sales have been a benefit to American agriculture. We have achieved a five and three quarter year uh—sale of a minimum six million metric tons, which means that they have already bought about four million metric tons this year and are bound to buy another two million metric tons to take the grain and corn and wheat that the American farmers have produced in order to uh—have full production. And these grain sales to the Soviet Union have helped us tremendously in meeting the costs of the additional oil and—the oil that we have bought from overseas. If we turn to Helsinki—I'm glad you raised it, Mr. uh—Frankel. In the case of Helsinki, thirty-five nations signed an agreement, including the secretary of state for the Vatican—I can't under any circumstances believe that the—His Holiness, the Pope would agree by signing that agreement that the thirty-five nations have turned over to the Warsaw Pact nations the domination of the—Eastern Europe. It just isn't true. And if Mr. Carter alleges that His Holiness by signing that has done it, he is totally inaccurate. Now, what has been accomplished by the Helsinki agreement? Number one, we have an agreement where they notify us and we notify them of any uh—military maneuvers that are to be undertaken. They have done it. In both cases where they've done so, there is no Soviet domination of Eastern Europe and there never will be under a Ford administration.

Here was the so-called gaffe heard around the world. After World War II and certainly into the 1970s, the very apex of Soviet domination was Eastern Europe. Several nations in this region, most notably Poland, Romania, Yugoslavia, and Hungry, were considered Soviet satellite states. In other words, they were nations controlled by the Soviet Union, even though there was a veneer of independence. The very nature of the Cold War involved the expanding influence of the Soviet Union throughout the world but particularly in Eastern Europe. As president and former minority leader of the U.S. House of Representatives, Gerald Ford understood this dynamic, but for some reason he made this mistake.

"[T]here is no Soviet domination of Eastern Europe and there never will be under a Ford administration."

MR. FRANKEL: I'm sorry, I—could I just follow—did I understand you to say, sir, that the Russians are not using Eastern Europe as their own sphere of influence in occupying most of the countries there and in—and making sure with their troops that it's a—that it's a Communist zone, whereas on our side of the line the Italians and the French are still flirting with the possibility of Communism?

This left many observers stunned. Undoubtedly the Romanians and the Poles considered themselves to be dominated by the Soviet Union. The odd thing was that Ford refused to back down from this statement during the debate and for several days after.

It is hard to know the weight of the gaffe. Ford's statement certainly was talked about for several weeks and put him on the defensive. After the election, Carter suggested that "If it hadn't been for the debates, I would have lost. They established me as competent on foreign and domestic affairs." The reality, nevertheless, was that Ford confronted an uphill battle after pardoning Nixon. Most experts agree that the slipup at the debate was embarrassing, but it probably had a modest impact on the final outcome of the election.

MR. FORD: I don't believe, uh—Mr. Frankel that uh—the Yugoslavians consider themselves dominated by the Soviet Union. I don't believe that the Romanians consider themselves dominated by the Soviet Union. I don't believe that the Poles consider themselves dominated by the Soviet Union. Each of those countries is independent, autonomous: it has its own territorial integrity and the United States does not concede that those countries are under the domination of the Soviet Union. As a matter of fact, I visited Poland, Yugoslavia and Romania to make certain that the people of those countries understood that the president of the United States and the people of the United States are dedicated to their independence, their autonomy and their freedom.

Source: "Gerald R. Ford: 854—Presidential Campaign Debate, October 6, 1976." The American Presidency Project, http://www.presidency.ucsb.edu/ws/?pid=6414.

Election of 1980

Carter's "Crisis of Confidence" Speech

Address to the Nation
on the Energy Situation

July 15, 1979

INTRODUCTION

On Independence Day 1979, the Office of the President alerted the television networks to set aside time in their broadcasts that evening for an address by President Jimmy Carter. For weeks, the nation had been struggling through an energy crisis exacerbated by the decision by the Organization of the Petroleum Exporting Countries (OPEC) to cut off shipments of oil to the United States. Lines at gas stations stretched for blocks, as gas was in short supply. Many gas stations shut down. The president's staff was insistent that Carter address the nation regarding the energy crisis.

Instead of using the blocked time that night, Carter disappeared for several days to Camp David, the presidential retreat close to Washington, D.C. Nobody outside of his staff seemed to know where he had gone. While he was away, he redrafted the energy speech that had been written for him. Before he gave the speech, he was quoted as having told his staff that "I just don't want to b***sh*t the American people." When he returned to public view, he gave an address that was initially well received but later was roundly derided by many critics, including Ronald Reagan. As a boon to the Reagan campaign, the media dubbed the address the "Malaise" speech.

At the time, there was escalating inflation and rising gas prices. As a consequence, there was a real concern among many Americans that the United States was being held hostage to the interests of foreign nations. The nation's mood was foul. At the time, some critics— and even a few supporters—of the president argued that it was less an energy crisis than a crisis in leadership. In this speech, Carter framed the issue as a crisis in confidence. "This is not a message of happiness or reassurance," Carter told the country that night, "but it is the truth and it is a warning."

. . . I want to talk to you right now about a fundamental threat to American democracy. . . .

The threat is nearly invisible in ordinary ways. It is a crisis of confidence. It is a crisis that strikes at the very heart and soul and spirit of our national will. We can see this crisis in the growing doubt about the meaning of our own lives and in the loss of a unity of purpose for our nation.

The erosion of our confidence in the future is threatening to destroy the social and the political fabric of America.

. . . In a nation that was proud of hard work, strong families, close-knit communities, and our faith in God, too many of us now tend to worship self-indulgence and consumption. Human identity is no longer defined by what one does, but by what one owns. But we've discovered that owning things and consuming things does not satisfy our longing for meaning.

125

We've learned that piling up material goods cannot fill the emptiness of lives which have no confidence or purpose.

The symptoms of this crisis of the American spirit are all around us. . . .

As you know, there is a growing disrespect for government and for churches and for schools, the news media, and other institutions. This is not a message of happiness or reassurance, but it is the truth and it is a warning.

These changes did not happen overnight. They've come upon us gradually over the last generation, years that were filled with shocks and tragedy.

We were sure that ours was a nation of the ballot, not the bullet, until the murders of John Kennedy and Robert Kennedy and Martin Luther King Jr. We were taught that our armies were always invincible and our causes were always just, only to suffer the agony of Vietnam. We respected the presidency as a place of honor until the shock of Watergate.

We remember when the phrase "sound as a dollar" was an expression of absolute dependability, until ten years of inflation began to shrink our dollar and our savings. We believed that our nation's resources were limitless until 1973, when we had to face a growing dependence on foreign oil.

These wounds are still very deep. They have never been healed. . . .

We are at a turning point in our history. There are two paths to choose. One is a path I've warned about tonight, the path that leads to fragmentation and self-interest. Down that road lies a mistaken idea of freedom, the right to grasp for ourselves some advantage over others. . . . It is a certain route to failure.

All the traditions of our past, all the lessons of our heritage, all the promises of our future point to another path, the path of common purpose and the restoration of American values. That path leads to true freedom for our nation and ourselves. We can take the first steps down that path as we begin to solve our energy problem.

"This is not a message of happiness or reassurance, but it is the truth and it is a warning."

Many of the themes that Carter articulates are still with us. In fact, some people consider this a missed opportunity to heed a call that might have changed our dependence on oil in important fundamental ways.

Energy will be the immediate test of our ability to unite this nation, and it can also be the standard around which we rally. On the battlefield of energy we can win for our nation a new confidence, and we can seize control again of our common destiny.

Here Carter proposes a long series of policy solutions to the energy crisis.

. . . This intolerable dependence on foreign oil threatens our economic independence and the very security of our nation. The energy crisis is real. It is worldwide. It is a clear and present danger to our nation. These are facts and we simply must face them. . . .

Carter's admonition or exhortation to conserve, to forego consumption in favor of a new ethic of responsible citizenship, resonated with the public immediately. The country was being called together toward action for a common purpose. Carter's polling numbers spiked.

I'm asking you for your good and for your nation's security to take no unnecessary trips, to use carpools or public transportation whenever you can, to park your car one extra day per week, to obey the speed limit, and to set your thermostats to save fuel. Every act of energy conservation like this is more than just common sense—I tell you it is an act of patriotism.

[. . .]

Every gallon of oil each one of us saves is a new form of production. It gives us more freedom, more confidence, that much more control over our own lives.

So, the solution of our energy crisis can also help us to conquer the crisis of the spirit in our country. It can rekindle our sense of unity, our confidence in the future, and give our nation and all of us individually a new sense of purpose.

[. . .]

Although the address was initially well received, the Republicans turned the narrative on its head. In this new narrative, the speech was pessimistic and defeatist. Ronald Reagan's 1980 presidential campaign used Carter's speech to great effect to distinguish Reagan's optimism and hope for America's future.

The Reagan campaign sought to draw important distinctions between Carter's message of conservation, thrift, and shared sacrifice and Reagan's own message of hope, optimism, and the national unity necessary to be a "shining city on a hill." On the eve of the general election, Reagan again reminded voters of Carter's address in July:

"I find no national malaise, I find nothing wrong with the American people. . . . If you feel that Mr. Carter has faithfully served America with the kind of competence and distinction which deserve four more years in office, then you should vote for him. If he has given you the kind of leadership you are looking for, if he instills in you pride for our country and a sense of optimism about our future, then he should be reelected."

Little by little we can and we must rebuild our confidence. We can spend until we empty our treasuries. . . . But we can succeed only if we tap our greatest resources—America's people, America's values, and America's confidence.

[. . .]

Working together with our common faith we cannot fail.

Thank you and good night.

Source: Jimmy Carter, *Public Papers of the Presidents: Jimmy Carter, 1979, Book 2* (Washington, DC: U.S. Government Printing Office), 1235.

Ted Kennedy's "Mudd Moment"

Excerpt from Roger Mudd's Memoir
The Place to Be (2008)
November 4, 1979

INTRODUCTION

By the summer of 1979, Jimmy Carter's presidency seemed to be in a free fall. Gas and oil prices had shot through the roof; inflation was approaching double digits, as was the unemployment rate; and growing interest rates made the purchase of homes and cars much tougher for average Americans. Responding to growing criticism and his shrinking approval ratings, Carter gave an address to the nation—later to be called his "Malaise" speech. In short, Carter blamed the glum mood of the public on themselves. It was a "crisis of confidence," he said, and Americans should snap out of it. Needless to say, this did not go over well with the American public.

By about this same time, there was widespread recognition that Carter would be vulnerable in the following year's presidential election. Smelling blood in the water, Republican candidates were lining up. (Ronald Reagan would eventually be the nominee.) There were also movements in Democratic quarters; surely a better candidate could be found.

Soon a grassroots movement in support of Democrat Edward M. "Ted" Kennedy gathered steam. Kennedy, a Senator from Massachusetts and the last of the Kennedy brothers, was the darling of the liberal wing of the party—a group that never really trusted Carter. Kennedy was popular but was also scarred by a decade-old scandal: late one summer evening in 1969, his car veered off a bridge on Chappaquiddick Island, Massachusetts, and a young woman with him had drowned.

On the occasion of this excerpt, Kennedy agreed to give a one-hour live interview with CBS reporter Roger Mudd. Lengthy live interviews are always risky for candidates, but Kennedy was well versed on myriad policy questions, and he did not expect too many tough questions from Mudd, who was thought to be somewhat of a Kennedy family friend.

But to the surprise of many, Kennedy slipped up. Mudd had asked the simplest of questions: Why do you want to be president of the United States? Presented here are Mudd's recollections of the interview.

What attracted the most attention was the senator's helpless, hopeless answer to the question "Why do you want to be president?" It was probably the slowest pitch I'd ever thrown at a presidential candidate, slow enough that the senator could have seen the stitches on the ball. So basic was the question and so easy should have been the answer that most reporters never asked it, for fear of being labeled pushovers. The question gained notoriety—Daniel Schorr henceforth referred to it as "the Roger Mudd Question"—because of

"I had again hit the Kennedy stonewall, and there seemed no way to get over, around, under, or through it. So I changed the subject."

the answer, almost a parody of a politician's circumlocution. If Kennedy had been a southerner, his answer would have come right out of the mouth of Senator Claghorn.

My question, which I asked during our interview in his Senate office on October 12, came after I had gone back over Chappaquiddick, over Judge James Boyle's findings in the case, over whether the public feared he might panic again, and the suggestion in the Manchester Guardian that he would choke during a nuclear crisis. The senator's answers were a virtual replay of what he'd said to me back in August on Cape Cod. I had again hit the Kennedy stone wall, and there seemed no way to get over, around, under, or through it. So I changed the subject:

MUDD: Why do you want to be president?

KENNEDY: Well, I'm—were I to make the announcement, and to run, the reasons I would run is because I have a great belief in this country. That it is—there's more natural resources than any nation in the world; there's the greatest education population in the world; the greatest technology of any country in the world; the greatest capacity for innovation in the world; and the greatest political system in the world. And yet I see at the current time that most of the industrial nations of the world are exceeding us in terms of productivity and are doing better than us in terms of meeting the problems of inflation; that they're dealing with their problems of energy and their problems of unemployment. It just seems to me that this nation can cope and deal with its problems in a way that it has in the past; we're facing complex issues and problems in this nation at this time and that we have faced similar challenges at other times. And the energies and resourcefulness of this nation, I think, should be focused on these problems in a way that brings a sense of restoration in this country by its people to—in dealing with the problems that we face: primarily the issues on the economy, the problems of inflation, and the problems of—energy. And I would basically feel that—it's imperative for this country to either move forward; that it can't stand still or otherwise it moves backward. And that leadership for this nation can galvanize a—a—an effort with a team to try and deal with these problems that we're facing in our nation, and can be effective in trying to cope with the problems that we'd face. And I think that'd be the real challenge in—in the 1980s. I think it's a watershed period in our country, from a variety of different points, primarily from an energy point of view and from an economic point of view.

His answer contained 336 words and we used the first 242 of them, stopping with the sentence that ended with "or otherwise it moves backward."

"Oh, my God," I thought. "He doesn't know. He doesn't know why he's running." His sentences did not parse, his words walked over themselves as he kept repeating that the country had problems of energy, and inflation, and unemployment, and inflation, and energy, and unemployment. It never got much better than that.

Source: Roger Mudd, *The Place to Be: Washington, CBS, and the Glory Days of Television News* (New York: PublicAffairs, 2008), 355–356. Used by permission.

When candidates for the presidency approach the arduous task of running for more than a year, of meeting reporters and voters day in and day out, the very first and most essential step is to be able to clearly and powerfully articulate why they would want to be president. Kennedy was not able to do that in this interview. His vague, unprepared response suggested that either he did not have the fire in his gut to run for the presidency or that he had somehow assumed that he would be ordained the Democratic nominee, that he would not have to work for it.

Kennedy announced his candidacy a few months later. He was able to win several primaries against Jimmy Carter, but the last Kennedy presidential campaign never really got off the ground. Kennedy's response to Mudd's simple question proved to be prophetic.

Failed Rescue Mission

President Jimmy Carter's Address to the Nation on the Failed Attempt to Rescue American Embassy Hostages Held in Iran

April 25, 1980

INTRODUCTION

On November 4, 1979, a group of Islamist students and militants took over the American embassy in Tehran, Iran. This was part of the so-called Iranian Revolution in which the secular monarchy was replaced by religious fundamentalists. The outrage of the students and militants centered on what they perceived to be the influence of the United States on Iranian politics and culture. As part of the takeover, they captured and held hostage 66 American men and women; 13 of the hostages were released later that month, and another hostage was released in July 1980. The following is an excerpt from a speech delivered by President Jimmy Carter.

At the time, it seemed that freeing the hostages would be a simple matter. These rebels were mostly students and ragtag elements of an already weak military, and the United States was the world's military superpower. But the hostages were kept in the recesses of the embassy, and storming the facility would have likely led to their death. Carter and the American military were stymied, and as the days and weeks of the hostages' captivity continued, a call for action grew. On April 24, President Carter authorized a small-scale military rescue operation.

This announcement stunned the American public. How could such a small and seemingly insignificant nation stymie the United States, and how could American military lives be lost? Keep in mind that we were still in the Cold War with the Soviet Union, and perceptions regarding each nation's military prowess seemed to have serious repercussions.

Late yesterday, I cancelled a carefully planned operation which was underway in Iran to position our rescue team for later withdrawal of American hostages, who have been held captive there since November 4. Equipment failure in the rescue helicopters made it necessary to end the mission.

As our team was withdrawing, after my order to do so, two of our American aircraft collided on the ground following a refueling operation in a remote desert location in Iran. Other information about this rescue mission will be made available to the American people when it is appropriate to do so.

There was no fighting; there was no combat. But to my deep regret, eight of the crewmen of the two aircraft which collided were killed, and several other Americans were hurt in the accident. Our people were immediately airlifted from Iran. Those who were injured have gotten medical treatment, and all of them are expected to recover.

No knowledge of this operation by any Iranian officials or authorities was evident to us until several hours after all Americans were withdrawn from Iran.

Our rescue team knew and I knew that the operation was certain to be difficult and it was certain to be dangerous. We were all convinced that if and when the rescue operation had been commenced that it had an excellent chance of success. They were all volunteers; they were all highly trained. I met with their leaders before they went on this operation. They knew then what hopes of mine and of all Americans they carried with them.

To the families of those who died and who were wounded, I want to express the admiration I feel for the courage of their loved ones and the sorrow that I feel personally for their sacrifice.

The mission on which they were embarked was a humanitarian mission. It was not directed against Iran; it was not directed against the people of Iran. It was not undertaken with any feeling of hostility toward Iran or its people. It has caused no Iranian casualties.

There continued to be hopes that a wedge might develop between the Iranian people and the radicals at the embassy. These hopes would be dashed during the crisis and in the years and decades to follow.

Planning for this rescue effort began shortly after our Embassy was seized, but for a number of reasons, I waited until now to put those rescue plans into effect. To be feasible, this complex operation had to be the product of intensive planning and intensive training and repeated rehearsal. However, a resolution of this crisis through negotiations and with voluntary action on the part of the Iranian officials was obviously then, has been, and will be preferable.

This rescue attempt had to await my judgment that the Iranian authorities could not or would not resolve this crisis on their own initiative. With the steady unraveling of authority in Iran and the mounting dangers that were posed to the safety of the hostages themselves and the growing realization that their early release was highly unlikely, I made a decision to commence the rescue operations plans.

This attempt became a necessity and a duty. The readiness of our team to undertake the rescue made it completely practicable. Accordingly, I made the decision to set our long-developed plans into operation. I ordered this rescue mission prepared in order to safeguard American lives, to protect

America's national interests, and to reduce the tensions in the world that have been caused among many nations as this crisis has continued.

One of the toughest parts of being the president of the United States—and there are many—is making the final decision to put military personnel in harm's way. Lives are lost, and the burden of those deaths falls on the president. Carter surely felt anguish over the loss of life in the rescue attempt.

It was my decision to attempt the rescue operation. It was my decision to cancel it when problems developed in the placement of our rescue team for a future rescue operation. The responsibility is fully my own.

In the aftermath of the attempt, we continue to hold the Government of Iran responsible for the safety and for the early release of the American hostages, who have been held so long. The United States remains determined to bring about their safe release at the earliest date possible.

As President, I know that our entire Nation feels the deep gratitude I feel for the brave men who were prepared to rescue their fellow Americans from captivity. And as President, I also know that the Nation shares not only my disappointment that the rescue effort could not be mounted, because of mechanical difficulties, but also my determination to persevere and to bring all of our hostages home to freedom.

It is difficult to know how this event contributed to Carter's loss to Ronald Reagan later that year. We do know that Reagan campaigned on the idea of restoring American prestige and renewing our position as a global military leader. The failed mission to rescue the hostages in Iran was certainly an aspect of that appeal. It should be noted, however, that Carter continued to work tirelessly on the release of the hostages and was able to secure their freedom, after 444 days of captivity, on the day of Reagan's inauguration.

We have been disappointed before. We will not give up in our efforts. Throughout this extraordinarily difficult period, we have pursued and will continue to pursue every possible avenue to secure the release of the hostages. In these efforts, the support of the American people and of our friends throughout the world has been a most crucial element. That support of other nations is even more important now.

We will seek to continue, along with other nations and with the officials of Iran, a prompt resolution of the crisis without any loss of life and through peaceful and diplomatic means.

Thank you very much.

Source: Jimmy Carter, *Public Papers of the Presidents of the United States: Jimmy Carter, 1980–1981,* Book 1 (Washington, DC: U.S. Government Printing Office, 1981), 772–773.

"The Dream Will Never Die" Speech

Senator Ted Kennedy's Address to the Democratic National Convention

August 12, 1980

INTRODUCTION

Jimmy Carter was elected in the wake of the Watergate Scandal in 1976. There were high hopes that he would bring the nation together after more than two decades of strife that involved the Civil Rights Movement, the Vietnam War, and the near impeachment of a president. Yet other issues, both foreign and domestic, crippled Carter's presidency. By the spring of 1980, there was a call for a Democratic alternative, and Massachusetts senator Edward M. Kennedy jumped into the race.

Kennedy did rather well in many Democratic primaries and caucuses, but he fell short of Carter. As noted elsewhere in this volume, sitting presidents nearly always receive their party's nomination for a second term.

This speech at the Democratic National Convention was Kennedy's concession—the recognition that he fell short and that Carter would lead the party in November.

Well, things worked out a little different from the way I thought, but let me tell you, I still love New York.

My fellow Democrats and my fellow Americans, I have come here tonight not to argue as a candidate but to affirm a cause. I'm asking you—I am asking you to renew the commitment of the Democratic Party to economic justice.

I am asking you to renew our commitment to a fair and lasting prosperity that can put America back to work.

This is the cause that brought me into the campaign and that sustained me for nine months across 100,000 miles in 40 different states. We had our losses, but the pain of our defeats is far, far less than the pain of the people that I have met.

We have learned that it is important to take issues seriously, but never to take ourselves too seriously.

The serious issue before us tonight is the cause for which the Democratic Party has stood in its finest hours, the cause that

Kennedy's two older brothers, John and Robert, were both assassinated, and there was a deep emotional affinity for the last brother. He was a beloved Democrat. However, Ted was implicated in a scandal a decade earlier. In July 1969, he was driving a car late at night on Chappaquiddick Island, Massachusetts; his passenger was a young woman, Mary Jo Kopechne. The car veered off a bridge, and Kopechne was drowned. Kennedy did not report the incident for nearly 10 hours. A great deal of mystery surrounded the event. Was Kennedy intoxicated? Why was he with a young woman (he was married at the time)? And did he try to cover up the accident? Beyond the tragedy of a lost life, most agreed that the senator's chances of becoming president ended that summer night.

keeps our Party young and makes it, in the second century of its age, the largest political party in this republic and the longest lasting political party on this planet.

Our cause has been, since the days of Thomas Jefferson, the cause of the common man and the common woman.

More so than his brother John and perhaps even more than his brother Robert, Ted Kennedy championed the cause of the common man. What is interesting about this is that the Kennedy family was extremely affluent—surely one of the blue-blooded families of New England.

Our commitment has been, since the days of Andrew Jackson, to all those he called "the humble members of society—the farmers, mechanics, and laborers." On this foundation we have defined our values, refined our policies and refreshed our faith. . . .

I speak out of a deep belief in the ideals of the Democratic Party, and in the potential of that Party and of a President to make a difference. And I speak out of a deep trust in our capacity to proceed with boldness and a common vision that will feel and heal the suffering of our time and the divisions of our Party. . . .

The 1980 Republican convention was awash with crocodile tears for our economic distress, but it is by their long record and not their recent words that you shall know them.

Ronald Reagan, the charismatic former governor of California, would be the Republican nominee that year.

The same Republicans who are talking about the crisis of unemployment have nominated a man who once said, and I quote, "Unemployment insurance is a prepaid vacation plan for freeloaders." And that nominee is no friend of labor.

The same Republicans who are talking about the problems of the inner cities have nominated a man who said, and I quote, "I have included in my morning and evening prayers every day the prayer that the Federal Government not bail out New York." And that nominee is no friend of this city and our great urban centers across this Nation.

The same Republicans who are talking about security for the elderly have nominated a man who said just four years ago that "Participation in social security should be made voluntary." And that nominee is no friend of the senior citizens of this Nation.

The same Republicans who are talking about preserving the environment have nominated a man who last year made the preposterous statement, and I quote, "Eighty percent of our air pollution comes from plants and trees."

And that nominee is no friend of the environment. . . .

The vast majority of Americans cannot afford this panacea from a Republican nominee who has denounced the progressive income tax as the invention of Karl Marx. I am afraid he has confused Karl Marx with Theodore Roosevelt—that obscure Republican president who sought and fought for a tax system based on ability to pay. Theodore Roosevelt was not Karl Marx, and the Republican tax scheme is not tax reform.

Finally, we cannot have a fair prosperity in isolation from a fair society. So I will continue to stand for a national health insurance. . . .

This became one of Kennedy's signature issues—a system whereby all Americans would have access to affordable health care. In fact, when Barack Obama signed into law the Affordable Health Care Act on March 23, 2010, he made reference to Kennedy's long battle for meaningful reform.

I say again, as I have before, if health insurance is good enough for the President, the Vice President and the Congress of the United States, then it is good enough for you and every family in America. . . .

Democrats can be proud that we chose a different course and a different platform. We can be proud that our Party stands for investment in safe energy instead of a nuclear future that may threaten the future itself. . . .

We can be proud that our Party stands for a fair housing law to unlock the doors of discrimination once and for all. The American house will be divided against itself so long as there is prejudice against any American buying or renting a home.

And we can be proud that our Party stands plainly and publicly and persistently for the ratification of the Equal Rights Amendment. . . .

Kennedy was also a strong champion of women's rights.

In closing, let me say a few words to all those that I have met and to all those who have supported me, at this convention and across the country. . . .

Among you, my golden friends across this land, I have listened and learned.

Tonight, in their name, I have come here to speak for them. And for their sake, I ask you to stand with them. On their behalf I ask you to restate and reaffirm the timeless truth of our Party.

All observers knew that Kennedy and Carter did not get along. But unlike nearly all party nomination concession speeches in which the loser heaps praise on the victor, Kennedy mentions Carter just this once. Kennedy does not reference any of Carter's accomplishments or highlight any shining character traits. It was a very tepid endorsement.

I congratulate President Carter on his victory here.

I am confident that the Democratic Party will reunite on the basis of Democratic principles, and that together we will march towards a Democratic victory in 1980. . . .

And may it be said of us, both in dark passages and in bright days, in the words of Tennyson that my brothers quoted and loved, and that have special meaning for me now:

"I am a part of all that I have met; . . .

Tho' much is taken, much abides; . . .

. . . that which we are, we are:

One equal temper of heroic hearts,

. . . strong in will

To strive, to seek, to find, and not to yield."

Kennedy would return to the Senate and by all accounts became one of the greatest legislators in American history. His presidential aspirations would end at this convention, but not his drive to create a more humane, just society. This would continue until his death on August 25, 2009. Kennedy had become the fourth longest-serving senator in U.S. history.

For me, a few hours ago, this campaign came to an end. For all those whose cares have been our concern, the work goes on, the cause endures, the hope still lives, and the dream shall never die.

Source: Edward M. Kennedy, "Address to the Democratic National Convention." John F. Kennedy Presidential Library and Museum, http://www.jfklibrary.org/Research/Ready-Reference/EMK-Speeches/Address-to-the-Democratic-National-Convention.aspx.

"Are You Better Off Than You Were Four Years Ago?"

The Second Carter-Reagan Presidential Debate

October 28, 1980

INTRODUCTION

Prior to the 1980 election, only two presidents in the 20th century had lost reelection bids. Woodrow Wilson, a Democrat, was able to oust William Howard Taft, a Republican, because minor party candidate Teddy Roosevelt took many votes away from Taft. Franklin D. Roosevelt defeated Herbert Hoover at the dawn of the Great Depression. Generally speaking, incumbent presidents win reelection.

But in the autumn of 1980, Jimmy Carter's prospects of a second term looked grim. Some 52 American civilian and military personnel were still being held hostage in the American embassy in Iran, and perhaps more important, the nation's economy seemed to be in shambles. He also confronted a strong challenger in Ronald Reagan. This document is an excerpt from the second presidential debate that year.

MR. SMITH, ABC NEWS: Thank you, Mrs. Hinerfeld. The League of Women Voters is pleased to welcome to the Cleveland, Ohio, Convention Center Music Hall President Jimmy Carter, the Democratic Party's candidate for reelection to the Presidency. and Governor Ronald Reagan of California, the Republican Party's candidate for the Presidency. . . .

MR. ELLIS, CHRISTIAN SCIENCE MONITOR: Mr. President, when you were elected in 1976, the Consumer Price Index stood at 4.8%. It now stands at more than 12%. Perhaps more significantly, the nation's broader, underlying inflation rate has gone up from 7% to 9%. Now, a part of that was due to external factors beyond U.S. control, notably the more than doubling of oil prices by OPEC last year. Because the United States remains vulnerable to such external shocks, can inflation in fact be controlled? If so, what measures would you pursue in a second term?

These figures were staggering. Prices were shooting up, particularly the cost of gas, and unemployment had soared to nearly 10 percent. Not mentioned here but also significant was growing interest rates. The very stability of the nation's economic foundation seemed off center.

MR. CARTER: Again it's important to put the situation in perspective. In 1974, we had a so-called oil shock, wherein the

138

price of OPEC oil was raised to an extraordinary degree. We had an even worse oil shock in 1979. In 1974, we had the worst recession, the deepest and most penetrating recession since the Second World War. The recession that resulted this time was the briefest since the Second World War. In addition, we've brought down inflation. Earlier this year, in the first quarter, we did have a very severe inflation pressure brought about by the OPEC price increase. It averaged about 18% in the first quarter of this year. In the second quarter, we had dropped it down to about 13%. The most recent figures, the last three months, on the third quarter of this year, the inflation rate is 7%—still too high, but it illustrates very vividly that in addition to providing an enormous number of jobs—nine million new jobs in the last three and a half years—that the inflationary threat is still urgent on us. I notice that Governor Reagan recently mentioned the Reagan-Kemp-Roth proposal, which his own running mate, George Bush, described as voodoo economics, and said that it would result in a 30% inflation rate. And Business Week, which is not a Democratic publication, said that this Reagan-Kemp-Roth proposal—and I quote them, I think—was completely irresponsible and would result in inflationary pressures which would destroy this nation. So our proposals are very sound and very carefully considered to stimulate jobs, to improve the industrial complex of this country, to create tools for American workers, and at the same time would be anti-inflationary in nature. So to add nine million new jobs, to control inflation, and to plan for the future with an energy policy now intact as a foundation is our plan for the years ahead. . . .

MR. SMITH: Now, the same question goes to Governor Reagan. Governor Reagan, would you like to have the question repeated?

Reagan's reference to blaming the American people was a sharp attack. Earlier in his administration, President Carter gave an address in which he suggested that much of the nation's problems were due to a "crisis of confidence." The "Malaise" speech, as it came to be known, did not go over well with voters or members of the media. The nation's problems weren't the president's fault; they were our fault!

MR. REAGAN: Mr. Ellis, I think this idea that has been spawned here in our country that inflation somehow came upon us like a plague and therefore it's uncontrollable and no one can do anything about it, is entirely spurious and it's dangerous to say this to the people. When Mr. Carter became President, inflation was 4.8%, as you said. It had been cut in two by President Gerald Ford. It is now running at 12.7%. President Carter also has spoken of the new jobs created. Well, we always, with the normal growth in our country and increase in population, increase the number of jobs. But that can't hide the fact that there are eight million men and women out of work in America today, and two million of those lost their jobs in just the last few months. Mr. Carter had also promised that he would not use unemployment as a tool to fight against inflation. And yet, his 1980 economic message stated that we would reduce productivity and gross national product and increase unemployment in order to get a handle on inflation, because in January, at the beginning of the year, it was more than 18%. Since then, he has blamed the people for inflation, OPEC, he has blamed the Federal Reserve system, he has blamed the lack of productivity of the American people, he has then accused the people of living too well and that we must share in scarcity, we must sacrifice and get used to doing with less.

We don't have inflation because the people are living too well. We have inflation because the Government is living too well. And the last statement, just a few days ago, was a speech to the effect that we have inflation because Government revenues have not kept pace with Government spending. I see my time is running out here. I'll have to get this out very fast. Yes, you can lick inflation by increasing productivity and by decreasing the cost of government to the place that we have balanced budgets, and are no longer grinding out printing press money, flooding the market with it because the Government is spending more than it takes in. And my economic plan calls for that. The President's economic plan calls for increasing the taxes to the point that we finally take so much money away from the people that we can balance the budget in that way. But we will have a very poor nation and a very unsound economy if we follow that path. . . .

MR. REAGAN: . . . Next Tuesday all of you will go to the polls, will stand there in the polling place and make a decision.

This line—"are you better off than you were four years ago?"—summed up the rationale for kicking Carter from office. The statement was simple, straightforward, and incredibly effective. Reagan knew the answer for most voters, of course, and it was his ticket to the White House. From this debate onward, challengers at all levels have attempted to tap this retrospective evaluation whereby the past seems better than the present.

I think when you make that decision, it might be well if you would ask yourself, are you better off than you were four years ago? Is it easier for you to go and buy things in the stores than it was four years ago? Is there more or less unemployment in the country than there was four years ago? Is America as respected throughout the world as it was? Do you feel that our security is as safe, that we're as strong as we were four years ago? And if you answer all of those questions yes, why then, I think your choice is very obvious as to whom you will vote for. If you don't agree, if you don't think that this course that we've been on for the last four years is what you would like to see us follow for the next four, then I could suggest another choice that you have. . . .

Source: "Jimmy Carter: Presidential Debate in Cleveland, October 28, 1980." The American Presidency Project, http://www.presidency.ucsb.edu/ws/?pid=29408.

Election of 1984

Mondale and Paying Higher Taxes

Walter Mondale's Acceptance Speech at the Democratic National Convention

July 19, 1984

INTRODUCTION

Candidates for public office must find a balance between promising what is possible in government and what the voters want during a campaign. Some scholars have even suggested that it is in the very nature of democratic elections that candidates make promises they cannot deliver. Occasionally some candidate will take a different route, using bluntness and realism to suggest that he or she is serious and has integrity. Straight talk has always had some appeal.

Yet astute politicians gauge the public's appetite for frank talk and austerity. By 1984, it had become clear that the budget deficit was ballooning and that changes were needed. But with the country having gone through serious economic problems a few years earlier during Jimmy Carter's administration, voter enthusiasm for sacrifice was meager, to say the least. In other words, voters were in no mood to pay higher taxes.

The following is an excerpt from Walter Mondale's Democratic presidential nomination acceptance speech. Here Mondale, Carter's vice president, tells the crowd that if elected, he would get the federal deficit under control by cutting spending and raising taxes.

My fellow Democrats, my fellow Americans:

I accept your nomination. Behind us now is the most wide open race in political history.

It was not a particularly close nomination battle, however. Early in the race, there was some speculation that Massachusetts senator Ted Kennedy would once again jump into the contest. But once Kennedy declined, Mondale faced only modest challenges from a few other candidates.

It was noisy—but our voices were heard. It was long—but our stamina was tested. It was hot—but the heat was passion, and not anger. It was a roller coaster—but it made me a better candidate, and it will make me a stronger president of the United States.

I do not envy the drowsy harmony of the Republican Party. They squelch debate; we welcome it. They deny differences; we bridge them. They are uniform; we are united. They are a portrait of privilege; we are a mirror of America.

Just look at us at here tonight: Black and white, Asian and Hispanic, Native and immigrant, young and old, urban and rural, male and female—from yuppie to lunchpail, from sea to shining sea. We're all here tonight in this convention speaking for America. And when we in this hall speak for America, it is America speaking. . . .

I'm Walter Mondale. You may have heard of me—but you may not really know me. I grew up in the farm towns of southern Minnesota. My dad was a preacher, and my mom was a music teacher. We never had a dime. But we were rich in the values that were important; and I've carried those values with me ever since.

They taught me to work hard; to stand on my own; to play by the rules; to tell the truth; to obey the law; to care for others; to love our country; to cherish our faith.

My story isn't unique.

In the last few weeks, I've deepened my admiration for someone who shares those same values. Her immigrant father loved our country. Her widowed mother sacrificed for her family. And her own career is an American classic: Doing your work. Earning your way. Paying your dues. Rising on merit.

My presidency will be about those values. My vice president will be Geraldine Ferraro.

Here Mondale made history. For the first time, a major party would nominate a woman to be on a presidential election ticket. New York congresswomen Geraldine Ferraro would run as the Democratic nominee for the vice presidency. Ferraro would prove to be a strong campaigner and a rather good debater, but her husband would be caught in a financial scandal, bringing unwanted publicity to the ticket.

Tonight, we open a new door to the future. Mr. Reagan calls it "tokenism." We call it America. . . .

We are wiser, stronger, and focused on the future. If Mr. Reagan wants to re-run the 1980 campaign: Fine. Let them fight over the past. We're fighting for the American future—and that's why we're going to win this campaign.

Here Mondale was doing his best to distance himself from Carter by suggesting that the 1984 Democratic platform was much different than the 1980 platform.

One last word to those who voted for Mr. Reagan.

I know what you were saying. But I also know what you were not saying.

You did not vote for a $200 billion deficit.

You did not vote for an arms race.

You did not vote to turn the heavens into a battleground.

You did not vote to savage Social Security and Medicare.

You did not vote to destroy family farming.

You did not vote to trash the civil rights laws.

You did not vote to poison the environment.

You did not vote to assault the poor, the sick, and the disabled.

And you did not vote to pay fifty bucks for a fifty-cent light bulb.

Four years ago, many of you voted for Mr. Reagan because he promised you'd be better off. And today, the rich are better off. But working Americans are worse off, and the middle class is standing on a trap door. . . .

Here is the truth about the future: We are living on borrowed money and borrowed time. These deficits hike interest rates, clobber exports, stunt investment, kill jobs, undermine growth, cheat our kids, and shrink our future.

Whoever is inaugurated in January, the American people will have to pay Mr. Reagan's bills. The budget will be squeezed. Taxes will go up. And anyone who says they won't is not telling the truth to the American people.

I mean business. By the end of my first term, I will reduce the Reagan budget deficit by two-thirds.

This was the shocker. Mondale had just admitted that if elected, he would move to raise taxes. Few candidates before or since have been so bold about this issue. He received applause at the convention, but the reaction of average voters was surely less enthusiastic.

Here and elsewhere in the speech, Mondale was taking on Reagan's supply-side economic policies. This view holds that all prosper when taxes on the affluent and the business class are lowered. The idea is that prosperity will trickle down to the working class. Then as now, this is a controversial approach.

Let's tell the truth. It must be done, it must be done. Mr. Reagan will raise taxes, and so will I. He won't tell you. I just did.

There's another difference. When he raises taxes, it won't be done fairly. He will sock it to average-income families again, and leave his rich friends alone. And I won't stand for it. And neither will you and neither will the American people. . . .

I challenge tonight, I challenge Mr. Reagan to put his plan on the table next to mine—and then let's debate it on national television before the American people. Americans want the truth about the future—not after the election. . . .

We will launch a renaissance in education, in science, and learning. A mind is a terrible thing to waste. And this must be the best-educated, best-trained generation in American history. And I will lead our nation forward to the best system that this nation has ever seen. We must do it, we must do it. . . .

My friends, America is a future each generation must enlarge; a door each generation must open; a promise each generation must keep.

For the rest of my life, I want to talk to young people about their future.

And whatever their race, whatever their religion, whatever their sex, I want to hear some of them say what I say—with joy and reverence—tonight: "I want to be president of the United States."

Thank you very much.

Source: "Walter F. Mondale: Address Accepting the Presidential Nomination at the Democratic National Convention in San Francisco, July 19, 1984." The American Presidency Project, http://www.presidency.ucsb.edu/ws/?pid=25972.

It seems that Americans were not particularly interested in austerity measures in 1984, certainly not for higher taxes. Mondale was defeated in a landslide. In fact, he won just one state—his home state of Minnesota.

Reagan's Age Issue

The Second Reagan-Mondale Presidential Debate

October 21, 1984

INTRODUCTION

On October 21 near the end of the 1984 presidential campaign, Walter Mondale and Ronald Reagan faced each other in a nationally broadcast debate about foreign policy. Reagan's performance in the most recent debate had generated talk about his fitness to continue in the campaign, speculation that was clearly related to his ability to keep up with the daily demands of serving in the White House. In this excerpt from the debate, the moderator, Henry Trewhitt of the *Baltimore Sun* newspaper, poses a very difficult question to President Reagan. His question frames Reagan's age as a national security concern and suggests that even John F. Kennedy—a most youthful president—was exceedingly taxed during a critical international crisis. The age issue portended grave difficulties for Reagan. Given its salience to voters, the president was surely prepared to address the issue.

MR. TREWHITT: Mr. President, I want to raise an issue that I think has been lurking out there for two or three weeks and cast it specifically in national security terms. You already are the oldest President in history. And some of your staff say you were tired after your most recent encounter with Mr. Mondale. I recall yet that President Kennedy had to go for days on end with very little sleep during the Cuban missile crisis. Is there any doubt in your mind that you would be able to function in such circumstances?

Doing no service to Mondale, the moderator senses the moment and pauses to recognize—even praise—the rhetorical brilliance of Reagan's retort.

PRESIDENT REAGAN: Not at all, Mr. Trewhitt, and I want you to know that also I will not make age an issue of this campaign. I am not going to exploit, for political purposes, my opponent's youth and inexperience. [Laughter and applause]

If I still have time, I might add, Mr. Trewhitt, I might add that it was Seneca or it was Cicero, I don't know which, that said, "If it was not for the elders correcting the mistakes of the young, there would be no state."

149

MR. TREWHITT: Mr. President, I'd like to head for the fence and try to catch that one before it goes over, but I'll go on to another question.

Mr. Mondale, I'm going to hang in there. Should the President's age and stamina be an issue in the political campaign?

MR. MONDALE: No. And I have not made it an issue, nor should it be. What's at issue here is the President's application of his authority to understand what a President must know to lead this nation, secure our defense, and make the decisions and the judgments that are necessary.

A minute ago the President quoted Cicero, I believe. I want to quote somebody a little closer to home, Harry Truman. He said, "The buck stops here."

[. . .]

A President has to lead his government or it won't be done. Different people with different views fight with each other. For three and a half years, this administration avoided arms control. . . . And a recent book that just came out by perhaps the nation's most respected author in this field, Strobe Talbott, called *Deadly Gambits*, concludes that this President has failed to master the essential details needed to command and lead us, both in terms of security and [in] terms of arms control. That's why they call the President the Commander in Chief. Good intentions, I grant. But it takes more than that. You must be tough and smart.

It was as if nobody heard Mondale; his response didn't matter. Reagan's quip stole the show, was the lead story in the reporting of the debate, and completely erased the age issue as an important concern for voters. Reagan's polling numbers began a steady ascent that night, never to return to their nadir prior to the debate. He successfully defused a critical point of leverage that Mondale had in the waning days of the campaign. Reagan went on to secure a landslide victory just two weeks later.

Source: "Ronald Reagan: Debate between the President and Former Vice President Walter F. Mondale in Kansas City, Missouri, October 21, 1984." The American Presidency Project, http://www.presidency.ucsb.edu/ws/?pid=39296.

"Morning in America" Ad

Campaign Ad for Ronald Reagan
1984

INTRODUCTION

The 1984 general election pitted incumbent president Ronald Reagan against the Democratic nominee, Walter Mondale. Mondale had been President Jimmy Carter's vice president and running mate in the 1980 election. Reagan's reelection campaign used this political commercial to great effect in 1984. In soft tones and with images that evoke optimism, hope, patriotism, and prosperity, Reagan was able to remind voters of the pessimism of the Carter years (recall the narrative that the Reagan campaign developed for the "Malaise" speech). That message was particularly resonant given Mondale's role in the Carter administration.

NARRATOR: It's morning again in America.

Today more men and women will go to work than ever before in our country's history. With interest rates at about half the record highs of 1980, nearly 2,000 families today will buy new homes, more than at any time in the past four years.

This language picked up on another common theme from the 1980 campaign when at the end of a presidential debate against Jimmy Carter, Reagan asked voters "are you better off than you were four years ago? Is it easier for you to go and buy things in the stores than it was four years ago? Is there more or less unemployment in the country than there was four years ago? Is America as respected throughout the world as it was? Do you feel that our security is as safe, that we're as strong as we were four years ago?"

It was such a success in 1980 that Reagan's 1984 campaign brought it back again. This time around, though, it was employed to invite voters to consider Reagan's own economic policies in the most positive light.

This afternoon 6,500 young men and women will be married, and with inflation at less than half of what it was just four years ago, they can look forward with confidence to the future.

It's morning again in America, and under the leadership of President Reagan, our country is prouder and stronger and better.

Why would we ever want to return to where we were less than four short years ago?

Again, the invitation of a favorable comparison to the economic policies of the Carter administration was clear. The ad was exceedingly successful in drawing distinctions between the incumbent, Reagan, and Mondale by linking Mondale to what the Reagan campaign saw as the failed policies of the Carter administration. It was a deft campaign strategy that ultimately succeeded in securing Reagan's second term in office. The election wasn't close. Mondale would go on to win only one state in the general election: his home state of Minnesota.

Source: "Historical Campaign Ads: Morning in America/Reagan-Bush '84." YouTube, http://www.youtube.com/watch?v=XMJ90T2rwXU.

Election of 1988

Hart and Donna Rice

"Newspaper Stakeout Infuriates Hart: Report on Female House Guest Called 'Character Assassination'"
James R. Dickenson and Paul Taylor, *Washington Post*

May 4, 1987

INTRODUCTION

Throughout much of American history, there was an unwritten rule about the press coverage of candidates: while official business would be fair game, personal issues were out. Voters were not entitled to behind-the-scenes events and occurrences. At times, this rule was taken to extremes. All the reporters who covered Franklin D. Roosevelt understood that polio had caused partial paralysis in his legs and that he could not walk without assistance and could not stand without braces. But Roosevelt was anxious to keep this a secret from the public, so it was never reported in the news. There are only three existing photos of Roosevelt in his wheelchair. He was also a rather heavy drinker and was estranged from his wife, Eleanor, but this was not covered in the news. The same was true regarding John Kennedy's recurrent extramarital affairs and his chronic back pain. Most reporters knew of his sexual liaisons with numerous women but kept it out of their stories.

For a number of reasons—primarily the Watergate Scandal, the Vietnam War, and growing competitive pressures—the privacy norm began to change in the 1970s. Hard-core investigative journalism became ever popular, and soon the private lives of politicians were being covered. Congresswoman Geraldine Ferraro, the 1984 Democratic vice presidential candidate, seemed set aback at the coverage of her husband's financial dealings. More and more seemed to be on the table when it came to covering candidates. But would the media cover extramarital affairs?

The matter was settled decisively in the 1988 presidential campaign. A young, popular, and articulate senator from Colorado, Gary Hart, emerged as the clear front-runner for the Democratic nomination. He had thrown his hat into the ring four years earlier, but most observers thought that he was not quite ready. By the autumn of 1987, it seemed that Hart was destined for the nomination.

Yet there were persistent rumors of extramarital affairs. This following news account, first published in the *Washington Post,* details one of the most dramatic turnarounds in modern electoral history.

The Miami Herald reported yesterday that a news team that staked out Democratic presidential front-runner Gary Hart's Capitol Hill town house determined that a young woman from Miami spent Friday night and Saturday with him while his wife was in Denver.

Hart, whose campaign has been debating for three weeks how to deal with questions of alleged "womanizing," denounced the story as "preposterous" and "inaccurate." He said he is the victim of "character assassination" by unethical and "outrageous" journalism that is "reduced to hiding in bushes, peeking in windows and personal harassment."

The paper, which spread the story across the top of its front page, said that a team of five Herald and Knight-Ridder reporters kept the front and rear entrances of Hart's town house under surveillance from Friday evening until Saturday night, except for a period between 3 a.m. and 5 a.m. They said they saw Hart and the woman enter the house about 11:15 p.m. Friday and saw no one leave or enter until Hart and the woman came out at about 8:40 p.m. Saturday.

Reporters hiding in the bushes seemed a bit much to most Americans, but *Herald* and Knight Ridder reporters argued that Hart brought it on himself. Earlier in the campaign, Hart had dared reporters to follow him around in an effort to show that he was not having an affair. It would seem that his dare backfired.

Members of the Herald team said they would have seen anyone entering or leaving the house during those hours, except for the predawn period. According to one of them, they "napped" during that time.

Approached by the reporters later Saturday night, Hart denied having any "personal relationship" with the woman, denied that she had spent the night at his house and said that she had come to Washington to visit friends. He said that the woman, identified by the Hart campaign as Donna Rice, was in his town house for only a few minutes and that she and a female friend from Miami had stayed at the home of William Broadhurst, a Washington attorney and friend of Hart. Telephones at Broadhurst's office and home were not answered yesterday.

Hart told the reporters, however, that he had called Rice in Miami several times in the past two months from campaign stops around the country. He described the calls as "casual, political." Hart said he did not know what Rice's occupation is.

"The story in its facts and in its inferences is totally inaccurate," Hart's campaign manager, William Dixon, said in a statement. "Gary Hart will not dignify it with a comment because it's character assassination. It's harassment. He's offended and he's outraged. He's furious. He's a victim. Someone has got to say at some point that enough is enough. . . ."

"As you know, Mr. Hart has suggested the press follow him to disprove the allegations on womanizing," Herald Executive Editor Heath Meriwether replied in a statement. "We observed Hart's town house for more than 24 hours from a respectable distance and we conducted ourselves in a professional manner throughout. We never engaged in the practices suggested by Mr. Dixon. The womanizing issue has become a major one in Hart's campaign because it raises questions concerning the candidate's judgment and integrity. That's why we reported on this story."

The story appeared just three weeks after Hart formally announced his candidacy. During that time, he was faced with questions about womanizing and his unpaid $1.3 million debt from his 1984 presidential race. His advisers had hoped that the focus would move on to substantive issues.

Clearly Hart was the front-runner and would have likely captured the nomination if not for the media reports of his relationship with Donna Rice.

The story's publication also coincided with an Iowa Poll showing that Hart has increased his enormous lead over rivals in that state, which will hold the first 1988 presidential caucus. His share of the vote increased to 65 percent from 59 percent, followed by Jesse L. Jackson with 9 percent, Rep. Richard A. Gephardt (D-Mo.) with 7 percent and Gov. Michael S. Dukakis of Massachusetts with 3 percent.

Yesterday's New York Times magazine also featured a cover story about Hart that quotes him on the womanizing issue:

"Follow me around. . . . I'm serious. If anybody wants to put a tail on me, go ahead. They'd be very bored."

Hart supporters speculated that a great deal now depends on the reaction of Hart's wife, Lee.

"If it's true, it's incredibly self-destructive because it means he's been womanizing all the time he was denying it," said one supporter and contributor.

They did not, of course.

Dixon, Hart's campaign manager, expressed confidence that the voters would see the story as false and react accordingly.

"If fair people are given the opportunity to reach a fair conclusion, then we're not afraid of it," he said. "This raises the whole question of journalistic ethics. It raises a question of at what point the question becomes character assassination."

Dixon said yesterday that Hart apparently met Rice last New Year's Eve in Aspen, Colo., at a party hosted by Don Henley, a member of the Eagles rock group. He said that Lee Hart was with Hart at the party.

Hart and Rice met again in March—March 1, according to the Miami Herald—when Hart and Broadhurst were in Miami, where Hart had a fund-raising event. They were on a chartered boat, and Rice and a friend, Lynn Armandt, came on board for about an hour, Dixon said. He said Hart did not remember Rice from the first meeting, so she said to him, "Hey, I know you, you're Senator Hart."

At the time, Armandt told Broadhurst that she was looking for a job in Washington and he offered to interview her as a caretaker for the town houses he owns on Capitol Hill, Dixon said. Armandt came up last Friday for the interview and asked Rice to accompany her because she wasn't comfortable staying alone in the home of a stranger.

According to Dixon, Armandt's job interview took place mid-afternoon Friday, then Broadhurst drove her to the airport to meet Rice. Coincidentally, Hart flew in to National Airport about the same time and the four of them drove back to Broadhurst's house where they had dinner together.

At about 11:15 p.m. the four walked to Hart's Capitol Hill town house, which is about three blocks away on 6th Street SE, according to Dixon. He said they wanted to see a deck being built on the top of Hart's town house; then Broadhurst, Armandt and Rice returned to Broadhurst's apartment while Hart stayed at his house alone.

This statement contradicts the Herald report.

"This raises the whole question of journalistic ethics. It raises a question of at what point the question becomes character assassination."

The Herald said it was told by a "confidential source" that Hart was interested in a Miami woman and that she planned to go to Washington for the weekend. The Herald did not know Rice's name and had no information beyond a general description of her as an attractive blond actress in her late 20s, according to Jim Savage, a Knight-Ridder editor who was on the surveillance team.

Shortly afterward, Hart withdrew from the race. It was the first time in American history that a declared presidential candidate was force to withdraw from a campaign because of a media report of an extramarital affair. Shockwaves were sent throughout the political landscape. If this could happen to a presidential candidate, could it also happen to a congressional candidate? What about a mayoral candidate? The line between the public and private lives of politicians had vanished.

Investigative reporter Jim McGee boarded Eastern flight 996 last Friday afternoon and saw two women on the plane who met the general description. One was "lovingly" met in Washington by a boyfriend, and McGee lost track of the second. After checking in with the Knight-Ridder bureau, he went to Hart's house and saw the second woman emerge with Hart at about 9:15 p.m., according to Savage. . . .

Source: James R. Dickenson and Paul Taylor Washington, "Newspaper Stakeout Infuriates Hart; Report on Female House Guest Called 'Character Assassination,'" *Washington Post,* May 4, 1987, Section A1, p. 2. Used by permission.

Bush's "Read My Lips" Pledge

George Bush's Acceptance Speech at the Republican National Convention

August 18, 1988

INTRODUCTION

The idea of raising taxes has never been popular, and this was particularly true in the 1980s. Ronald Reagan was reelected by a landslide in 1984 due in no small measure to a statement made by his opponent, former vice president Walter Mondale, that he would support higher taxes to offset a growing federal deficit; Mondale's statement was a crisis point in the 1984 election. In 1988 the deficit was growing, but the economy had stalled. There was growing inflation, and many Americans saw their purchasing power dwindle. Few seemed willing to accept new taxes.

It thus made perfect sense that George H. W. Bush would include a finely honed line in his Republican nomination acceptance speech in August 1988. This text provides an excerpt of that speech.

Thank you, ladies and gentlemen. Thank you very, very much.

I have many friends to thank tonight. I thank the voters who supported me. I thank the gallant men who entered the contest for the presidency this year, and who have honored me with their support. And, for their kind and stirring words, I thank Governor Tom Kean of New Jersey—Senator Phil Gramm of Texas—President Gerald Ford—and my friend, President Ronald Reagan.

There is much evidence to suggest that Reagan and Bush were friends. But it also made good political sense to remind voters of their long relationship; Reagan had selected Bush as his vice president eight years earlier. By the end of Reagan's second term, his job approval among all Americans was a modest 53 percent, but among Republicans it was considerably higher.

I accept your nomination for President. I mean, I mean to run hard, to fight hard, to stand on the issues—and I mean to win.

There are a lot. There are a lot of great stories in politics about the underdog winning—and this is going to be one of them.

And we're going to win with the help of Senator Dan Quayle of Indiana—a young leader who has become a forceful voice in preparing America's workers for the labor force of the future. What a superb job he did here tonight. Born in the middle of the century, in the middle of America, and holding

160

the promise of the future—I'm proud to have Dan Quayle at my side.

Many of you have asked, many of you have asked, "When will this campaign really begin?" We'll I've come to this hall to tell you, and to tell America: Tonight is the night.

For seven and a half years I have helped the President conduct the most difficult job on earth. Ronald Reagan asked for, and received, my candor. He never asked for, but he did receive, my loyalty. Those of you who saw the President's speech this week, and listened to the simple truth of his words, will understand my loyalty all these years.

But now, now, you must see me for what I am: The Republican candidate for President of the United States. And now I turn to the American people to share my hopes and intentions, and why—and where—I wish to lead. . . .

"But I'll try to be fair to the other side. I'll try to hold my charisma in check."

And so tonight is for big things. But I'll try to be fair to the other side. I'll try to hold my charisma in check. And uh, no I reject the temptation to engage in personal references. My approach this evening is, as Sergeant Joe Friday used to say, "Just the facts, ma'am."

And after all, after all, the facts are on our side.

I seek the presidency for a single purpose, a purpose that has motivated millions of Americans across the years and the ocean voyages. I seek the presidency to build a better America. It is that simple—and that big. . . .

Some say, you know some say, this isn't an election about ideology, it's an election about competence. Well, it's nice of them to want to play on our field. But this election isn't only about competence, for competence is a narrow ideal. Competence makes the trains run on time but doesn't know where they're going. Competence is the creed of the technocrat who makes sure the gears mesh but doesn't for a second understand the magic of the machine.

The truth is, the truth is, this election is about the beliefs we share, the values that we honor, and the principles we hold dear. . . .

This is America: the Knights of Columbus, the Grange, Hadassah, the Disabled American Veterans, the Order of Ahepa, the Business and Professional Women of America, the union hall, the Bible study group, LULAC, "Holy Name"—a brilliant diversity spread like stars, like a thousand points of light in a broad and peaceful sky. . . .

The reference to a "thousand points of light" would be picked up again in Bush's inaugural address. The passage in that speech, penned by conservative speech writer Peggy Noonan, is as follows: "I have spoken of a thousand points of light, of all the community organizations that are spread like stars throughout the Nation, doing good. . . . The old ideas are new again because they are not old, they are timeless: duty, sacrifice, commitment, and a patriotism that finds its expression in taking part and pitching in."

Should public school teachers be required to lead our children in the pledge of allegiance? My opponent says no—and I say yes.

Should society be allowed to impose the death penalty on those who commit crimes of extraordinary cruelty and violence? My opponent says no—but I say yes.

And should our children have the right to say a voluntary prayer, or even observe a moment of silence in the schools? My opponent says no—but I say yes.

The Republican Party had taken the mantle of a host of social conservative causes in the 1980s, and Bush was merely echoing his endorsement of these policies. This was particularly important for Bush, given that most followers viewed the vice president as a moderate on most of these issues.

And should, should free men and women have the right to own a gun to protect their home? My opponent says no—but I say yes.

The gun lobby then, as now, was quite powerful.

And is it right to believe in the sanctity of life and protect the lives of innocent children? My opponent says no—but I say yes.

You see, we must, we must change, we've got to change from abortion—to adoption. And let me tell you this: Barbara and I have an adopted granddaughter. And the day of her christening we wept with joy. I thank God that her parents chose life.

I'm, I'm the one who believes it is a scandal to give a weekend furlough to a hardened first degree killer who hasn't even served enough time to be eligible for parole.

I'm the one, I'm the one, who says a drug dealer who is responsible for the death of a policeman should be subject to capital punishment.

And I'm the one who will not raise taxes. My opponent, my opponent now says, my opponent now says, he'll raise them as a last resort, or a third resort. But when a

By the end of Reagan's second term, there was growing worry about a rising federal debt. One approach to tightening the nation's fiscal belt would be to cut the size of government, and the other would be to raise revenue. Conservatives are anxious to cut government spending.

politician talks like that, you know that's one resort he'll be checking into. My opponent won't rule out raising taxes. But I will. And the Congress will push me to raise taxes, and I'll say no, and they'll push, and I'll say no, and they'll push again, and I'll say, to them, "Read my lips: no new taxes." . . .

With Bush having lukewarm support from conservative voters early in the race, this statement, repeated as a sound bite throughout the autumn campaign, proved to be an important part of his eventual victory. But of course it also meant that there would be no leeway on this issue, a reality that would come back to bite Bush four years later. That is to say, many observers wondered if his fellow Republicans let the broken promise slide. Many voters in both parties did not, and this may have cost him reelection.

Thank you. You know, one, you know it is customary to end an address with a pledge or a saying that holds a special meaning.

And I've chosen one that we all know by heart, one that we all learned in school. And I ask everyone in this great hall to stand and join me in this, we all know it.

"I pledge allegiance to the flag of the United States of America, and to the republic for which it stands, one nation, under God, indivisible, with liberty and justice for all."

Thank you, and God bless you.

Source: "George Bush: Address Accepting the Presidential Nomination at the Republican National Convention in New Orleans, August 18, 1988." The American Presidency Project, http://www.presidency.ucsb.edu/ws/?pid=25955.

Dukakis and the "Tank Ride" Ad

Anti–Michael Dukakis Campaign Ad
1988

INTRODUCTION

The 1988 presidential election was generally perceived to be a referendum on the Reagan presidency. George H. W. Bush was the incumbent vice president, had significant national security policy experience, was a former member of Congress and ambassador to China, was a World War II combat pilot, and was the former director of the Central Intelligence Agency. As governor of Massachusetts, Michael Dukakis could not boast such self-evident familiarity with foreign policy, national security issues, and military preparedness.

In some respects, Dukakis was lucky that the general election campaign was largely devoid of substance. Had foreign policy and defense been more salient, perhaps Dukakis's appeal would have been comparatively more limited. Due to this lack of substantive policy debate, the campaign came to be very candidate-centered as opposed to being focused on policy issues or economic conditions. Moreover, without the influence of salient national issues and themes, it is very hard for challengers to provide voters a justification for tossing our incumbents. Where substance is lacking, symbols can become valuable tools for campaigns. Dukakis's "Tank Ride" ad came to define a campaign struggling to overcome a perception that it lacked foreign policy experience.

MALE NARRATOR: Michael Dukakis has opposed virtually every defense system we developed.

MALE NARRATOR [and TEXT]: He opposed new aircraft carriers. He opposed anti-satellite weapons. He opposed four missile systems, including the Pershing II missile deployment. Dukakis opposed the stealth bomber, a ground emergency warning system against nuclear testing. He even criticized our rescue mission to Grenada and our strike on Libya. And now he wants to be our commander in chief. America can't afford that risk.

Source: "1988 Bush vs. Dukakis: Tank Ride (Bush, 1988)." Museum of the Living Image: The Living Room Candidate, http://www.livingroomcandidate.org/commercials/1988.

While the Bush team struggled to overcome a deficit of 17 points in national opinion polls, negative campaign tactics proved successful. Sometimes, though, the Dukakis campaign was an unwitting accomplice. The images from this ad of Dukakis in a tank were filmed by the Dukakis people in September 1988 as their candidate attempted to make the argument that he was not weak on defense. You can see what attracted the Bush campaign to this footage. Dukakis just looked a little too goofy sitting in the tank, smiling at the camera in an oversized helmet. In fact, the image resembled Snoopy, the begoggled beagle as the World War I flying ace, the Red Baron, so much so that the ad came to be known as Dukakis's "Snoopy moment." Clearly this did not generate confidence in the Democrat's foreign policy and defense credentials.

"Senator, You Are No Jack Kennedy"

Bentsen-Quayle Vice Presidential Debate
October 5, 1988

INTRODUCTION

One of the most difficult choices thrust on presidential nominees is their choice of a running mate. There are many factors to consider and numerous potential pitfalls in picking a vice presidential candidate. Most nominees seek to use the selection to a vice presidential candidate to balance the ticket, often in terms of geography but many times by picking someone with a different background, different elected office experiences, or a different ideology. There is no magic formula, but most scholars agree that the foremost criteria in the selection must be that the vice presidential candidate will be ready to assume office in an emergency and that the choice must do no harm. That is, although the selection might not add very much to the ticket, the vice presidential candidate cannot hurt the presidential nominee's chances.

George H. W. Bush's selection of the junior senator from Indiana, Dan Quayle, in 1988 proved somewhat controversial. Quayle had been first elected to the Senate in 1980, and he won reelection rather easily 6 years later. He was a true conservative, which seemed to balance Bush's more moderate history, and came from an important swing state. But Quayle was also relatively young (just 42 years old) and by most accounts had done little to distinguish himself in Congress.

The following is an excerpt of the vice presidential debate from that election in which Quayle's age and lack of experience became issues.

WOODRUFF: [Senator Quayle,] your leader in the Senate Bob Dole said that a better qualified person could have been chosen. Other Republicans have been far more critical in private. Why do you think that you have not made a more substantial impression on some of these people who have been able to observe you up close?

Dukakis was the governor of Massachusetts and the Democratic presidential nominee. He had never served in Washington and thus had very little foreign policy experience.

QUAYLE: The question goes to whether I am qualified to be Vice President, and in the case of a tragedy, whether I'm qualified to be President. Qualifications for the office of Vice President or President are not age alone. You must look at accomplishments, and you must look at experience. I have more experience than others that have sought the office of Vice President. Now let's look at qualifications, and let's look at the three biggest issues

165

that are going to be confronting America in the next presidency. Those three issues are national security and arms control; jobs and education; and the Federal budget deficit. On each one of those issues I have more experience than does the Governor of Massachusetts. In national security and arms control, you have to understand the difference between a ballistic missile, a warhead, what throwweight, what megatonnage is. You better understand about telemetry and encryption. And you better understand that you have to negotiate from a position of strength. These are important issues, because we want to have more arms control and arms reductions. In the area of jobs and education, I wrote the Job Training Partnership Act, a bipartisan bill, a bill that has trained and employed over three million economically disadvantaged youth and adults in this country. On the area of the Federal budget deficit, I have worked eight years on the Senate Budget Committee. And I wish that the Congress would give us the line item veto to help deal with that. And if qualifications alone are going to be the issue in this campaign, George Bush has more qualifications than Michael Dukakis and Lloyd Bentsen combined. [Applause]

WOODRUFF: Senator Bentsen—I'm going to interrupt at this point and ask once again that the audience please keep your responses as quiet as possible. We know that many of you here are for one candidate or another. But you are simply taking time away from your candidate, and more likely than not, you'll be causing the partisans for the other candidate to react again when their candidate speaks. So please. Senator Bentsen, you have one minute to respond.

Because Dukakis had little Washington experience, it made sense that he would tap a veteran lawmaker as his vice presidential candidate—Senator Lloyd Bensten of Texas. Bensten was very well respected by those on both sides of the aisle; he was a serious, seasoned lawmaker. He had a good bit of campaign experience too, having thrown his hat into the presidential race in 1976, and was considered a moderate in the party (whereas Dukakis was thought of as a liberal). Also of no little consequence, the so-called Boston-Austin ticket had proved successful a few decades earlier when John Kennedy tapped a Texan, Lyndon B. Johnson, as his running mate.

BENTSEN: This debate tonight is not about the qualifications for the Vice Presidency. The debate is whether or not Dan Quayle and Lloyd Bentsen are qualified to be President of the United States. Because Judy, just as you have said, that has happened too often in the past. And if that tragedy should occur, we have to step in there without any margin for error, without time for preparation, to take over the responsibility for the biggest job in the world, that of running this great country of ours; to take over the awesome responsibility for commanding the nuclear weaponry that this country has. No, the debate tonight is a debate about the presidency itself, and a presidential decision that has to be made by you. The stakes could not be higher. . . .

BROKAW: Senator Quayle, I don't mean to beat this drum until it has no more sound in it. But to follow up on Brit Hume's question, when you said that it was a hypothetical situation, it is, sir, after all, the reason that we're here tonight, because you are running not just for Vice President—[Applause]

BROKAW: And if you cite the experience that you had in Congress, surely you must have some plan in mind about what you would do if it fell to you to become President of the United States, as it has to so many Vice Presidents just in the last 25 years or so.

The issues of Quayle's youth and inexperience would follow him throughout the campaign.

QUAYLE: Let me try to answer the question one more time. I think this is the fourth time that I've had this question.

BROKAW: The third time.

QUAYLE: Three times that I've had this question—and I will try to answer it again for you, as clearly as I can, because the question you are asking is what kind of qualifications does Dan Quayle have to be president, what kind of qualifications do I have and what would I do in this kind of a situation. And what would I do in this situation? I would make sure that the people in the cabinet and the people that are advisors to the president are called in, and I would talk to them, and I will work with them. And I will know them on a firsthand basis, because as vice president I will sit on the National Security Council. And I will know them on a firsthand basis, because I'm going to be coordinating the drug effort. I will know them on a firsthand basis because Vice President George Bush is going to re-create the Space Council, and I will be in charge of that. I will have day-to-day activities with all the people in government. And then, if that unfortunate situation happens—if that situation, which would be very tragic, happens, I will be prepared to carry out the responsibilities of the presidency of the United States of America. And I will be prepared to do that. I will be prepared not only because of my service in the Congress, but because of my ability to communicate and to lead. It is not just age; it's accomplishments, it's experience. I have far more experience than many others that sought the office of vice president of this country. I have as much experience in the Congress as Jack Kennedy did when he sought the presidency. I will be prepared to deal with the people in the Bush administration, if that unfortunate event would ever occur.

WOODRUFF: Senator Bentsen.

BENTSEN: Senator, I served with Jack Kennedy, I knew Jack Kennedy, Jack Kennedy was a friend of mine. Senator, you are no Jack Kennedy. [Prolonged shouts and applause] What has to be done in a situation like that is to call in the—

These lines were delivered slowly, and by the time Bensten suggested that "you are no Jack Kennedy," the statement seemed to be a fatal blow. And it did not help that Quayle seemed to be thunderstruck.

WOODRUFF: Please, please, once again you are only taking time away from your own candidate.

QUAYLE: That was really uncalled for, Senator. [Shouts and applause]

BENTSEN: You are the one that was making the comparison, Senator—and I'm one who knew him well. And frankly I think you are so far apart in the objectives you choose for your country that I did not think the comparison was well-taken.

This exchange became the great sound bite of the debate and one of the most memorable lines in modern electoral history. But it is also fair to say that the impact was probably minimal. Yes, most agreed that Quayle was a bit young and inexperienced, but voters rarely modify their choice because of the vice president. Indeed, bear in mind that Bush defeated Dukakis rather handily a month later.

Source: "Presidential Debates: Vice-Presidential Debate in Omaha, Nebraska, October 5, 1988." The American Presidency Project, http://www.presidency.ucsb.edu/ws/?pid=29424.

Dukakis and the Death Penalty Question

The Second Bush-Dukakis Presidential Debate

October 13, 1988

INTRODUCTION

The 1988 Republican nominee for president was George H. W. Bush, the sitting vice president for two terms under Ronald Reagan. Michael Dukakis, governor of Massachusetts, was the Democratic nominee. The political and economic environment was a boon to the incumbent party. There were no major economic issues, nor did foreign affairs crises dominate the nation's attention.

The challenge for Dukakis was to make the case against the incumbent. Dukakis tried to draw Bush out on his involvement in the Iran-Contra Affair, but Bush refused to engage the issue. Dukakis argued that Bush was too bellicose in foreign affairs and too insensitive to the needs of the poor and the rights of disadvantaged groups in society. In making these arguments, Dukakis was then exposing himself to Bush's countercharge that Dukakis was too weak on defense, too liberal in domestic policy, and too ill-prepared in foreign affairs.

In addition to the distinctions that arose from their policy disputes, Dukakis was further distinguished for his lack of emotion during the campaign. He struggled to show sincerity and deep empathy and understanding that is so often necessary in candidate-centered (rather than issue-centered) campaigns. As the candidates met for their second debate, Dukakis needed to overcome the sense that voters had about his icy demeanor.

Kitty Dukakis, Governor Dukakis's wife, would later remark that she thought the question was unfair and in poor taste. In Bernard Shaw's judgment, it was precisely the kind of question that ought to have been asked. It forced the well-rehearsed candidate into an uncomfortable position by demanding an answer to a question that needled him right where he was most sensitive. For Bush, it was his selection of Dan Quayle as his running mate. For Dukakis, it was his image that he was soft on crime and was also emotionless. The audience was prepared for an emotional reaction, but Dukakis did not abide.

SHAW: On behalf of the Commission on Presidential Debates, I am pleased to welcome you to the second presidential debate. I am Bernard Shaw of CNN, Cable News Network. My colleagues on the panel are Ann Compton of ABC NEWS; Margaret Warner of Newsweek magazine; and Andrea Mitchell of NBC NEWS. The candidates are Vice President George Bush, the Republican nominee; and Governor Michael Dukakis, the Democratic nominee. [Applause]

SHAW: For the next 90 minutes we will be questioning the candidates following a format designed and agreed to by representatives of the two campaigns. However, there are no restrictions on the questions that my colleagues and I can ask this evening, and the candidates have no prior knowledge of our questions. By agreement between the candidates, the first question goes to Gov. Dukakis. You have two minutes to respond. Governor, if Kitty Dukakis were raped and murdered, would you favor an irrevocable death penalty for the killer?

DUKAKIS: No, I don't, Bernard. And I think you know that I've opposed the death penalty during all of my life. I don't see any evidence that it's a deterrent, and I think there are better and more effective ways to deal with violent crime. We've done so in my own state. And it's one of the reasons why we have had the biggest drop in crime of any industrial state in America; why we have the lowest murder rate of any industrial state in America.

The question was fraught with drama, but Dukakis's response seemed as though he didn't think it terribly dramatic—just another policy where he'd had a long-standing and deeply held position. Having settled that issue, Dukakis turns the focus of his remarks to the war on drugs that he feels is an issue on which Bush has not made a particularly compelling case.

But we have work to do in this nation. We have work to do to fight a real war, not a phony war, against drugs. And that's something I want to lead, something we haven't had over the course of the past many years, even though the Vice President has been at least allegedly in charge of that war. We have much to do to step up that war, to double the number of drug enforcement agents, to fight both here and abroad, to work with our neighbors in this hemisphere. And I want to call a hemispheric summit just as soon after the 20th of January as possible to fight that war. But we also have to deal with drug education prevention here at home. And that's one of the things that I hope I can lead personally as the President of the United States. We've had great success in my own state. And we've reached out to young people and their families and been able to help them by beginning drug education and prevention in the early elementary grades. So we can fight this war, and we can win this war. And we can do so in a way that marshals our forces, that provides real support for state and local law enforcement officers who have not been getting that support, and do it in a way which will bring down violence in this nation, will help our youngsters to stay away from drugs, will stop this avalanche of drugs that's pouring into the country, and will make it possible for our kids and our families to grow up in safe and secure and decent neighborhoods.

SHAW: Mr. Vice President, your one-minute rebuttal.

Dukakis responded to the moderator's question in the same way he dealt with most any other policy question put to him. How the question was asked didn't matter; it was at its root a death penalty question. Dukakis had long maintained a consistent and, in his view, principled view of the policy. To change his mind on that policy simply because the hypothetical involved his spouse in a particularly graphic way would violate that principled position. The problem was that voters weren't particularly sensitive to arguments from principle; they wanted to see the candidate react with emotion. Who wouldn't want to seek vengeance for such a deed? Dukakis's consistency at the price of showing emotion was devastating for his appeal to voters. The Republican Party went on to win another landslide election.

BUSH: Well, a lot of what this campaign is about, it seems to me Bernie, goes to the question of values. And here I do have, on this particular question, a big difference with my opponent. You see, I do believe that some crimes are so heinous, so brutal, so outrageous, and I'd say particularly those that result in the death of a police officer, for those real brutal crimes, I do believe in the death penalty, and I think it is a deterrent, and I believe we need it. And I'm glad that the Congress moved on this drug bill and have finally called for that related to these narcotics drug kingpins. And so we just have an honest difference of opinion: I support it and he doesn't.

Source: "Presidential Debates: Presidential Debate at the University of California in Los Angeles, October 13, 1988." The American Presidency Project, http://www.presidency.ucsb.edu/ws/?pid=29412.

"Willie Horton" Ad

Anti–Michael Dukakis Campaign Ad

1988

INTRODUCTION

The 1988 presidential race between George Bush (the sitting vice president) and Michael Dukakis (former governor of Massachusetts) was remarkable among modern presidential campaigns for its almost complete lack of substantive issues dominating the national conversation. This is not to say that the candidates did not differ on policy issues—they surely did. But aside from the pledge "no new taxes," Bush never fully articulated exactly what policy would be prioritized in his adminis-tration. Bush was Reagan's vice president, and the Republican Party was unified heading into the general election. The Democratic primary, however, was wide open. Multiple candidates vied for the nomination and the opportunity to win the presidential election—something that Democrats hadn't done very often since 1948.

Immediately after Dukakis received the Democratic nomination, the Bush campaign trailed Dukakis by 17 points in national polls. With the time to the general election dwindling, the Bush campaign was able to pull back within reach of the Dukakis camp through a very effective negative campaign strategy. Although it was paid for by an unaffiliated political action committee (PAC), the "Willie Horton" ad was the centerpiece of the highly effective—and controversial—campaign to paint Dukakis as soft on crime.

MALE NARRATOR and TEXT: Bush and Dukakis On Crime

TEXT: Supports Death Penalty

MALE NARRATOR: Bush supports the death penalty for first degree murderers.

TEXT: Opposes Death Penalty

MALE NARRATOR: Dukakis not only opposes the death penalty,

TEXT: Allowed Murderers to Have Weekend Passes

MALE NARRATOR: he allowed first-degree murderers to have weekend passes from prison. One was Willie Horton,

Dukakis had inherited the furlough program from a previous Republican administration. He did, however, preside over the program that allowed those convicted of first-degree murder, such as Willie Horton, to participate in the furlough program. As Dukakis's campaign for president got under way, he abolished the program. He later called it "99% effective."

As Horton's image fills the screen, the viewer is in effect asked whether Dukakis was complicit in the tragedy. The implication is that had Dukakis been less soft on crime, the tragedy would have been averted.

The ad was an independent expenditure by an unaffiliated PAC called National Security Political Action Committee (NSPAC) and was immediately reviled by many observers for being laced with overt racist imagery and implicit racist commentary. At the vice presidential debate, Senator Lloyd Bentsen demanded the Bush campaign denounce the ad. Bush argued that his campaign had nothing to do with the ad, even though it fit the campaign's overall strategy to make up the 17-point deficit.

The "Willie Horton" ad was soon pulled in favor of an ad that used the image of a revolving prison door to describe the furlough program. The overall soft-on-crime theme resonated with voters, and the Bush campaign used it to great effect, even if it retained implicit appeals to latent racism. Just a month or so after the initial airing of the "Willie Horton" ad, Bush received 53.9 percent of the popular vote to 46.1 percent for the Dukakis campaign.

TEXT: **Willie Horton**

MALE NARRATOR: who murdered a boy in a robbery, stabbing him 19 times. Despite a life sentence,

MALE NARRATOR and TEXT: Horton Received 10 Weekend Passes From Prison

MALE NARRATOR: **Horton fled, kidnapped a young couple, stabbing the man and repeatedly raping his girlfriend.**

TEXT: Kidnapping Stabbing Raping

MALE NARRATOR and TEXT: **Weekend Prison Passes. Dukakis On Crime.**

Source: "Willie Horton 1988 Attack Ad." YouTube, www.youtube.com/watch?v=Io9KMSSEZ0Y.

Reagan, Bush, and the Iran-Contra Affair

Excerpt from the *Final Report of the Independent Counsel for Iran/Contra Matters* (August 4, 1993)

1987–1988

INTRODUCTION

In the summer of 1987, Americans were enthralled by a television spectacle from the Senate chambers—an indicted criminal, Lieutenant Colonel Oliver North, lecturing the U.S. Congress on duty, security, and morality. His argument was largely that yes, the Reagan administration lied to Congress and to the country, but that lie was justified by the ends we sought.

North's testimony revealed that in 1986, President Reagan and his administration—including his vice president and soon to be presidential candidate, George H. W. Bush—had unsuccessfully orchestrated a complicated scheme to serve two distinct goals. First, the administration wanted to free U.S. hostages taken by a terrorist group in Lebanon. Second, the administration wanted to provide military assistance to anticommunist forces, called Contras, in Nicaragua. There were at least two real problems with such goals, however.

The first goal—to release the hostages—ultimately led the administration to negotiate with terrorists and sell high-tech weapons to Iran in exchange for Iran's effort to persuade the terrorists to release the hostages, in direct contradiction of U.S. policy. The profits from the illicit sale of the weapons to Iran were then used to provide support for the Contras, which was the second goal of the administration. But the difficulty was that the second goal was illegal. It was in direct violation of the Boland Amendment, an act passed by Congress to prohibit such support.

During his 1988 campaign for president, George H. W. Bush refused to answer queries regarding his involvement. He did, however, deny that he had any knowledge of the affair, although there was some evidence that he was indeed familiar with the events as they unfolded. As president, he subsequently pardoned several of the officials involved.

Executive Summary

In October and November 1986, two secret U.S. Government operations were publicly exposed, potentially implicating Reagan Administration officials in illegal activities. These operations were the provision of assistance to the military activities of the Nicaraguan contra rebels during an October 1984 to October 1986 prohibition on such aid, and the sale of U.S. arms to Iran in contravention of stated U.S. policy and in possible violation of arms-export controls. In late November 1986, Reagan Administration officials announced that some of the proceeds from the sale of U.S. arms to Iran had been diverted to the contras.

As a result of the exposure of these operations, Attorney General Edwin Meese III sought the appointment of an independent counsel to investigate and, if necessary, prosecute possible crimes arising from them.

The Special Division of the United States Court of Appeals for the District of Columbia Circuit appointed Lawrence E. Walsh as Independent Counsel on December 19, 1986, and charged him with investigating:

(1) the direct or indirect sale, shipment, or transfer since in or about 1984 down to the present, of military arms, materiel, or funds to the government of Iran, officials of that government, persons, organizations or entities connected with or purporting to represent that government, or persons located in Iran;

(2) the direct or indirect sale, shipment, or transfer of military arms, materiel or funds to any government, entity, or person acting, or purporting to act as an intermediary in any transaction referred to above;

(3) the financing or funding of any direct or indirect sale, shipment or transfer referred to above;

(4) the diversion of proceeds from any transaction described above to or for any person, organization, foreign government, or any faction or body of insurgents in any foreign country, including, but not limited to Nicaragua;

(5) the provision or coordination of support for persons or entities engaged as military insurgents in armed conflict with the government of Nicaragua since 1984.

This is the final report of that investigation.

Overall Conclusions

The investigations and prosecutions have shown that high-ranking Administration officials violated laws and executive orders in the Iran/contra matter.

As a result of the Iran-Contra Affair, more members of the Reagan administration were indicted or convicted or resigned than in any other presidential administration in U.S. history. Although he had signed relevant documents and a few conspirators mentioned his interest in the arms for hostages deal, Reagan himself didn't reveal much information as to his own involvement: "Try as I might, I cannot recall anything whatsoever. . . . My answer therefore, and the plain and simple truth is, I don't remember, period."

Independent Counsel concluded that:

—the sales of arms to Iran contravened United States Government policy and may have violated the Arms Export Control Act [Independent Counsel is aware that the Reagan Administration Justice Department took the position, after the November 1986 revelations, that the 1985 shipments of United States weapons to Iran did not violate the law. This post hoc position does not correspond with the contemporaneous advice given the President. As detailed within this report, Secretary of Defense Caspar W. Weinberger (a lawyer with an extensive record in private practice and the former general counsel of the Bechtel Corporation) advised President Reagan in 1985 that the shipments were illegal. Moreover, Weinberger's opinion was shared by attorneys within the Department of Defense and the White House counsel's office once they became aware of the 1985 shipments. Finally, when Attorney General Meese conducted his initial inquiry into the Iran arms sales, he expressed concern that the shipments may have been illegal.]

—the provision and coordination of support to the contras violated the Boland Amendment ban on aid to military activities in Nicaragua;

—the policies behind both the Iran and contra operations were fully reviewed and developed at the highest levels of the Reagan Administration;

—although there was little evidence of National Security Council level knowledge of most of the actual contra-support operations, there was no evidence that any NSC member dissented from the underlying policy—keeping the contras alive despite congressional limitations on contra support;

—the Iran operations were carried out with the knowledge of, among others, President Ronald Reagan, Vice President George Bush, Secretary of State George P. Shultz, Secretary of Defense Caspar W. Weinberger, Director of Central Intelligence William J. Casey, and national security advisers Robert C. McFarlane and John M. Poindexter; of these officials,

In his 1992 reelection campaign, Bush's involvement in Iran-Contra was again in the news, as prosecutors reindicted Caspar Weinberger just four days prior to the election. Records uncovered since the initial investigation revealed that Bush had known and approved of the arms for hostages deal since 1985. After the election but before Bill Clinton took office, Bush pardoned Weinberger for his involvement. Lawrence Walsh believed that the pardon was an attempt to conceal Bush's own involvement in the affair.

only Weinberger and Shultz dissented from the policy decision, and Weinberger eventually acquiesced by ordering the Department of Defense to provide the necessary arms; and

—large volumes of highly relevant, contemporaneously created documents were systematically and willfully withheld from investigators by several Reagan Administration officials.

—following the revelation of these operations in October and November 1986, Reagan Administration officials deliberately deceived the Congress and the public about the level and extent of official knowledge of and support for these operations.

Considering the passage of the Boland Amendment, Congress acted in a very specific way to limit presidential unilateral action in foreign affairs. Yet the president continued to pursue a policy in direct contradiction with the law. As Bush hit the campaign trail, there was no doubt that he had good reason to avoid discussing his involvement in the largest scandal in the executive branch since Watergate.

In addition, Independent Counsel concluded that the off-the-books nature of the Iran and contra operations gave line-level personnel the opportunity to commit money crimes.

Source: Lawrence E. Walsh, *Final Report of the Independent Counsel for Iran/Contra Matters* (Washington, DC: U.S. Government Printing Office, 1993), xiii.

Election of 1992

The *Star* Publishes Gennifer Flowers' Allegations

**"PRESIDENTIAL CAMPAIGN: Allegations of
Clinton Affairs May Recast Democrats' Race"
Rhodes Cook, *CQ Weekly***

January 25, 1992

INTRODUCTION

Almost precisely four years after Democratic presidential candidate Gary Hart was forced to withdraw from the race because of reports of an extramarital affair, another front-runner seemed destined for the same fate. Bill Clinton, then a popular governor of Arkansas, quickly emerged as a strong contender for the nomination. He too was young, articulate, and ideologically moderate. It helped that he was a southerner (always an important strategic consideration) and that his wife, Hillary Rodham Clinton, was smart and articulate. They seemed to be the perfect campaign couple.

Then rumors emerged regarding Bill Clinton's affairs. At first he denied the allegations. But two weeks before the New Hampshire primary, the first in the nation, an Arkansas state employee and part-time cabaret singer, Gennifer Flowers, held a press conference about her relationship with the governor. In a tightly packed room, Flowers detailed a 12-year affair with Clinton and even played voice mail messages from him to her. The evidence, it seemed, was unambiguous.

The fledgling front-runner status of Arkansas Gov. Bill Clinton came under attack the week of Jan. 20 as a supermarket tabloid published allegations that he had extramarital affairs.

The initial stories were in wide circulation before they arrived on newsstands Jan. 21 in the edition of the tabloid *Star*, dated Jan. 28.

Clinton not only denied the accusations but also said the women named had denied them as well. But the story was revived on Jan. 23 when the *Star* announced a follow-up focusing on one woman who was voicing the allegations herself.

The woman, Gennifer Flowers, is a former singer and TV reporter who now works for the Arkansas state government. She was said to have had an affair with Clinton from 1977 through 1989. She was also said to have tape-recorded recent conversations with Clinton in which they discussed her earlier denials of the *Star*'s first story.

Rumors of marital infidelity have dogged Clinton for years, but he had deflected them with some success since launching his campaign Oct. 3.

At a Claremont, N.H., campaign stop Jan. 23, Clinton called the *Star* allegations "outright lies" and charged that Flowers was paid to change her story. The *Star*'s editor, Richard Kaplan, confirmed that his paper had paid Flowers for her story.

Years later it would be revealed that Clinton did in fact have an affair with Flowers. Whether or not the precise allegations, such as the 12-year duration of the affair, were true continues to be a mystery.

Both Clinton and his wife, Hillary, have said the standard for media coverage of their personal life should be their marriage's current status.

"If we had just walked away from our marriage, I could be up here running for president, and you would not be here tonight talking to me about this," Clinton said Jan. 23.

The spasm of reporting on Clinton's private life recalled the questions of character that sank the presidential candidacies of former Sen. Gary Hart of Colorado and Delaware Sen. Joseph R. Biden Jr., both Democrats, in 1987.

Both the Hart and Biden campaigns unraveled quickly—Hart's under charges of marital infidelity, Biden's after accusations of plagiarism.

Most observers assumed that Clinton would go the way of Gary Hart. Yet Clinton and his wife refused to withdraw from the race. Instead, they held an intimate live interview with CBS's *60 Minutes* reporter Steve Kroft on January 26. It was a special edition of the program, and many Americans tuned in.

It was by no means clear at week's end that Clinton's situation would follow a similarly swift downward spiral. If it did, other Democrats now on the sidelines might be encouraged to reconsider their positions.

But entering the race at this point is not so simple. Access to the ballot has already closed in more than a dozen primary states, including all those that vote before mid-March except South Carolina (March 7). There, the Democratic filing deadline is Feb. 1.

That means it is already too late for a new Democratic candidate to run in New Hampshire (Feb. 18), South Dakota (Feb. 25), the March 3 contests in Colorado, Georgia and Maryland, and all the Super Tuesday (March 10) primaries—Florida, Louisiana, Mississippi, Oklahoma, Tennessee and Texas in the South, plus Massachusetts and Rhode Island.

In the Clintons' *60 Minutes* interview, Bill Clinton would portray the media in this light: *"I think what the press has to decide is: Are we going to engage in a game of 'gotcha'? . . . I can remember a time when a divorced person couldn't run for president, and that time, thank goodness, has passed. Nobody's prejudiced against anybody because they're divorced. Are we going to take the reverse position now that if people have problems in their marriage and there are things in their past which they don't want to discuss which are painful to them, that they can't run?"*

Clinton was taking on the media. He was saying that matters of this sort are personal, between the two people in a marriage, and are not the media's business. Hillary Clinton, appearing side by side with her husband, also argued that the private lives of politicians are no different than the private lives of everyone else:

"There isn't a person watching this who would feel comfortable sitting on this couch detailing everything that ever went on in their life or their marriage. And I think it's real dangerous in this country if we don't have some zone of privacy for everybody."

Clinton would go on to come in second in the New Hampshire primary, good enough for the media to dub him the "Comeback Kid." Many scholars view the Clintons' performance on *60 Minutes* as shifting the perception of Bill's alleged affairs and turning the tide in his favor, as illustrated in an exchange between Kroft and Bill Clinton.

Kroft stated that "I think most Americans would agree that it's very admirable that you've stayed together—that you've worked your problems out and that you've seemed to reach some sort of understanding and arrangement."

Clinton said in response: "Wait a minute, wait a minute, wait a minute. You're looking at two people who love each other. This is not an arrangement or an understanding. This is a marriage. That's a very different thing."

Undoubtedly this approach worked for Clinton. Sitting next to his wife, holding her hand, Clinton was saying that they were having some troubles but were still in love, still in a marriage. The issue was essentially dead after this interview. America had gotten its first taste of the tenacity and style of Bill and Hillary Clinton.

The filing deadline for the Michigan primary (March 17) has also passed, and the filing period for Democratic candidates in Illinois (another March 17 primary) closes Jan. 28.

By the day after New Hampshire's Feb. 18 primary, the available primaries left for a late-starting candidate to enter would be a relative handful in May and early June. The filing periods would have closed by then for primaries in delegate-rich New York (April 7), Wisconsin (April 7), Pennsylvania (April 28) and North Carolina (May 5).

To be sure, the womanizing charges might not sink Clinton's candidacy at all; they might even help him if voters see him as the victim of unscrupulous attackers and a gossipy press.

To Clinton's advantage, the basic ground rules of media reporting seem to have changed since 1987. Then, the burden of proof was on Hart and Biden to prove the charges against them were false. This year, the media—with the exception of the sensational tabloids—seem to be taking the opposite position; that the accuser must prove the charges correct.

When the *New York Post* on Jan. 17 trumpeted alleged womanizing by Clinton in a headline that screamed "Wild Bill," the *New York Times* buried the accusation in a small item deep in the newspaper. The *Times* did the same with the *Star*'s follow-up on Jan. 24.

The issue has gained new salience at a time when Clinton was opening a clear lead over his rivals in New Hampshire polls. A variety of surveys taken in mid-to-late January showed Clinton with the support of roughly 30 percent of likely Democratic primary voters.

Most New Hampshire polls also show Bush with a wide lead over conservative columnist Patrick J. Buchanan. But the state's political scene is particularly volatile this year, and even Bush supporters acknowledge that voters could be influenced by upcoming events such as the president's State of the Union speech Jan. 28.

Source: Rhodes Cook, "PRESIDENTIAL CAMPAIGN: Allegations of Clinton Affairs May Recast Democrats' Race." *CQ Weekly* (January 25, 1992), 187. Used by permission.

Is Bill Clinton a Draft Dodger?

Bill Clinton's 1969 Letter to the Head of the University of Arkansas's Army Reserve Program

February 12, 1992

INTRODUCTION

In many respects, the Vietnam War was very different from previous wars. Our engagement escalated slowly, almost without notice by the general public, and the rationale for our commitment was not accepted by many Americans. The horrific nature of modern warfare was played out on the evening news. As such, the military draft was unpopular, and many young men balked at the prospects of going to war in Vietnam. Some of these men would simply refuse to go, occasionally leaving the United States altogether, while others did what they could to avoid being called to duty.

Yet being accused of not serving one's country during wartime has always been a serious charge in electoral politics; one must answer the call of duty. So when men of the Vietnam War era began to run for high political office, the Vietnam question moved front and center. Because the war was unpopular, this issue became complicated.

Bill Clinton did not go to Vietnam and did not serve in the military. Precisely how he was able to avoid the draft became an issue in his race for the White House. The letter presented here, uncovered by the media in February 1992, was sent by Clinton, then a Rhodes scholar at Oxford University in England, on December 3, 1969. Clinton was 22 years old at the time. The letter was directed to Colonel Eugene Holmes, who headed up the Army Reserve program at the University of Arkansas. Needless to say, its disclosure, along with Clinton's statement about being saved from the draft, became a major issue when the letter was made public on February 12, 1992, one week before the New Hampshire primary election.

Dear Colonel Holmes,

I am sorry to be so long in writing. I know I promised to let you hear from me at least once a month, and from now on you will, but I have had to have some time to think about this first letter. Almost daily since my return to England I have thought about writing, about what I want to and ought to say. First, I want to thank you, not just for saving me from the draft, but for being so kind and decent to me last summer, when I was as low as I have ever been. One thing which made the bond we struck in good faith somewhat palatable to me was my high regard for you personally. In retrospect, it seems that the

To Republican operatives, Clinton's open admission that his educational deferment saved him from the draft confirmed that he was a so-called draft dodger. How could the public support someone who did all he could to avoid military service?

admiration might not have been mutual had you known a little more about me, about my political beliefs and activities. At least you might have thought me more fit for the draft than for ROTC. Let me try to explain.

Being an outspoken critic of our war in Vietnam would later be less problematic for Democratic candidates and in fact would likely help in many primaries and caucuses. However, working the system to avoid the draft, regardless of one's antiwar sentiments, was controversial.

As you know, I worked for two years in a very minor position on the Senate Foreign Relations Committee. I did it for the experience and the salary, but also for the opportunity, however small, of working every day against a war I opposed and despised with a depth of feeling I had reserved solely for racism in America before Vietnam. I did not take the matter lightly, but studied it carefully, and there was a time when not many people had more information about Vietnam at hand than I did. I have written and spoken and marched against the war. One of the national organizers of the Vietnam Moratorium is a close friend of mine. After I left Arkansas last summer, I went to Washington to work in the national headquarters of the Moratorium, then to England to organize the Americans here for demonstrations here October 15th and November 16th.

Interlocked with the war is the draft issue, which I did not begin to consider separately until early 1968. For a law seminar at Georgetown I wrote a paper on the legal arguments for and against allowing, within the Selective Service System, the classification of selective conscientious objection, for those opposed to participation in a particular war, not simply to, quote, participation in war in any form, end quote. From my work I came to believe that the draft system itself is illegitimate. No government really rooted in limited, parliamentary democracy should have the power to make its citizens fight and kill and die in a war they may oppose, a war which even possibly may be wrong, a war which, in any case, does not involve immediately the peace and freedom of the nation.

The draft was justified in World War II because the life of the people collectively was at stake. Individuals had to fight if the nation was to survive, for the lives of their countrymen and their way of life. Vietnam is no such case. Nor was Korea, an example where, in my opinion, certain military action was justified but the draft was not, for the reasons stated above.

Because of my opposition to the draft and the war, I am in great sympathy with those who are not willing to fight, kill, and maybe die for their country, that is, the particular policy of a particular government, right or wrong. Two of my friends at Oxford are conscientious objectors. I wrote a letter of recommendation for one of them to his Mississippi draft board, a letter which I am more proud of than anything else I wrote at Oxford last year. One of my roommates is a draft resister who is possibly under indictment and may never be able to go home again. He is one of the bravest, best men I know. His country needs men like him more than they know. That he is considered a criminal is an obscenity. . . .

When the draft came, despite political convictions, I was having a hard time facing the prospect of fighting a war I had been fighting against, and that is why I contacted you. ROTC was the one way left in which I could possibly, but not positively, avoid both Vietnam and resistance. Going on with my education, even coming back to England, played no part in my decision to join ROTC. I am back here, and would have been at Arkansas Law School, because there is nothing else I can do. In fact, I would like to have been able to take a year out perhaps to teach in a small college or work on some community action project and in the process to decide whether to attend law school or graduate school and how to be putting what I have learned to use. But the particulars of my personal life are not nearly as important to me as the principles involved.

A common route for many men to avoid being shipped to Vietnam was to join the Reserve Officers' Training Corps (ROTC) at their colleges. Young men trained for leadership positions in the military, but they did so on college campuses. Occasionally these men were sent to Vietnam, but more often than not they were kept at home—in reserve.

After I signed the ROTC letter of intent I began to wonder whether the compromise I had made with myself was not more objectionable than the draft would have been, because I had no interest in the ROTC program in itself and all I seemed to have done was to protect myself from physical harm. Also, I began to think I had deceived you, not by lies—there were none—but by failing to tell you all the things I'm writing now. I doubt that I had the mental coherence to articulate them then. At that time, after we had made our agreement and you had sent my 1-D deferment to my draft board, the anguish and loss of self-regard and self-confidence really set in. I hardly slept for weeks and kept going by eating compulsively and reading until exhaustion brought sleep. Finally on September 12th, I stayed up all night writing a letter to the chairman of my draft board, saying basically what is in the preceding paragraph, thanking him for trying to help me in a case where he really couldn't, and stating that I couldn't do the ROTC after all and would he please draft me as soon as possible.

I never mailed the letter, but I did carry it on me every day until I got on the plane to return to England. I didn't mail the letter because I didn't see, in the end, how my going in the Army and maybe going to Vietnam would achieve anything except a feeling that I had punished myself and gotten what I deserved. So I came back to England to try to make something of this second year of my Rhodes scholarship.

And that is where I am now, writing to you because you have been good to me and have a right to know what I think and feel. I am writing too in the hope that my telling this one story will help you to understand more clearly how so many fine people have come to find themselves still loving their country but loathing the military, to which you and other good men have devoted years, lifetimes, of the best service you could give. To many of us, it is no longer clear what is service and what is disservice, or if it is clear, the conclusion is likely to be illegal. Forgive the length of this letter. There was much to say. There is still a lot to be said, but it can wait. Please say hello to Colonel Jones for me. Merry Christmas.

Sincerely,

Bill Clinton

Source: "Bill Clinton's Draft Letter." PBS.org, http://www.pbs.org/wgbh/pages/frontline/shows/clinton/etc/draftletter.html.

Clinton never served in the ROTC, and of course he never went to Vietnam. Many observers had assumed that when this letter was revealed, Clinton's candidacy would crumble. In fact, polling data at the time suggested that the governor's chances were fading. Yet Clinton seemed to handle the issue deftly, reminding voters that while patriotic, many young men of that generation worked diligently to avoid being sent to Vietnam. In the end Clinton came in second in the New Hampshire primary, doing well enough to be dubbed the "Comeback Kid." He would pick up speed and easily win the Democratic nomination.

Buchanan at the Republican National Convention

Pat Buchanan's Address to the Republican National Convention

August 17, 1992

INTRODUCTION

We generally think of key moments in presidential campaigns as specific to individual races, not having an impact on future contests. But this was not the case with President George H. W. Bush's 1988 tax pledge.

Bush, saying that he refused to consider raising taxes, won the 1988 election rather easily. Yet the budget process stalled because the House and Senate were controlled by Democrats, and they believed that raising revenue should be used to help reduce the budget deficit. Eventually Bush agreed to provisions that raised some taxes as part of a 1990 budget compromise bill. While he was praised by many for averting a budget crisis and for finding a middle-ground solution, he had broken his "no new taxes" pledge.

With waning approval numbers, particularly among fellow Republicans, it was probably not a surprise that Bush would confront a challenge for the Republican nomination in 1992. At the center of this attack was former Republican presidential adviser and media commentator Pat Buchanan. Buchanan, a darling of social conservatives, forged a relentless assault on Bush, reminding Republicans that the president had broken his pledge.

Buchanan eventually dropped out of the race, but because of his strong showing in early primaries (38 percent of the vote in New Hampshire, for instance), he was granted a prime-time address at the Republican National Convention later that summer. The excerpt presented here is from that speech.

What a terrific crowd this is. What a terrific crowd.

This may even be larger than the crowd I had in Ellijay, Georgia. Don't laugh. We carried Ellijay.

Listen, my friends, we may have taken the long way home, but we finally got here to Houston. And the first thing I want to do tonight is to congratulate President George Bush and to remove any doubt about where we stand. The primaries are over; the heart is strong again; and the Buchanan brigades are enlisted—all the way to a great Republican comeback victory in November.

Buchanan's assault on Bush during the primaries and caucuses was relentless, so one might wonder why he would suggest that his brigades were enlisted to help Bush win. It is customary for candidates to mend fences when one secures the nomination. The making up is easier in some instances than in others.

My friends—My friends, like many of you—like many of you last month, I watched that giant masquerade ball up at Madison Square Garden, where 20,000 liberals and radicals came dressed up as moderates and centrists in the greatest single exhibition of cross-dressing in American political history.

You know, one—one by one—one by one the prophets of doom appeared at the podium. The Reagan decade, they moaned, was a terrible time in America, and they said the only way to prevent worse times is to turn our country's fate and our country's future over to the Party that gave us McGovern, Mondale, Carter, and Michael Dukakis. Where do they find these leaders? No way, my friends. The American people are not going to go back to the discredited liberalism of the 1960s and the failed liberalism of the 1970s, no matter how slick the package in 1992. . . .

Buchanan offered a tough fire-and-brimstone speech that seemed to resonate with hard-line conservatives and drew enthusiastic applause from those at the convention center.

The presidency, my friends—The presidency is also an office that Theodore Roosevelt called America's "bully pulpit." Harry Truman said it was "preeminently a place of moral leadership." George Bush is a defender of right-to-life, and a champion of the Judeo-Christian values and beliefs upon which America was founded.

But the speech also set aback, perhaps even scared, many moderate voters—the very same voters whom the Bush-Quayle ticket would need to secure a general election victory. While it was surely true then, as it is today, that a large majority of Republican followers opposed abortion and expansive gay rights, it was also true that many moderates were less strident. Presidential candidates understand the necessity of moving to the middle after the nomination process, but Buchanan was no longer a candidate. In a sense, he was going rogue.

Mr. Clinton—Mr. Clinton however, has a different agenda. At its top is unrestricted—unrestricted abortion on demand. When the Irish-Catholic Governor of Pennsylvania, Robert Casey, asked to say a few words on behalf of the 25 million unborn children destroyed since Roe v Wade, Bob Casey was told there was no room for him at the podium at Bill Clinton's convention, and no room at the inn. Yet—Yet a militant leader of the homosexual rights movement could rise at that same convention and say: "Bill Clinton and Al Gore represent the most pro-lesbian and pro-gay ticket in history." And so they do. Bill Clinton says he supports "school choice"—but only for state-run schools. Parents who send their children to Christian schools, or private schools, or Jewish schools, or Catholic schools, need not apply.

Elect me, and you get "two for the price of one," Mr. Clinton says of his lawyer-spouse. And what—And what does Hillary believe? Well, Hillary believes that 12-year-olds should have the right to sue their parents. And Hillary has compared marriage and the family, as institutions, to slavery and life on an Indian reservation. Well, speak for yourself, Hillary.

Friends—Friends, this—This, my friends—This is radical feminism. The agenda that Clinton & Clinton would impose on America: abortion on demand, a litmus test for the Supreme Court, homosexual rights, discrimination against religious schools, women in combat units. That's change, all right. But that's not the kind of change America needs. It's not the kind of change America wants. And it's not the kind of change we can abide in a nation we still call "God's country."

Buchannan was rallying the conservative base, to be sure, but he also offered a perspective that did not seem to match the growing views of many voters—particularly moderate voters. This was especially true with his comments about women's rights and his frequent robust criticism of those who sought to ensure the rights of gay men and women.

. . . You know up at that great—at that great big costume party they held up in New York, Mr. Gore made a startling declaration. Henceforth, Albert Gore said, the "central organizing principle" of governments everywhere must be: the environment. Wrong, Albert. The central organizing principle of this republic is: freedom. And from the ancient— And from the ancient forests—from the ancient forests of Oregon and Washington, to the Inland Empire of California, America's great middle class has got to start standing up to these environmental extremists who put birds and rats and insects ahead of families, workers, and jobs. . . .

Yes, we disagreed with President Bush, but we stand with him for the freedom to choose religious schools, and we stand with him against the amoral idea that gay and lesbian couples should have the same standing in law as married men and women. We stand with President Bush—We stand with President Bush for right-to-life and for voluntary prayer in the public schools. And we stand against putting our wives and daughters and sisters into combat units of the United States Army. And we stand, my—my friends—We also stand with President Bush in favor of the right of small towns and communities to control the raw sewage of pornography that so terribly pollutes our popular culture. We stand with President Bush in favor of federal judges who interpret the law as written, and against would-be Supreme Court justices like Mario Cuomo who think they have a mandate to rewrite the Constitution.

Buchanan's speech proved to be one of the most dramatic and memorable moments at the convention. There was a great deal of talk afterward regarding a shrinking Republican tent. In other words, would the party be able to win in November simply by energizing the conservative base? Would moderates feel comfortable voting for the Republican ticket? Drawing a direct causal connection between this speech and Bush's defeat to Bill Clinton would be difficult. But few scholars would dispute that Buchanan's convention address was a key part of the election.

God bless you, and God bless America.

Source: Patrick J. Buchanan, "1992 Republican National Convention Speech, August 17, 1992." Patrick J. Buchanan Official Website, http://buchanan.org/blog/1992-republican-national-convention-speech-148. Used by permission of the Republican National Committee.

Election of 1996

Colin Powell Declines to Run

Press Conference in Washington, D.C.

November 8, 1995

INTRODUCTION

Retired general Colin Powell was an exceptionally popular public figure in the early 1990s. Having served as the youngest general in the nation's history and as national security adviser and chairman of the Joint Chiefs of Staff, Powell had both the foreign policy experience that the office of the presidency often demands as well as the nonpartisan sensibility that evoked comparisons to President Dwight D. Eisenhower. Amid speculation that Powell would be invited to replace Dan Quayle on the 1992 Republican ticket, Powell chose instead to retire from the military. During the first Bill Clinton administration, Powell stayed out of governmental service but remained politically active. Many observers soon began suggesting that he would be a successful presidential candidate in the 1996 election. National opinion polls bore that out. As Clinton's first term progressed, however, the likelihood of a Republican victory in 1996 diminished.

After many weeks of intense attention by the national media, Powell had come to a decision. He began this November 8, 1995, press conference with the announcement that he would not seek the Republican nomination for president. Moreover, he added, he would not be willing to consider running as vice president either. Although he had served his country in the military for more than 35 years, the difficulties of a political campaign in an era of increasing incivility and polarization weighed heavily in his decision.

The possibility of Powell's candidacy was very exciting for many reasons. In particular, though, was the chance that he would be the first African American presidential nominee from either major party. As a Republican, citing the legacy of Abraham Lincoln seemed appropriate. However, since well before the Civil Rights era, the Republican Party had distanced itself from most African American voters through electoral strategies designed to appeal to disaffected southern white voters as well as through policies that seemed to run counter to African American voters' preferences.

GEN. COLIN POWELL, (RET.): I know that this is the right decision for me. It was not reached easily or without a great deal of personal anguish. For me and my family, saying no was even harder than saying yes. I will remain in private life and seek other ways to serve. I have a deep love for this country that has no bounds. I will find other ways to contribute to the important work needed to keep us moving forward. I know my decision will disappoint many who have supported me. . . .

I will continue to speak out forcefully in the future on the issues of the day, as I have been doing in recent weeks. I will do so as a member of the Republican Party and try to assist the party in broadening its appeal. I believe I can help the party of Lincoln move once again closer to the spirit of Lincoln. I will give my talent and energy to charitable and educational activities.

I will also try to find ways for me to help heal the racial divides that still exist within our society. Finally, let me say how honored I am that so many of you thought me worthy of your support. It says more about America than it says about me. In one generation, we have moved from denying a black man service at a lunch counter to elevating one to the highest military office in the nation and to being a serious contender for the Presidency. This is a magnificent country, and I am proud to be one of its sons. Thank you very much. Mr. Donaldson.

SAM DONALDSON: General, you say it's a calling you did not feel, but some people are going to say that you backed away from the fight you should have made because as a general used to having your way, and not used to be criticized, and in the hurly-burly, the down-and-dirty of American politics, you just didn't have the stomach for it.

GEN. COLIN POWELL, (RET.): I understand the down and dirty of American politics, and that's the way it should be. I mean, you should run this test of fire if you wish this highest office. But at this point in my life, and knowing what I know about myself, my talent, my energies, and what I'm capable of doing, this was not the right thing for me to do at this time. . . .

It was clear that this was a very difficult decision. The campaign would surely create many personal difficulties for the Powells. At this point in the press conference, General Powell reflected on the revelations that his wife, Alma, suffered from depression. Powell's responses to questions about her treatment were forthright and terse. "My wife has depression. She's had it for many, many years, and we have told many people about it. It is not a family secret. It is very easily controlled with proper medication, just as my blood pressure is sometimes under control with proper medication."

REPORTER: What do you think of the conservative opposition that surfaced publicly last week?

GEN. COLIN POWELL, (RET.): Well, I expected opposition, conservative opposition to some of the views I took, and it has come, but I have also received some support from conservatives that essentially said the party ought to be broad enough to, to accept and listen to many views. The particular meeting last week that you're talking about, the views expressed concerning my views, I expected to get. We all should be concerned, however, about the nature of that meeting and the nature of the attack. When you move away from just disagreeing with

Like Eisenhower before him, Powell was perceived by many as someone who could transcend politics. He was, after all, an African American Republican war hero who cared about inequalities in society.

somebody's views and you move into ad hominem attacks to destroy character, you're adding to the incivility that exists in our political life right now, which we ought to do something about.

[. . .]

The Contract with America was a set of conservative policies proposed by the new Republican majority in the U.S. House of Representatives. Democrats had controlled the House for more than 40 years before the 1994 takeover by Republicans.

REPORTER: You said many times that you were fearful of the Republicans' Contract With America as being too harsh. How do you see the Republican Party as it's now shaping up, particularly now they're cutting—they're going to change welfare, they're going to change Medicare, they're going to change Medicaid, what are your thoughts on those viewpoints?

GEN. COLIN POWELL, (RET.): The harshness I spoke of and which I will continue to speak of is that we have to be absolutely sure that we have on our mind at all times that with these changes we are fundamentally changing the social safety net people have relied upon. And at the end of this chain, there are children who may be in need and at risk. Yes, sir. . . .

REPORTER: Many Americans who respect you greatly will reach the conclusion from this that you have to be out of your mind to seek the presidency.

The coarsening of the political debate seems to have been at the heart of Powell's decision to not run in 1996. Incivility in politics is not new, but the heightened polarization between the parties and the increasing cohesion within the parties has certainly contributed to the advantage gained by demonizing one's political opponents—even if those opponents are within the same political party. Moderates such as Powell were beginning to disappear from the political landscape.

GEN. COLIN POWELL, (RET.): No. No. Let me say first of all, this gives me a chance to say I applaud and congratulate those candidates who are out there now fighting for the right to be President of the United States. And we should be proud that such people do come forward and always have come forward. It is a needed process. You have to have that kind of fighting and debate. It's called democracy. I would say to the American people that they should start to draw the line, however, on some of the incivility that we see in our national debate and in our political debate. We have to start remembering that I'm very fond of saying we are all a family, we have to work together. Yes, sir. . . .

Source: "Bowing Out: Powell's Announcement." General Colin Powell, Press Conference in Washington, D.C., November 8, 1995. PBS News Hour, http://www.pbs.org/newshour/bb/politics/july-dec95/election_11-08a.html.

Dole Retires from the Senate

Address on the Senate Floor

June 11, 1996

> ### INTRODUCTION
>
> On June 11, 1996, Senator Bob Dole (R-KS) resigned his Senate seat after 27 years of distinguished service in the chamber. At the time of his resignation, he had been the Senate majority leader since 1995. He had indicated earlier that he would continue to serve as majority leader even as he pursued the presidential nomination, so this announcement was a surprise that shocked many observers and even some Senate colleagues.
>
> At 73 years of age, Dole was the oldest person to ever seek the presidency. The issue of his age would become a central theme of the 1996 campaign. Bill Clinton, the Democratic incumbent, routinely reminded voters of the age issue by developing the "Bridge to the Future" campaign theme. The implication was clear—Senator Dole was an aging lion of the Senate, not a dynamic, energetic problem solver.
>
> As a senator, Dole was able to forge many bipartisan coalitions to move important legislation forward. In this address to the Senate chamber, he clearly seemed to emphasize the importance of compromise, comity, and cross-partisan cooperation. In reflecting upon his long tenure in the Senate, the announcement was an emotional occasion.

. . . I am very honored to have my wife Elizabeth and my daughter Robin in the gallery today. Thank you very much.

And I know they join me in expressing our deep appreciation to everyone here and to the people of Kansas. And as all of us go back who are leaving this year, or thinking about leaving in a couple of years, whatever, you think about the people who sent you here—and the people who tried not to send you here.

But once you're here, you forget about those—and they're all your constituents, whether Democrats, Republicans or independents. And four times my friends in Kansas, Republicans and Democrats and independents, I believe, gave me their votes in the House of Representatives, and five times they've given me their votes in the United States Senate.

And I think to all of us, such trust is perhaps the greatest gift that can come to any citizen in our democracy. And I know I'll be forever grateful, as everyone here will be forever grateful to our friends and our supporters who never gave up on us, who never lost their confidence in us. Maybe they didn't like some of our votes, or maybe they didn't like other things, but when the chips were down, they were there.

[. . .]

And I always thought the differences were a healthy thing, and that's why we're all so healthy because we have a lot of differences in this chamber. I've never seen a healthier group in my life.

[. . .]

Few sitting members of the Senate had served longer than Dole. Senator Robert Byrd, Democrat from West Virginia, was one of them. Byrd was widely acknowledged to be the Senate's unofficial historian and parliamentarian. He was also among the most frequent (and long-winded) speakers in the chamber.

The reference to Senator Byrd evokes a theme of bipartisanship, comity, and collaboration that by 1996 was in short supply.

So I would say that it's been a great ride. A few bumps along the way. I've learned a lot from people in this room. I've even gone to Sen. Byrd when I was the majority leader to ask his advice on how to defeat him on an issue.

And if you know Robert Byrd as I do, he gave me the answer! But it wasn't easy. I mean, this man's determined! And I know that in his book, in his great works about the Senate, in the first book, when I became the majority leader he very candidly writes in his book, he had his doubts about this Bob Dole because I might be too partisan, or I might not work with the minority leader.

But as I've heard him say a number of times since, I demonstrated that I wasn't that partisan; and B, if I understood one thing, as my successor will understand, is that unless the two leaders are working together, nothing is going to happen in this place.

We have to trust each other, as Sen. Daschle and I have, as Sen. Mitchell and I have, as Sen. Byrd and I have. And I have also great respect for Sen. Mansfield, Sen. Baker, though I didn't have the privilege of—I wasn't in the leadership at that time. And I would say to all those who have been in the leadership positions, it's a difficult life.

[. . .]

And I'm looking at one of the giants in the Senate right now, Sen. Thurmond. And I looked at others on the way in—Sen. Byrd. And I thought about Sen. Baker and Sen. Dirksen and Sen. Russell, and many, many more, Democrats and Republicans, who loved this place, who made it work.

[. . .]

And I could go on and on and I could—I'm not as—not like Sen. Byrd, because nobody can do the—the way Sen. Byrd does it. But you think of all these people who have come and gone, and all the new bright stars that are here today on both sides of the aisle. And one thing you know for certain, it's a great institution.

As far as I know, everybody that I know on either side has observed that rule. It's true in any business, any profession, but it's more true in politics, because the American people are looking at us and they want us to tell the truth. Doesn't mean we have to agree. Doesn't mean we can't have different motivations. And I learned that leadership is a combination of background and backbone.

And I learned a lot, as I said, from the likes of Sen. Byrd and others I'd watched and watched. . . .

So I would just say that we all know how the political process works. And some people are cynical and some people think it's awful and some people don't trust us. But the people who watch us, I think, day in and day out have a better understanding.

[. . .]

And I think sometimes around here we think we have to have everything, we've got to have total victory. 'I won't settle for less, it's got to be my way or no way.' Well, Ronald Reagan said once, if I can get 90 percent of what I want, I'd call that a pretty good deal. Ninety percent isn't bad, you get the other 10 percent later.

It's a small amendment then. Some people never understand that—take the 90, then work on the 10.

Dole goes on to give a long list of Democrats and Republicans he collaborated with on important policy issues, many of whom were of an era when bipartisan coalitions were more common. With the Republican primary behind him, Dole seems to be making the case that his willingness to cross the aisle to work with Democrats is a good thing as he pursues the presidency.

I want to say, too, that I—and I've read that my resignation and my decision to leave caused astonishment in some quarters. And I don't begrudge anybody their surprise. But I just want to disabuse anybody about the Senate. This is a great opportunity. There are hundreds and hundreds and thousands and thousands of people who would give anything they had to be a member of this body. And that's the way it should be—very competitive.

So, I said the truth is that I would no more distance myself from the Senate than I would from the United States itself. This—the body—is a reflection of America. It's what America is all about. We come from different states and different backgrounds, different opportunities, different challenges in our life.

And, yes, the institution has its imperfections and our occasional—or occasional inefficiency. And we're like America. We're still a work in progress in the United States Senate.

[. . .]

The senator cites a long list of examples of bipartisanship legislative successes, including veterans' health care and changes to Social Security, among others. In deliberately citing occasions where he crossed party lines, he is attempting to limit criticism for being too close to the unpopular Republican Speaker of the House, Newt Gingrich. The Clinton campaign would come to successfully link Dole and Gingrich together in voters' minds.

And I remember the first time I was ever approached by a reporter. Here I was a brand new—I was a law student, a brand-new. . . . I didn't know anything about anything. And he said, 'Well, what are you going to do now for your district?' or something on that case. I said, 'Ah, I'm going to sit around, watch for a couple of days, and then stand up for what's right.' Well, that's what we all do around there. And I hope I've done it over the years.

And so, I would close with, again, thanking all of my colleagues. I don't believe—I'm just trying to think back—I don't think we've ever had any real disagreements. I remember one time—I'll remind the Democratic leader—that I offered an amendment that you thought you were going to offer. And I made a mistake. I wasn't trying to one up the senator from South Dakota, so I withdrew my amendment. Then he offered the amendment. I think that's called civility.

The imagery evoked by the Eisenhower quote is reflective of the Clinton campaign's "Bridge to the Future" theme. Clinton's use of the metaphor is meant to draw attention to, among other things, Dole's age and the need for change. Here Dole speaks of a sense of hope for the future, as if to suggest that he's also capable of thinking about tomorrow.

So, I would close with—my hero was Dwight Eisenhower because he was our supreme commander. He also came from Abilene, Kansas; born in Texas, but quickly moved to Kansas.

[. . .]

'As we peer into society's future—we, you and I and our government must avoid the impulse to live only for today, plundering for our own ease and convenience the precious resources of tomorrow. We cannot mortgage the material assets of our grandchildren without risking the loss of their political and spiritual heritage. We want democracy to survive for all generations to come, not to become the insolvent phantom of tomorrow.'

And I think those words are just as good today as they were 35 years ago when President Eisenhower spoke them. We can lead or we can mislead, as the people's representatives, but whatever we do, we will be held responsible.

[. . .]

So the Bible tells us to everything there is a season, and I think my season in the Senate is about to come to an end. But the new season before me makes this moment far less the closing of one chapter than the opening of another. And we all take pride in the past, but we all live for the future. . . . And like everybody here, I'm an optimist. I believe our best tomorrows are yet to be lived. So again, thank you. God bless America, and God bless the United States Senate.

Comity, civility, bipartisanship, and history. Each was a point of emphasis for Senator Dole's farewell address. Those emphases were coincidentally helpful in convincing voters that Dole was not simply an extension of the House Republicans' conservative agenda. The Clinton campaign painted a picture of the Dole-Kemp ticket as reflective of the excesses of the House Republicans' Contract with America. That unflattering portrayal of the senator's record (along with concerns about his age) would resonate with voters, even though this address documents many bipartisan successes that provide counterevidence of that narrative. Dole would go on to lose in a landslide, garnering only 40 percent of the popular vote.

Source: Congressional Record, 104th Congress (1995–1996), pp. S6043–S6046.

Election of 2000

Clinton, Gore, and the Monica Lewinsky Affair

Excerpt from the Starr Report

September 9, 1998

INTRODUCTION

It is often the case that presidential campaigns take place against a backdrop of highly salient events or themes. While Vice President Al Gore was not implicated in the Monica Lewinsky affair, he chose not to appear at campaign events with President Bill Clinton. Some political observers suggest that the charges of impeachment faced by President Clinton created a kind of moral fatigue among voters. This amounted to a significant headwind into which Gore's candidacy had to appeal to voters with misgivings about another Democratic presidency.

In 1994 after the Republican takeover of the U.S. House and Senate, the investigation of Ken Starr (the appointed independent counsel) into multiple charges against Bill and Hillary Clinton (e.g., Whitewater, White House files on Republican members of Congress, the White House Travel Office, Vince Foster's suicide) revealed the absence of any criminal activity. However, Starr argued that Clinton had perjured himself in a recent sexual harassment civil suit brought against him by a former Arkansas state employee named Paula Jones. That perjury charge was ultimately one of two charges identified by Starr as impeachable offenses.

In the course of the Paula Jones investigation, Linda Tripp revealed information to Starr that a former White House intern named Monica Lewinsky had engaged in oral sex with the president. The revelation that the president had participated in such activities in the White House was shocking. Clinton himself testified that the meaning of the term "sexual relations," provided by the independent counsel, did not include actions he had taken with Lewinsky.

As you can see from this excerpt from the report submitted by the independent counsel, this amounted to perjury. Furthermore, Starr argued, Clinton had obstructed justice in the Jones case by encouraging Lewinsky to be evasive in her responses to investigators.

Clinton's response to this accusation came at the very end of a speech on education policy given on January 26, 1998:
"Now, I have to go back to work on my State of the Union speech. And I worked on it until pretty late last night. But I want to say one thing to the American people. I want you to listen to me. I'm going to say this again. I did not have sexual relations with that woman, Miss Lewinsky. I never told anybody to lie, not a single time—never. These allegations are false. And I need to go back to work for the American people."

There is Substantial and Credible Information that President Clinton Committed Acts that May Constitute Grounds for an Impeachment

Introduction

Pursuant to Section 595(c) of Title 28, the Office of Independent Counsel (OIC) hereby submits substantial and credible information that President Clinton obstructed justice during the *Jones v. Clinton* sexual harassment lawsuit by lying under oath and concealing evidence of

his relationship with a young White House intern and federal employee, Monica Lewinsky. After a federal criminal investigation of the President's actions began in January 1998, the President lied under oath to the grand jury and obstructed justice during the grand jury investigation. There also is substantial and credible information that the President's actions with respect to Monica Lewinsky constitute an abuse of authority inconsistent with the President's constitutional duty to faithfully execute the laws.

There is substantial and credible information supporting the following eleven possible grounds for impeachment:

1. President Clinton lied under oath in his civil case when he denied a sexual affair, a sexual relationship, or sexual relations with Monica Lewinsky.

2. President Clinton lied under oath to the grand jury about his sexual relationship with Ms. Lewinsky.

3. In his civil deposition, to support his false statement about the sexual relationship, President Clinton also lied under oath about being alone with Ms. Lewinsky and about the many gifts exchanged between Ms. Lewinsky and him.

4. President Clinton lied under oath in his civil deposition about his discussions with Ms. Lewinsky concerning her involvement in the *Jones* case.

5. During the *Jones* case, the President obstructed justice and had an understanding with Ms. Lewinsky to jointly conceal the truth about their relationship by concealing gifts subpoenaed by Ms. Jones's attorneys.

6. During the *Jones* case, the President obstructed justice and had an understanding with Ms. Lewinsky to jointly conceal the truth of their relationship from the judicial process by a scheme that included the following means: (i) Both the President and Ms. Lewinsky understood that they would lie under oath in the *Jones* case about their sexual relationship; (ii) the President suggested to Ms. Lewinsky that she prepare an affidavit that, for the President's purposes, would

"Both the President and Ms. Lewinsky understood that they would lie under oath ..."

memorialize her testimony under oath and could be used to prevent questioning of both of them about their relationship; (iii) Ms. Lewinsky signed and filed the false affidavit; (iv) the President used Ms. Lewinsky's false affidavit at his deposition in an attempt to head off questions about Ms. Lewinsky; and (v) when that failed, the President lied under oath at his civil deposition about the relationship with Ms. Lewinsky.

7. President Clinton endeavored to obstruct justice by helping Ms. Lewinsky obtain a job in New York at a time when she would have been a witness harmful to him were she to tell the truth in the *Jones* case.

8. President Clinton lied under oath in his civil deposition about his discussions with Vernon Jordan concerning Ms. Lewinsky's involvement in the *Jones* case.

9. The President improperly tampered with a potential witness by attempting to corruptly influence the testimony of his personal secretary, Betty Currie, in the days after his civil deposition.

In 1974, the House Judiciary Committee decided that impeachment proceedings against a sitting president are justified only in cases where the president's actions threaten our democratic system. In 1992 before Clinton was elected president, Starr argued before the U.S. Supreme Court that the president could be impeached for any illegal or immoral activity. Ultimately, though, it is up to Congress to determine what constitutes an impeachable offense.

When the formal impeachment trial began in the Senate, a two-thirds vote was needed to convict President Clinton. Ultimately several Republicans voted with Democrats (who were the minority party) as the Senate rejected both impeachment charges of perjury and obstruction of justice.

In the end, the fallout from the affair was rather limited for Clinton, as his approval ratings remained quite high. Nonetheless, Al Gore sought to keep Clinton at a substantial distance during Gore's campaign in 2000, lest Clinton's involvement remind voters of the moral failings of the incumbent president.

10. President Clinton endeavored to obstruct justice during the grand jury investigation by refusing to testify for seven months *and* lying to senior White House aides with knowledge that they would relay the President's false statements to the grand jury—and did thereby deceive, obstruct, and impede the grand jury.

11. President Clinton abused his constitutional authority by (i) lying to the public and the Congress in January 1998 about his relationship with Ms. Lewinsky; (ii) promising at that time to cooperate fully with the grand jury investigation; (iii) later refusing six invitations to testify voluntarily to the grand jury; (iv) invoking Executive Privilege; (v) lying to the grand jury in August 1998; and (vi) lying again to the public and Congress on August 17, 1998—all as part of an effort to hinder, impede, and deflect possible inquiry by the Congress of the United States.

Source: Kenneth Starr, "Referral to the United States House of Representatives pursuant to Title 28, United States Code, § 595(c)." Library of Congress Thomas, http://www.gpo.gov/fdsys/pkg/GPO-CDOC-106sdoc3/pdf/GPO-CDOC-106sdoc3-2.pdf.

Push Polls and Whispers: South Carolina Primary

Republican Primary Debate
in South Carolina
February 16, 2000

INTRODUCTION

Senator John McCain (R-AZ) was not the front-runner but had appeared in recent days to claim a share of the lead in the Republican primaries. After deciding not to participate in Iowa, McCain set his campaign's sights on a strong showing in New Hampshire. There, he beat George W. Bush by 19 points and took his powerful momentum into the next challenge in South Carolina. The Bush campaign was reeling from the loss in New Hampshire and was forced to design a strategy to stop McCain's momentum.

In New Hampshire, McCain was able to appeal to moderate and liberal voters as an alternative to the conservatism of Bush. Such an approach worked for McCain in New Hampshire, but South Carolina would present a very different Republican base. The Christian Coalition, a powerful core of conservative evangelical voters, was particularly strong in South Carolina. Bush needed their support as well as their organizational capacities to overcome his defeat in New England. In an effort to negatively define Bush in South Carolina, the McCain campaign released an ad (later pulled) that linked Bush to President Clinton in terms of Bush's inability to tell the truth. The Bush campaign responded with a powerful but subtle attack. This exchange during the Republican debate in South Carolina reveals the tension between the two camps.

LARRY KING: All right, Governor, what do you make of all these past two weeks, the charges and counter-charges? You go, and then the Senator.

GOV. GEORGE W. BUSH: Well, it's kind of politics, and John and I shook hands and we said we weren't going to run ads, and I kind of smiled my way through the early primaries and got defined. I'm not going to let it happen again. And we shook hands, and unfortunately he ran an ad that equated me to Bill Clinton. He questioned my trustworthiness.

LARRY KING: Are you saying he broke the agreement with you?

GOV. GEORGE W. BUSH: No, I'm just saying you can disagree on issues. . . . We'll debate issues. But whatever you do, don't equate my integrity and trustworthiness to Bill Clinton. That's about as low a blow as you can give in a Republican primary. [Applause]

The dramatic shift in strategy was evident to the McCain campaign quite quickly. The first indications of a whisper campaign against McCain emerged in an email from a conservative Christian evangelical professor at Bob Jones University in Greenville, South Carolina, who was not affiliated with the Bush campaign. Soon afterward, voters reported being push-polled. Voters claimed to have received calls asking them "Would you be more likely or less likely to vote for John McCain for president if you knew he had fathered an illegitimate black child?" The push poll was apparently a reference to the McCains' adopted Bangladeshi daughter, Bridget.

Other rumors were circulating as well, including the charge that his spouse, Cynthia McCain, was a drug addict; that John McCain was a Manchurian candidate sent to destroy the Republican Party from within; and that he was mentally unstable from his time as a prisoner of war in Vietnam. In this debate, another issue arose—that of a Vietnam War veteran's disparaging remarks toward McCain at a Bush campaign rally.

The point of smear tactics, negative campaigning, and push polling is to raise questions about a candidate in the voter's mind. The fact that the tactics used in the push polling were false, racist, and highly unethical was not a concern for those conducting the polls. This apparently was not a concern for McCain's political opponent, either. Although the origin of the push poll was never determined, it was also never condemned by anyone associated with the Bush campaign. As you might imagine, McCain and his wife were enraged by the tactics.

The smears worked as intended, as McCain lost in South Carolina. Bush won by 11 points, with Bush taking the conservative evangelical vote by a margin of 2 to 1 over McCain. Although McCain would go on to win Michigan and a handful of other states, any momentum that his campaign had after New Hampshire effectively ended in South Carolina.

> **LARRY KING: That's what got you mad to sort of fight back?**

GOV. GEORGE W. BUSH: Well, I stand by my ads.

LARRY KING: Senator McCain, did you break a promise?

SEN. JOHN MCCAIN: Well, let me tell you what happened. There was an ad run against me. We ran a counter-ad in New Hampshire. Governor Bush took the ad down. But let me tell you what really went over the line. Governor Bush had an event and he paid for it, and stood next to a spokesman for a fringe veterans group. That fringe veteran said that John McCain had abandoned the veterans. Now, I don't know how, if you can understand this, George, but that really hurts.

GOV. GEORGE W. BUSH: Yeah.

SEN. JOHN MCCAIN: That really hurts. And so five United States Senators, Vietnam veterans, heroes, some of them really incredible heroes, wrote George a letter and said, "apologize."

GOV. GEORGE W. BUSH: Let me . . .

SEN. JOHN MCCAIN: You should be ashamed.

GOV. GEORGE W. BUSH: Yeah, let me speak to that.

SEN. JOHN MCCAIN: You should be ashamed. . . .

[. . .]

SEN. JOHN MCCAIN: . . . [Y]ou're putting out stuff that is unbelievable, George, and it's got to stop. And your answer's got to stop.

> **GOV. GEORGE W. BUSH: I'm going to see about what I'm putting on TV. And what I put on TV was looking in that camera and saying, "you can disagree with me on issues, John, but do not question . . . do not question my trustworthiness, and do not compare me to Bill Clinton."**

Source: "GOP Debate, February 16, 2000." PBS.org, http://www.pbs.org/newshour/bb/politics/jan-june00/sc_debate_2-16.html.

Nader at the Green Party Convention

Ralph Nader's Acceptance Speech at the Green Party Convention

June 25, 2000

INTRODUCTION

There are several reasons why we seem grounded in a two-party model. At the top of the list would be the system of the first-past-the-post single-member district. Unlike other democracies where legislative seats are allotted in proportion of votes netted by each party, in the United States we send just one winner to office. This means that as minor party candidates struggle year after year without any sort of payoff, they eventually merge with the ideologically closest major party. In other words, left-leaning minor parties eventually merge with Democrats, and right-leaning minor parties usually merge with Republicans.

Occasionally, minor party presidential candidates become a spoiler. Here the candidate draws off enough votes from a major party candidate to ensure the victory of the other major party candidate. For example, in 1912 former Republican Teddy Roosevelt ran as a Bull Moose Party candidate, thereby splitting the Republican vote with Republican Howard Taft. This ensured Democrat Woodrow Wilson's victory. That is to say, Roosevelt played the role of a spoiler.

The same process occurred in the 2000 election. Ralph Nader, a longtime progressive and consumer rights advocate, decided to run for the presidency as a Green Party candidate. Presented here is his Green Party acceptance speech.

On behalf of all Americans who seek a new direction, who yearn for a new birth of freedom to build the just society, who see justice as the great work of human beings on Earth, who understand that community and human fulfillment are mutually reinforcing, who respect the urgent necessity to wage peace, to protect the environment, to end poverty and to preserve values of the spirit for future generations, who wish to build a deep democracy by working hard for a regenerative progressive politics, as if people mattered—to all these citizens and the Green vanguard, I welcome and am honored to accept the Green Party nomination for President of the United States.

Nader had been a powerful liberal activist since the 1960s. His landmark book, *Unsafe at Any Speed* (1965), drew attention to the failings of the automobile industry and its thirst for profits at the expense of safety. Many Democrats thought that Nader was the conscience of the party.

The Green Party stands for a nation and a world that consciously advances the practice of deep democracy. A deep democracy facilitates people's best efforts to achieve social justice, a sustainable and bountiful environment and an end to systemic bigotry and discrimination against law-abiding people merely because they are different. Green goals place community and self-reliance over dependency on ever larger absentee corporations and their media, their technology, their capital, and their politicians. Green goals aim at preserving the commonwealth of assets that the people of the United States already own so that the people, not big business, control what they own, and using these vast resources of the public lands, the public airwaves and trillions of worker pension dollars to achieve healthier environments, healthier communities and healthier people.

These goals are also conservative goals. Don't conservatives, in contrast to corporatists, want movement toward a safe environment, toward ending corporate welfare and the commercialization of childhood? Don't they too want a voice in shaping a clean environment rooted in the interests of the people? Don't they too want a fair and responsive marketplace, for their health needs and savings? Let us not in this campaign prejudge any voters, for Green values are majoritarian values, respecting all peoples and striving to give greater voice to all voters, workers, individual taxpayers and consumers. As with the right of free speech, we may not agree with others, but we will defend their right to free speech as strongly as we do for ourselves.

Nader had shown interest in running for the presidency as a Democrat, but his position at the far left of the political spectrum coupled with the fact that he had not held public office suggested that his chances were slim at best. As is often the case with unsuccessful major party candidates, Nader argued that the system was broken.

Earlier this year, I decided to seek your nomination because obstacles blocking solutions to our society's injustices and problems had to be overcome. Feelings of powerlessness and the withdrawal of massive numbers of Americans from both civic and political arenas are deeply troubling. This situation had to be addressed by fresh political movement arising from the citizenry's labors and resources and dreams about what America could become at long last. The worsening concentration of global corporate power over our government has turned that government frequently against its own people, denying its people their sovereignty to shape their future. Again and again, the will of the people has been thwarted and the voice of the people to protest has been muted.

In the past, citizens who led and participated in this country's social justice movements faced steep concentrations of power and overcame them. A brief look at American history is instructive today. Common themes occur from the Revolution of 1776 against King George III's empire to the anti-slavery drives and women's suffrage movements of the 19th century, to the farmers' revolt against the large banks and railroads that began in 1887, and on to the trade union, civil rights, environmental and consumer protection initiatives of the 20th century, culminating in the demands for equity by Americans who are discriminated against due to their race, gender, tribal status, class, disability or sexual preference....

Over the past twenty years we have seen the unfortunate resurgence of big business influence, generating its unique brand of wreckage, propaganda and ultimatums on American labor, consumers, taxpayers and most generically, American voters. Big business has been colliding with American democracy and democracy has been losing. The results of this democracy gap are everywhere to be observed by those who suffer these results and by those who employ people's yardsticks to measure the quality of the economy, not corporate yardsticks and their frameworks. What we must collectively understand about the prevalent inequalities is important because so many of these conditions have been normalized in our country.

Here too, Nader was the champion of organized labor. He had spent his career writing about and advocating the rights of workers.

Over the next four and one half months, this campaign must challenge the campaigns of the Bush and Gore duopoly in every locality by running with the people. When Americans go to work, wondering who will take care of their elderly parents or their children, irritated by the endless traffic jams, stifled by their lack of rights in the corporate workplace, ripped off by unscrupulous sellers and large companies, put on telephone hold for the longest times before you get an answer to a simple question—so much for this modern telecommunications age, beset by having to pay for health care you cannot afford or drug prices you shouldn't have to suffer, aghast at how little time your frenzied life leaves you for children, family, friends and community, overcome by the sheer ugliness

Nader had written nearly a dozen books. In addition to his work on consumer rights issues, many of his works centered on pollution and chemicals in the air, the water, and the food supply. These were important concerns of many Americans, particular those on the ideological Left.

of commercial strips and sprawls and incessantly saturating advertisements, repelled by the voyeurism of the mass media and the commercialization of childhood, upset at the rejection of the wisdoms of our elders and forebears, anxious over the ways your tax dollars are being misused, feeling that there needs to be more to life than the desperate rat race to make ends meet, then think about becoming a part of a progressive movement of Greens, of this citizens' campaign, to change the political economy so that healthy environments, healthy communities, and healthy people become its overwhelming reason for being. . . .

How badly do we want a just and decent society, a society that raises our expectation levels about ourselves and our community, a society that foresees and forestalls future risks, a society that has the people planning the future of their country, not global corporations as is the case now? A just and decent society is the dream of all those good citizens across our land who fight the good fight daily, it is the dream of the Green Party, it is the dream of a growing number of people seeking to involve themselves more actively in reclaiming this democracy of ours.

Clearly Nader was a strong writer and a powerful orator. Passages about dreams, liberty, justice, and equality warmed the hearts of many Americans.

This campaign is about strengthening our Republic with "liberty and justice for all" so that freedom is defined as participation in power: power to solve our problems and diminish our injustices that cause such pain and stultify so many Americans and their children. It is good to have such dreams, my mother would tell us, but she added a challenge. She taught us that determination puts your dream on wheels. Together we reviewed the problems and have understood that inequalities are getting worse. Together we can change the course of events as our forebears did. With commitment, dedication and determination we can put our dreams on wheels in this campaign. . . .

As the election grew near, many observers realized that the contest between Al Gore and George W. Bush would be close—extremely close. Many liberals and Gore supporters pushed Nader to withdraw from the race, fearing that even a few percentage points would spoil Gore's chances of a victory. This is precisely what happened. Nader netted just 3 percent of the overall vote. But in several states, his total was greater than Gore's loss. In Florida, Nader netted some 97,000 votes. Gore lost that state by a scant 537 votes and thus was defeated in the overall electoral college vote. Exit polling showed that a vast majority of the Nader voters in Florida and other close states would have voted for Gore if Nader had not been in the race. Simply stated, Nader's Green Party candidacy helped put George W. Bush in the White House.

With a new progressive movement, we the people have the ability to vastly improve our lives and to help shape the world's course to one of justice and peace for years to come.

Source: "Acceptance Statement of Ralph Nader for the Association of State Green Parties Nomination for President of the United States, Denver, Colorado, June 25, 2000." Ratical.org, http://www.ratical.org/co-globalize/RalphNader/062500.html. Used by permission of the Green Party of the United States.

Gore's Kiss

Image from the 2000 Democratic National Convention

August 17, 2000

INTRODUCTION

Here again, candidates must find a balance. On the one hand, we expect our elected officials to be earnest and eager to take the myriad responsibilities of the job seriously. But on the other hand, we expect them to be real and perhaps at times even spontaneous.

   Throughout much of his political career, Democrat Al Gore had the rap of being stiff and maybe boring. In fact, because he was widely known for coming across as dull, Gore poked fun at himself during campaign stops in 2000: "How can you tell Al Gore from his Secret Service agents? He's the stiff one." And "Al Gore is so boring his Secret Service code name is 'Al Gore.'"

▲ AP Photo/Stephen Savoia

Perhaps in an effort to combat the wooden tag or perhaps because it simply came upon him, Gore saw fit to give his wife, Tipper, a long, passionate kiss at the Democratic National Convention. Many applauded, many laughed, and many blushed. No candidate for the presidency had ever given his wife a more passionate kiss at a nominating convention.

   "The Kiss" was the talk at the so-called water cooler and was fodder for late-night comedians. In fact, there was even some polling done on the event. About half of men and women told Opinion Dynamics/Fox News that they saw Vice President Al Gore's famous kiss. Among the women who saw it, 27 percent thought that it was spontaneous, and 16 percent thought that it was a planned political move. Among the men who saw the kiss, 20 percent thought that it was spontaneous, and 24 percent thought that it was planned. But whether it did much to soften Gore's image is tough to know. He did get a bump in the polls after the convention, but that is quite common. How much of that bump can be attributed to the kiss is an open question.

Bush v. Gore

**George W. Bush, et al., Petitioners
v. Albert Gore, Jr., et al. On Writ of
Certiorari to the Florida Supreme Court**

December 12, 2000

INTRODUCTION

Vice President Al Gore won the popular vote in the 2000 election by more than half a million votes, while Bush took the electoral college votes 271 to 266. Florida's slate of 25 electors put Bush over the limit and into the White House. But those 25 electoral votes did not come easily—or quickly. The nation's eyes were turned to Florida as local election officials tried to fathom the intent of voters whose punch card ballots did not register in the tabulation machines.

The initial margin of Bush's victory in Florida was so slim that it triggered an automatic recount per state law. The initial recount showed significant gains for Gore, further reducing the margin of Bush's victory. The Gore campaign then petitioned the Florida secretary of state (a Republican) to count by hand ballots from those areas where machines did not register a vote for president. The campaign argued that machines were unable to accurately read ballots that the stylus (punch card instrument) failed to puncture properly. The secretary of state rejected the petition, and the Gore campaign sought relief in state court.

In court, the Gore team argued that Florida state law provided for a hand recount when there was a "receipt of a number of illegal votes or rejection of a number of legal votes sufficient to change or place in doubt the result of the election." Hand counts got under way, and previously unrecorded Gore votes continued to accumulate. The Florida Supreme Court directed local election officials to count by hand every legal vote where "there is a clear indication of the intent of the voter." Any votes that were counted by this standard were then tabulated and added to the state totals. As Gore's total votes increased, the Bush campaign sought a legal order preventing the recount from continuing. In petitioning the U.S. Supreme Court for review of their case, the Bush team argued that the injunction they sought would prevent Bush from suffering irreparable harm (in the form of denying him the slate of electors that the state had already certified was his).

Per Curiam.

. . . [W]e find a violation of the Equal Protection Clause.

The closeness of this election, and the multitude of legal challenges which have followed in its wake, have brought into sharp focus a common, if heretofore unnoticed, phenomenon. Nationwide statistics reveal that an estimated 2% of ballots cast do not register a vote for President for whatever reason, including deliberately choosing no candidate at all or some voter error, such as voting for two candidates or insufficiently marking a ballot. . . . In certifying election results, the votes eligible for inclusion in the certification are the votes meeting the properly established legal requirements.

This case has shown that punch card balloting machines can produce an unfortunate number of ballots which are not punched in a clean, complete way by the voter. After the current counting, it is likely legislative bodies nationwide will examine ways to improve the mechanisms and machinery for voting.

Having once granted the right to vote on equal terms, the State may not, by later arbitrary and disparate treatment, value one person's vote over that of another. The question before us . . . is whether the recount procedures the Florida Supreme Court has adopted are consistent with its obligation to avoid arbitrary and disparate treatment of the members of its electorate.

Here, the majority is making the argument that the lack of a clear standard by which to tabulate votes violates the Equal Protection clause. In essence, they are suggesting that different election boards will have different standards for determining what counts as a legal vote.

Much of the controversy seems to revolve around ballot cards designed to be perforated by a stylus but which, either through error or deliberate omission, have not been perforated with sufficient precision for a machine to count them. In some cases a piece of the card—a chad— is hanging, say by two corners. In other cases there is no separation at all, just an indentation.

Among the most memorable images of the strange events in Florida are the teams of election boards squinting at perforations, indentations, and hanging chads—tiny pieces of the ballots that should have completely separated from the ballot but for whatever reason did not. Were two unseparated perforations sufficient to count as a vote? Three? Six?

The Florida Supreme Court has ordered that the intent of the voter be discerned from such ballots. . . . Florida's basic command for the count of legally cast votes is to consider the "intent of the voter." This is unobjectionable as an abstract proposition and a starting principle. The problem inheres in the absence of specific standards to ensure its equal application.

The search for intent can be confined by specific rules designed to ensure uniform treatment. The want of those rules here has led to unequal evaluation of ballots in various respects. As seems to have been acknowledged at oral argument, the standards for accepting or rejecting contested ballots might vary not only from county to county but indeed within a single county from one recount team to another. . . . This is not a process with sufficient guarantees of equal treatment.

. . . The recount process, in its features here described, is inconsistent with the minimum procedures necessary to protect the fundamental right of each voter in the special instance of a statewide recount under the authority of a single state judicial officer.

When a court orders a statewide remedy, there must be at least some assurance that the rudimentary requirements of equal treatment and fundamental fairness are satisfied.

The Supreme Court then recognized the objections that were sure to arise, given its ruling. The Court effectively ended the recount, deciding the presidential election for George W. Bush. For an institution that prides itself on being politically independent, this decision more than most jeopardized that institutional integrity. The dissent from Justice John Paul Stevens makes this precise point.

Upon due consideration of the difficulties identified to this point, it is obvious that the recount cannot be conducted in compliance with the requirements of equal protection and due process without substantial additional work.

. . . None are more conscious of the vital limits on judicial authority than are the members of this Court, and none stand more in admiration of the Constitution's design to leave the selection of the President to the people, through their legislatures, and to the political sphere. When contending parties invoke the process of the courts, however, it becomes our unsought responsibility to resolve the federal and constitutional issues the judicial system has been forced to confront.

Justice Stevens in Dissent:

In the interest of finality . . . the majority effectively orders the disenfranchisement of an unknown number of voters whose ballots reveal their intent—and are therefore legal votes under state law—but were for some reason rejected by ballot-counting machines.

. . . [N]othing prevents the majority, even if it properly found an equal protection violation, from ordering relief appropriate to remedy that violation without depriving Florida voters of their right to have their votes counted. As the majority notes, "[a] desire for speed is not a general excuse for ignoring equal protection guarantees."

. . . [The Florida Supreme Court's] decisions were rooted in long-established precedent and were consistent with the relevant statutory provisions, taken as a whole. It did what courts do—it decided the case before it in light of the legislature's intent to leave no legally cast vote uncounted. In so doing, it relied on the sufficiency of the general "intent of the voter" standard articulated by the state legislature, coupled with a procedure for ultimate review by an impartial judge, to resolve the concern about disparate evaluations of contested ballots.

. . . What must underlie petitioners' entire federal assault on the Florida election procedures is an unstated lack of confidence in the impartiality and capacity of the state judges who would make the critical decisions if the vote count were to proceed. Otherwise, their position is wholly without merit. The endorsement of that position by the majority of this Court can only lend credence to the most cynical appraisal of the work of judges throughout the land. It is confidence in the men and women who administer the judicial system that is the true backbone of the rule of law. Time will one day heal the wound to that confidence that will be inflicted by today's decision. One thing, however, is certain. Although we may never know with complete certainty the identity of the winner of this year's Presidential election, the identity of the loser is perfectly clear. It is the Nation's confidence in the judge as an impartial guardian of the rule of law.

The action of the Court effectively ended the recount. Bush won Florida with 537 more votes than Gore. Compounding the difficulty of identifying voter intent was the design of the ballot in some precincts in Florida. The design of the so-called butterfly ballot presented difficulties for some voters who were reported to have mistakenly voted for Pat Buchanan instead of Al Gore. To make matters worse for the former vice president, Ralph Nader, the popular independent and progressive crusader for consumer rights, was reported to have pulled some—one might imagine at least 537—liberal Florida voters away from Gore's vote total.

As for the Court's decision, the warnings of the dissenters seemed prophetic, at least initially. Public opinion polls at the time of the decision revealed a deep division among voters regarding the legitimacy of the Court's action. Bush entered office after a shortened transition period with approximately half the country thinking that the Court had erred in its decision.

Source: U.S. Supreme Court, December 11, 2000, No. 00-949. Supreme Court of the United States, http://www.supremecourt.gov/oral_arguments/argument_transcripts/00-949.pdf.

Election of 2004

Bush and Same-Sex Marriage Initiatives in Competitive States

President Bush's Remarks Calling for a Constitutional Amendment Defining and Protecting Marriage

February 24, 2004

INTRODUCTION

In the 2004 election, conservative activists and legislatures in 11 states placed anti–gay marriage initiatives on the ballot. In each of the 11 states, those measures passed overwhelmingly with an average approval rate of 70 percent. Only in Oregon and Michigan were the votes on the ballot initiatives within 10 percentage points. The initiatives passed with such ease that many observers speculated that conservative turnout for Bush, especially among religious conservatives, was driven in large part by these ballot measures that appeared in many swing states.

The proliferation of state ballot initiatives may indeed have influenced turnout among evangelical voters, a core component of Bush's electoral support.

In addition to state initiatives and referenda, Congress considered a federal constitutional amendment to ban same-sex marriage. In this address, President Bush announced his support of the amendment, clearly signaling to state actors his views of attempts to amend state constitutions. The Bush campaign recognized the value of having these measures on the ballot in so many states, as they might energize people who would otherwise not turn out to vote. Given the number of voters opposed to gay marriage, it is clear that getting them to the polls would be a boon to Bush.

The ballot measures within the 11 states largely arose from recent state action by courts, legislatures, and city administrators to permit same-sex couples to marry or establish civil unions. Those actions within the states—whether by courts, legislators, or other public action—generated conservative countermobilizations that led to the large number of ballot initiatives.

In recent months . . . some activist judges and local officials have made an aggressive attempt to redefine marriage. In Massachusetts, four judges on the highest court have indicated they will order the issuance of marriage licenses to applicants of the same gender in May of this year. In San Francisco, city officials have issued thousands of marriage licenses to people of the same gender, contrary to the California Family Code. . . . A county in New Mexico has also issued marriage licenses to applicants of the same gender. And unless action is taken, we can expect more arbitrary court decisions, more litigation, more defiance of the law by local officials, all of which adds to uncertainty.

After more than two centuries of American jurisprudence and millennia of human experience, a few judges and local authorities are presuming to change the most fundamental institution of civilization. Their actions have created confusion on an issue that requires clarity.

On a matter of such importance, the voice of the people must be heard. Activist courts have left the people with one recourse. If we are to prevent the meaning of marriage from being changed forever, our Nation must enact a constitutional amendment to protect marriage in America.

The union of a man and woman is the most enduring human institution, honoring—honored and encouraged in all cultures and by every religious faith. Ages of experience have taught humanity that the commitment of a husband and wife to love and to serve one another promotes the welfare of children and the stability of society. Marriage cannot be severed from its cultural, religious, and natural roots without weakening the good influence of society. Government, by recognizing and protecting marriage, serves the interests of all.

Today I call upon the Congress to promptly pass and to send to the States for ratification an amendment to our Constitution defining and protecting marriage as a union of man and woman as husband and wife. The amendment should fully protect marriage while leaving the State legislatures free to make their own choices in defining legal arrangements other than marriage.

Prior to being submitted to the states for ratification, an amendment to the U.S. Constitution requires the support of two-thirds of both chambers in Congress. This proposed amendment failed to reach the necessary 290 votes in the House and did not come up for a vote in the Senate.

America is a free society which limits the role of government in the lives of our citizens. This commitment of freedom, however, does not require the redefinition of one of our most basic social institutions. Our Government should respect every person and protect the institution of marriage. There is no contradiction between these responsibilities.

Many postelection analyses and journalistic reports revealed that the ballot measures opposing same-sex marriage had demonstrable effects on turnout in key battleground states such as Ohio. For example, one study found that the roll-off (votes cast for president but not cast for ballot measures) was significantly higher in largely Democratic counties than in Republican counties. This reveals a higher degree of preference intensity for the initiatives among Republicans than Democrats. Rural areas, such as the Appalachian regions of southern Ohio, generated less roll-off than largely Democratic urban strongholds such as Cleveland-area counties. Similar stories emerged from other key states. Those additional votes mattered.

Source: "George W. Bush: Remarks Calling for a Constitutional Amendment Defining and Protecting Marriage, February 24, 2004." The American Presidency Project, http://www.presidency.ucsb.edu/ws/?pid=72554.

Kerry and the Swift Boat Veterans for Truth

Anti–John Kerry Campaign Ad

2004

INTRODUCTION

The candidates' military service records during the Vietnam War played a central role in the 2004 election. During the Vietnam War era, George W. Bush had stayed in the United States, opting to serve in the Air National Guard. John Kerry saw combat in Vietnam as a commander of a U.S. Navy swift boat. Questions about Bush's service record in Texas and Alabama had arisen during the 2000 campaign against Al Gore but really came under scrutiny in the 2004 election. Kerry, who received several medals for valor during his service in Vietnam, was targeted by a group of swift boat veterans who objected to the account that Kerry had given of his service. They also objected to Kerry's critique of U.S. policy in Vietnam when his tour of duty was over. In fact, one of the principal organizers of the Swift Boat Veterans for Truth was someone Kerry had confronted in a televised debate on *The Dick Cavett Show* in 1971.

Swift Boat Veterans for Truth was a so-called 527 group, which meant that it was organized under the authority of Section 527 of the Internal Revenue Code and subject to important restrictions in its activities. In particular, 527 groups could finance issue ads and target candidates so long as their activities were not coordinated with a campaign. There was no finding that Swift Boat Veterans for Truth activities were coordinated with the Bush campaign, although the group certainly aligned only against Kerry. At no time did Bush repudiate the claims made by the group, although he was under no legal obligation to do so.

The main thrust of the Swift Boat Veterans for Truth campaign against Kerry had to do with accounts that he and others had given of his heroism in combat. The campaign by the group included three ads targeting Kerry in competitive swing states as well as a book and many public appearances by the people affiliated with the group. As media outlets examined the claims made by the group, it appeared that many of them were unsubstantiated, incomplete, or wholly inaccurate. Nonetheless, the negative ads were successful in raising concerns among voters. The tactic of smearing a candidate for his or her lack of patriotism or truthfulness is now sometimes referred to as "swiftboating" the candidate.

The first ad by Swift Boat Veterans for Truth begins with a shot of vice presidential candidate Senator John Edwards (D-NC) speaking at a rally for Senator Kerry.

We now see on the screen a series of men who had served in some capacity on swift boats during the Vietnam War. Images of John Kerry are shown in the background, behind each interviewee.

John Edwards: "If you have any question about what John Kerry is made of, just spend 3 minutes with the men who served with him."

Al French: "I served with John Kerry."

Bob Elder: "I served with John Kerry."

George Elliott: "John Kerry has not been honest about what happened in Vietnam."

Al French: "He is lying about his record."

Louis Letson: "I know John Kerry is lying about his first Purple Heart because I treated him for that injury."

Van O'Dell: "John Kerry lied to get his bronze star. I know, I was there, I saw what happened."

Jack Chenoweth: "His account of what happened and what actually happened are the difference between night and day."

The Kerry campaign brought out several veterans who contradicted this version of events. Nonetheless, this drew the campaign into a dispute that drew it away from its core message. In fact, Kerry opened his address at the Democratic National Convention with a salute and the statement "I'm John Kerry and I'm reporting for duty." He then went on to emphasize patriotism and duty as a way to distinguish himself from Bush's service record.

Admiral Hoffman: "John Kerry has not been honest."

Adrian Lonsdale: "And he lacks the capacity to lead."

Larry Thurlow: "When the chips were down, you could not count on John Kerry."

Bob Elder: "John Kerry is no war hero."

Grant Hibbard: "He betrayed all his shipmates. He lied before the Senate."

Upon his return from Vietnam, Kerry had testified before the Senate as a leader of the group Vietnam Veterans Against the War.

Shelton White: "John Kerry betrayed the men and women he served with in Vietnam."

Joe Ponder: "He dishonored his country. He most certainly did."

Bob Hildreth: "I served with John Kerry."

Bob Hildreth (off-camera): "John Kerry cannot be trusted."

Announcer: "Swift Boat Veterans for Truth is responsible for the content of this advertisement."

Source: "Any Questions? (Swift Boat Veterans for Truth, 2004)." Museum of the Living Image: The Living Room Candidate, http://www.livingroomcandidate.org/commercials/2004.

Unlike the outcome in 2000, Bush won the popular vote in 2004. But he did so with the narrowest margin in history—50.7 percent to 48.3 percent. Part of the explanation for Bush's success in 2004 is attributable to incumbency advantage, economic conditions, and polarization among the electorate. Yes, many Democrats were vehemently opposed to the policies of the Bush administration, including the war in Iraq, but Republicans were aligned behind their candidate, and they turned out. Kerry captured the nomination early after Governor Howard Dean's poor showing in Iowa and didn't have to deal with a strong candidate (Ralph Nader) drawing from his left. Perhaps because of this, Democrats rallied to the Kerry campaign as their anyone-but-Bush candidate. Kerry's decision to make his military service in Vietnam the central theme of the convention—as opposed to, say, Bush's decision to go to war in Iraq—seems in retrospect to be rather odd, especially given that this allowed the Swift Boat Veterans for Truth to draw his attention away from his most resonant critique of Bush's handling of Iraq and the threat from terrorism.

Bush Air National Guard Allegations Surface

Alleged Air National Guard Memo
(August 18, 1973)

September 8, 2004

INTRODUCTION

In the 2004 presidential campaign, the candidates' military service during the Vietnam War became a salient issue. The nominees from both parties served in the military. Senator John Kerry (D-MA) was a highly decorated commander of a U.S. Navy swift boat in Vietnam. President George W. Bush served domestically in the Air National Guard.

As indicated in the previous analyses of the discussion of the Swift Boat Veterans for Truth campaign against Senator Kerry, many Republicans were suspicious of the accolades that Kerry received for his service in Vietnam. Kerry's later critique of U.S. policy in Vietnam, in their view, further undermined his patriotism and heroism.

Democrats responded with charges of their own against President Bush.

In the primary campaign in 2000, reporters had discovered that Bush received preferential treatment in being posted to the National Guard unit in Texas. Being placed in the unit meant that he would not have to serve in combat in Vietnam. It was a coveted position, attractive to many young men in the late 1960s interested in staying stateside. In the autumn of 2004, allegations arose again that Bush did not live up to the obligations of his National Guard service. Extensive searches of National Guard documents and interviews with Bush contemporaries in the National Guard revealed questions regarding his participation.

A CBS report, released by the popular show *60 Minutes,* focused on documents, including the memo reproduced on the following page, that were reportedly devastating to Bush's claims to have fulfilled all of his obligations that arose during his service in the Air National Guard. Days later, Dan Rather

of CBS was forced to apologize for his inability to confirm the authenticity of the documents. He later resigned, as did several others responsible for the report.

During a campaign that centered on national security and the military engagements in Iraq and Afghanistan, the candidates' records of their own military service gained a prominence that had not occurred during Bush's campaign against Al Gore in 2000.

Charges by the Swift Boat Veterans for Truth against Kerry's service record seemed to have more effect on voter preferences than the revelations about Bush's record in the Air National Guard. Part of the reason may be that the National Guard story quickly became a story about CBS News rather than President Bush's record. Soon after the CBS retractions, Bush established a commanding 14-point lead over Kerry that would prove insurmountable for the Democrat in November.

18 August 1973

Memo to File

SUBJECT: CYA

1. Staudt has obviously pressured Hodges more about Bush. I'm having trouble running interference and doing my job. Harris gave me a message today from Grp regarding Bush's OETR and Staudt is pushing to sugar coat it. Bush wasn't here during rating period and I don't have any feedback from 187th in Alabama. I will not rate. Austin is not happy today either.

2. Harris took the call from Grp today. I'll backdate but won't rate. Harris agrees.

Source: "Memo to File; Subject: CYA; 18 August 1973." CBS News, http://www.cbsnews.com/htdocs/pdf/BushGuardaugust18.pdf.

Election of 2008

Obama's Keynote Speech

Barack Obama's Speech at the Democratic National Convention, Boston, Massachusetts

July 27, 2004

INTRODUCTION

A candidate's fortunes are sometimes set well in advance of the actual campaign. In the case of Barack Obama, it is fair to say that his candidacy for the presidency sprang in large measure from the address that he gave at the 2004 Democratic National Convention. It was by all accounts a superb speech, a sermon that melted the hearts of the party's activists—the very group that would carry Obama's banner four years later. In the annals of national party convention speeches, this keynote address was a whopper!

Thank you so much. . . .

It is common for politicians to tout their humble origins, but Obama's story was truly different, and it quickly caught the attention of the convention and the millions watching on television.

Tonight is a particular honor for me because, let's face it, my presence on this stage is pretty unlikely. My father was a foreign student, born and raised in a small village in Kenya. He grew up herding goats, went to school in a tin-roof shack. His father—my grandfather—was a cook, a domestic servant to the British.

But my grandfather had larger dreams for his son. Through hard work and perseverance my father got a scholarship to study in a magical place, America, that shone as a beacon of freedom and opportunity to so many who had come before.

While studying here, my father met my mother. She was born in a town on the other side of the world, in Kansas. Her father worked on oil rigs and farms through most of the Depression. The day after Pearl Harbor my grandfather signed up for duty; joined Patton's army, marched across Europe. Back home, my grandmother raised a baby and went to work on a bomber assembly line. After the war, they studied on the G.I. Bill, bought a house through F.H.A., and later moved west all the way to Hawaii in search of opportunity.

And they, too, had big dreams for their daughter. A common dream, born of two continents.

My parents shared not only an improbable love, they shared an abiding faith in the possibilities of this nation. They would give me an African name, Barack, or "blessed," believing that in a tolerant America your name is no barrier to success. They imagined—They imagined me going to the best schools in the land, even though they weren't rich, because in a generous America you don't have to be rich to achieve your potential.

They're both passed away now. And yet, I know that on this night they look down on me with great pride.

They stand here—And I stand here today, grateful for the diversity of my heritage, aware that my parents' dreams live on in my two precious daughters. I stand here knowing that my story is part of the larger American story, that I owe a debt to all of those who came before me, and that, in no other country on earth, is my story even possible. . . .

This year, in this election we are called to reaffirm our values and our commitments, to hold them against a hard reality and see how we're measuring up to the legacy of our forbearers and the promise of future generations. . . .

People don't expect—People don't expect government to solve all their problems. But they sense, deep in their bones, that with just a slight change in priorities, we can make sure that every child in America has a decent shot at life, and that the doors of opportunity remain open to all.

They know we can do better. And they want that choice. . . .

You know, a while back—awhile back I met a young man named Shamus in a V.F.W. Hall in East Moline, Illinois. He was a good-looking kid—six two, six three, clear eyed, with an easy smile. He told me he'd joined the Marines and was heading to Iraq the following week. And as I listened to him explain why he'd enlisted, the absolute faith he had in our country and its leaders, his devotion to duty and service, I thought this young man was all that any of us might ever hope for in a child.

The recurrent reference to dreams came from Obama's memoir, *Dreams from My Father: A Story of Race and Inheritance,* first published in July 1995. By 2006 as buzz about an Obama candidacy grew louder, the book became a best seller.

American society was changing, becoming much more diverse. More so than any other candidate in American history, Obama represented the changing face of our nation.

But then I asked myself, "Are we serving Shamus as well as he is serving us?"

I thought of the 900 men and women—sons and daughters, husbands and wives, friends and neighbors, who won't be returning to their own hometowns. I thought of the families I've met who were struggling to get by without a loved one's full income, or whose loved ones had returned with a limb missing or nerves shattered, but still lacked long-term health benefits because they were Reservists.

Obama was referencing the faulty intelligence information at the center of George W. Bush's decision to invade Iraq. By this point in 2004, the American public remained somewhat supportive of the war. Yet within two years, opposition would swell. Unlike his Democratic rival Hillary Clinton, Obama had opposed the war from the beginning. In fact, his early opposition to the war was a critical aspect of his candidacy, a distinction that helped him nudge out Clinton for the nomination.

When we send our young men and women into harm's way, we have a solemn obligation not to fudge the numbers or shade the truth about why they're going, to care for their families while they're gone, to tend to the soldiers upon their return, and to never ever go to war without enough troops to win the war, secure the peace, and earn the respect of the world. . . .

It is that fundamental belief—It is that fundamental belief: I am my brother's keeper. I am my sister's keeper that makes this country work. It's what allows us to pursue our individual dreams and yet still come together as one American family.

E pluribus unum: "Out of many, one."

Now even as we speak, there are those who are preparing to divide us—the spin masters, the negative ad peddlers who embrace the politics of "anything goes." Well, I say to them tonight, there is not a liberal America and a conservative America—there is the United States of America. There is not a Black America and a White America and Latino America and Asian America—there's the United States of America.

This seemed to be the heart of his speech: that we are all together in the struggle to create a better nation. This theme—"We are one people"—would become an important call in Obama's run for the White House.

The pundits, the pundits like to slice-and-dice our country into red states and blue states; red states for Republicans, blue states for Democrats. But I've got news for them, too. We worship an "awesome God" in the blue states, and we don't like federal agents poking around in our libraries in the red states. We coach Little League in the blue states and yes, we've got some gay friends in the red states. There are patriots who opposed the war in Iraq

and there are patriots who supported the war in Iraq. We are one people, all of us pledging allegiance to the stars and stripes, all of us defending the United States of America. . . .

America! Tonight, if you feel the same energy that I do, if you feel the same urgency that I do, if you feel the same passion that I do, if you feel the same hopefulness that I do—if we do what we must do, then I have no doubt that all across the country, from Florida to Oregon, from Washington to Maine, the people will rise up in November, and John Kerry will be sworn in as President, and John Edwards will be sworn in as Vice President, and this country will reclaim its promise, and out of this long political darkness a brighter day will come.

Thank you very much everybody. God bless you. Thank you.

Source: "Transcript: Illinois Senate Candidate Barack Obama." Speech at the Democratic National Convention, Boston, Massachusetts, July 27, 2004. *Washington Post,* http://www.washingtonpost.com/wp-dyn/articles/A19751-2004 Jul27.html.

Every presidential race or two there are stand-out speeches, addresses that are both powerful and transformative. In 2004, that speech came from a little-known Illinois state senator named Barack Obama.

Obama, Race, and the South Carolina Democratic Primary

Barack Obama's Victory Speech following the South Carolina Primary

January 26, 2008

INTRODUCTION

The campaign for the Democratic nomination in 2008 was a particularly hard-fought contest. Both Barack Obama and Hillary Rodham Clinton had wins coming into the South Carolina primary in late January. Clinton seemed to be losing ground to the senator from Illinois, however. Just a week prior to South Carolina, Clinton had been leading in the polls by a large margin. Buoyed by success in Iowa, Obama turned his sights on South Carolina and began to broaden his appeal.

The issue of the breadth of Obama's appeal would become a central theme of the Democratic primary. To many observers, Obama's candidacy presaged a shift to a postracial society where African American candidates could appeal to broad swaths of the American electorate. But that theme stood in stark contrast to the sad history of racially polarized voting in the United States and in particular in the South. As the candidates descended upon South Carolina, the issue of race came to the fore.

Thank you, South Carolina! [Cheers, applause.]

[Chants of "Yes, We Can! Yes, We Can!"]

Thank you. Thank you.

[Continued chants of "Yes, We Can!"]

Thank you, everybody. Thank you. Thank you, South Carolina. [Cheers, applause.] Thank you. Thank you, South Carolina. Thank you to the rock of my life, Michelle Obama. [Cheers, applause.]

Thank you to Malia and Sasha Obama, who haven't seen their daddy in a week. [Cheers, applause.] Thank you to Pete Skidmore for his outstanding service to our country and being such a great supporter of this campaign. [Cheers, applause.]

You know, over two weeks ago we saw the people of Iowa proclaim that our time for change has come. [Cheers, applause.] But there were those who doubted this country's desire for something new, who said Iowa was a fluke, not to be repeated again. Well, tonight the cynics who believed that what began in the snows of Iowa was just an illusion were told a different story by the good people of South Carolina. [Cheers, applause.]

After four great contests in every corner of this country, we have the most votes, the most delegates—[cheers, applause]—and the most diverse coalition of Americans that we've seen in a long, long time. [Cheers, applause.]

You can see it in the faces here tonight. There are young and old, rich and poor. They are black and white, Latino and Asian and Native American. [Cheers, applause.] They are Democrats from Des Moines and independents from Concord and, yes, some Republicans from rural Nevada. And we've got young people all across this country who've never had a reason to participate until now. [Cheers, applause.]

And in nine days, in nine short days, nearly half the nation will have the chance to join us in saying that we are tired of business as usual in Washington. [Cheers, applause.] We are hungry for change, and we are ready to believe again. [Cheers, applause.]

[Chants of "We Want Change! We Want Change!"]

But if there's anything, though, that we've been reminded of since Iowa, it's that the kind of change we seek will not come easy. Now, partly because we have fine candidates in this field, fierce competitors who are worthy of our respect and our admiration—[applause]—and as contentious as this campaign may get, we have to remember that this is a contest for the Democratic nomination and that all of us share an abiding desire to end the disastrous policies of the current administration. [Cheers, applause.]

But there are real differences between the candidates. We are looking for more than just a change of party in the White House. We're looking to fundamentally change the status quo in Washington. [Cheers, applause.] It's a status quo that extends beyond any particular party. And right now that

"We are hungry for change, and we are ready to believe again."

status quo is fighting back with everything it's got, with the same old tactics that divide and distract us from solving the problems people face, whether those problems are health care that folks can't afford or a mortgage they cannot pay.

So this will not be easy. Make no mistake about what we're up against. We're up against the belief that it's all right for lobbyists to dominate our government, that they are just part of the system in Washington. But we know that the undue influence of lobbyists is part of the problem, and this election is our chance to say that we are not going to let them stand in our way anymore. [Cheers, applause.]

We're up against the conventional thinking that says your ability to lead as president comes from longevity in Washington or proximity to the White House. But we know that real leadership is about candor and judgment and the ability to rally Americans from all walks of life around a common purpose, a higher purpose. [Cheers, applause.]

We're up against decades of bitter partisanship that cause politicians to demonize their opponents instead of coming together to make college affordable or energy cleaner. It's the kind of partisanship where you're not even allowed to say that a Republican had an idea, even if it's one you never agreed with. That's the kind of politics that is bad for our party. It is bad for our country. And this is our chance to end it once and for all. [Cheers, applause.]

We're up against the idea that it's acceptable to say anything and do anything to win an election. But we know that this is exactly what's wrong with our politics. This is why people don't believe what their leaders say anymore. This is why they tune out. And this election is our chance to give the American people a reason to believe again. [Cheers, applause.]

But let me say this, South Carolina. What we've seen in these last weeks is that we're also up against forces that are not the fault of any one campaign but feed the habits that prevent us from being who we want to be as a nation.

During the primaries, Senator Clinton had remarked that Obama was unelectable because his candidacy relied so heavily on African American support. She had

It's a politics that uses religion as a wedge and patriotism as a bludgeon, a politics that tells us that we have to think,

act, and even vote within the confines of the categories that supposedly define us, the assumption that young people are apathetic, the assumption that Republicans won't cross over, the assumption that the wealthy care nothing for the poor and that the poor don't vote, the assumption that African-Americans can't support the white candidate, whites can't support the African-American candidate, blacks and Latinos cannot come together.

also remarked to voters that civil rights legislation was the result of action taken by Lyndon Johnson—a white president. Some observers had argued that Obama couldn't sustain African American support because he "wasn't black enough." Racially tinged statements became commonplace throughout the Democratic primary.

We are here tonight to say that that is not the America we believe in. [Cheers, applause.]

[Chants of "Yes, We Can! Yes, We Can!"]

I did not travel around this state over the last year and see a white South Carolina or a black South Carolina. I saw South Carolina—[cheers, applause]—because in the end, we're not up just against the ingrained and destructive habits of Washington. We're also struggling with our own doubts, our own fears, our own cynicism. The change we seek has always required great struggle and great sacrifice. And so this is a battle in our own hearts and minds about what kind of country we want and how hard we're willing to work for it.

So let me remind you tonight that change will not be easy. Change will take time. There will be setbacks and false starts, and sometimes we'll make mistakes. But as hard as it may seem, we cannot lose hope, because there are people all across this great nation who are counting on us, who can't afford another four years without health care. [Cheers.] They can't afford another four years without good schools. [Cheers.] They can't afford another four years without decent wages because our leaders couldn't come together and get it done.

Theirs are the stories and voices we carry on from South Carolina—the mother who can't get Medicaid to cover all the needs of her sick child. She needs us to pass a health care plan that cuts costs and makes health care available and affordable for every single American. That's what she's looking for. [Cheers, applause.]

The teacher who works another shift at Dunkin' Donuts after school just to make ends meet—she needs us to reform our education system so that she gets better pay and more support and that students get the resources that they need to achieve their dreams. [Cheers, applause.]

The Maytag worker who's now competing with his own teenager for a $7-an-hour job at the local Wal-Mart because the factory he gave his life to shut its doors—he needs us to stop giving tax breaks to companies that ship our jobs overseas and start putting them in the pockets of working Americans who deserve it—[cheers, applause]—and put them in the pockets of struggling homeowners who are having a tough time, and looking after seniors who should retire with dignity and respect.

That woman who told me that she hasn't been able to breathe since the day her nephew left for Iraq, or the soldier who doesn't know his child because he's on his third or fourth or even fifth tour of duty—they need us to come together and put an end to a war that should have never been authorized and should have never been waged. [Cheers, applause.]

So understand this, South Carolina. The choice in this election is not between regions or religions or genders. It's not about rich versus poor, young versus old, and it is not about black versus white.

[Cheers, applause.]

This election is about the past versus the future. [Cheers, applause.] It's about whether we settle for the same divisions and distractions and drama that passes for politics today or whether we reach for a politics of common sense and innovation, a politics of shared sacrifice and shared prosperity.

There are those who will continue to tell us that we can't do this, that we can't have what we're looking for, that we can't have what we want, that we're peddling false hopes. But here's what I know. I know that when people say we can't overcome all the big money and influence in Washington, I think of that elderly woman who sent me a contribution the other day, an envelope that had a money order for $3.01—[cheers, applause]—along with a verse of Scripture tucked inside the envelope. So don't tell us change isn't possible. That woman knows change is possible. [Cheers, applause.]

When I hear the cynical talk that blacks and whites and Latinos can't join together and work together, I'm reminded of the Latino brothers and sisters I organized with and stood with and fought with side by side for jobs and justice on the streets of Chicago. So don't tell us change can't happen. [Cheers, applause.]

When I hear that we'll never overcome the racial divide in our politics, I think about that Republican woman who used to work for Strom Thurmond, who's now devoted to educating inner-city children, and who went out into the streets of South Carolina and knocked on doors for this campaign. Don't tell me we can't change. [Cheers, applause.]

Yes, we can. Yes, we can change.

[Chants of "Yes, We Can! Yes, We Can!"]

Yes, we can.

[Continued chants of "Yes, We Can!"]

Yes, we can heal this nation. Yes, we can seize our future. And as we leave this great state with a new wind at our backs, and we take this journey across this great country, a country we love, with the message we've carried from the plains of Iowa to the hills of New Hampshire, from the Nevada desert to the South Carolina coast, the same message we had when we were up and when we were down, that out of many we are one, that while we breathe we will hope, and where we are met with cynicism and doubt and fear and those who tell us that we can't, we will respond with that timeless creed that sums up the spirit of the American people in three simple words: Yes, we can.

Thank you, South Carolina. I love you. [Cheers, applause.]

Source: "Barack Obama: Remarks Following the South Carolina Primary, January 26, 2008." The American Presidency Project, http://www.presidency.ucsb.edu/ws/?pid=76302.

After Obama won the South Carolina primary, Senator Clinton's spouse (former president Bill Clinton) would seek to downplay the victory, noting that "Jesse Jackson won South Carolina twice in '84 and '88. And he ran a good campaign, and Senator Obama's run a good campaign here. He's run a good campaign everywhere." By comparing Obama's win to that of an earlier African American presidential candidate who ultimately lost the nomination, Clinton seemed to suggest that the large African American population of South Carolina rather than the candidate's broad appeal contributed to Obama's success.

While Obama was unwilling to engage what at times seemed to be both Clintons aligned against him, his campaign advisers did. One key adviser later claimed that the Clintons were engaged in "the most shameful, offensive, fear-mongering" he'd seen.

In the general election, Obama's appeal to white voters was quite evident. In fact, polls suggested that white voters' support for Obama was even larger than support for John Kerry in 2004 or Al Gore in 2000. The racialized politics that characterized many previous elections may still have been in play, but Obama's success in appealing to white voters in addition to African American voters led many scholars to suggest that we had entered a new era in race and politics. Prior to Obama's success, the conventional wisdom was that African American candidates could only succeed in majority-minority districts.

"A More Perfect Union" Speech

Barack Obama's Speech on Race
March 18, 2008

INTRODUCTION

Some critical moments of presidential campaigns reignite a flagging candidacy or put to rest an unsettling narrative that has emerged to define the candidate. None better typifies that type of critical event than Barack Obama's "A More Perfect Union" speech. Obama gave this speech at the National Constitution Center in Philadelphia, Pennsylvania, located across the street from Independence Hall where the framers of the Constitution met in the summer of 1787. No doubt the occasion of the speech was one that the framers themselves would not have imagined: an African American candidate for president giving the central address of his ultimately successful primary campaign.

"We the people, in order to form a more perfect union." Two hundred and twenty one years ago, in a hall that still stands across the street, a group of men gathered and, with these simple words, launched America's improbable experiment in democracy. . . .

The document they produced was eventually signed but ultimately unfinished. It was stained by this nation's original sin of slavery, a question that divided the colonies and brought the convention to a stalemate until the founders chose to allow the slave trade to continue for at least twenty more years, and to leave any final resolution to future generations. . . .

This was one of the tasks we set forth at the beginning of this campaign—to continue the long march of those who came before us, a march for a more just, more equal, more free, more caring and more prosperous America. I chose to run for the presidency at this moment in history because I believe deeply that we cannot solve the challenges of our time unless we solve them together. . . .

In the weeks prior to his address, Senator Obama faced severe criticism from many quarters regarding the angry, racially tinged rhetoric espoused by his longtime pastor and confidant, Reverend Jeremiah Wright. Obama had previously denounced the words of Reverend Wright but continued to struggle to articulate his own view on race and distinguish that view from the anger and frustration felt by many in the black community, as evidenced by the reverend's remarks.

And yet, it has only been in the last couple of weeks that the discussion of race in this campaign has taken a particularly divisive turn. . . .

Reverend Wright's comments were not only wrong but divisive, divisive at a time when we need unity; racially charged at a time when we need to come together to solve a set of monumental problems—two wars, a terrorist threat, a falling economy, a chronic health care crisis and potentially devastating climate change; problems that are neither black or white or Latino or Asian, but rather problems that confront us all. . . .

Like other predominantly black churches across the country, Trinity embodies the black community in its entirety—the doctor and the welfare mom, the model student and the former gang-banger. Like other black churches, Trinity's services are full of raucous laughter and sometimes bawdy humor. They are full of dancing, clapping, screaming and shouting that may seem jarring to the untrained ear. The church contains in full the kindness and cruelty, the fierce intelligence and the shocking ignorance, the struggles and successes, the love and yes, the bitterness and bias that make up the black experience in America. . . .

I can no more disown him than I can disown the black community. I can no more disown him than I can my white grandmother—a woman who helped raise me, a woman who sacrificed again and again for me, a woman who loves me as much as she loves anything in this world, but a woman who once confessed her fear of black men who passed by her on the street, and who on more than one occasion has uttered racial or ethnic stereotypes that made me cringe. . . .

These people are a part of me. And they are a part of America, this country that I love.

The speech was a remarkable success in reasserting Obama's core principles, articulating a compelling view on issues of race, and demonstrating a sensitivity to the issue of race that no public official had before exhibited. Its sincerity and frankness and its deeply personal narrative coupled with constitutional themes and historical context added to its power and consequence.

[. . .]

. . . [W]e . . . need to remind ourselves that so many of the disparities that exist in the African-American community today can be directly traced to inequalities passed on from an earlier generation that suffered under the brutal legacy of slavery and Jim Crow.

[. . .]

This is the reality in which Reverend Wright and other African-Americans of his generation grew up. . . .

But for all those who scratched and clawed their way to get a piece of the American Dream, there were many who didn't make it. . . . That legacy of defeat was passed on to future generations. . . . Even for those blacks who did make it, questions of race, and racism, continue to define their worldview in fundamental ways. For the men and women of Reverend Wright's generation, the memories of humiliation and doubt and fear have not gone away; nor has the anger and the bitterness of those years. . . .

[. . .]

. . . That anger is not always productive; indeed, all too often it distracts attention from solving real problems; it keeps us from squarely facing our own complicity in our condition, and prevents the African-American community from forging the alliances it needs to bring about real change. But the anger is real; it is powerful; and to simply wish it away, to condemn it without understanding its roots, only serves to widen the chasm of misunderstanding that exists between the races. . . .

[. . .]

. . . I have never been so naive as to believe that we can get beyond our racial divisions in a single election cycle, or with a single candidacy—particularly a candidacy as imperfect as my own.

But I have asserted a firm conviction—a conviction rooted in my faith in God and my faith in the American people—that working together we can move beyond some of our old racial wounds, and that in fact we have no choice if we are to continue on the path of a more perfect union.

[. . .]

. . . It requires all Americans to realize that your dreams do not have to come at the expense of my dreams; that investing in the health, welfare, and education of black and brown and white children will ultimately help all of America prosper.

. . . **Let us find that common stake we all have in one another, and let our politics reflect that spirit as well.**

Source: "Barack Obama: Address at the National Constitution Center in Philadelphia: 'A More Perfect Union,' March 18, 2008." The American Presidency Project, http://www.presidency.ucsb.edu/ws/?pid=76710.

The next day, *The New York Times* compared the speech to the singular defining addresses of Abraham Lincoln and John F. Kennedy. Many contemporary observers noted that the "A More Perfect Union" address was a fundamental turning point in Barack Obama's candidacy.

Obama Rejects Public Financing

Letter to Barack Obama from Common Cause and the League of Women Voters (February 2008)

June 2008

INTRODUCTION

In June 2008, Democratic candidate Barack Obama made an unprecedented announcement: he would opt out of a federal campaign system that would provide public financing of his general election campaign. Obama was the very first major party candidate to have ever chosen to forego the more than $84 million in public funds. He opted to do so in large part because he expected to raise far, far more than $84 million on his own. In fact, his 2008 race broke all previous funding records. Had he accepted public financing, he would be obligated to observe federal campaign finance laws that limit expenditures during the general election. Moreover, by limiting his campaign to the $84 million, he essentially would be leaving hundreds of millions of dollars on the table.

Obama's announcement stood in stark contrast to earlier commitments that the candidate had made to supporters and campaign finance reform groups such as Common Cause. However, the Obama campaign had signaled earlier in the race that it would not commit to public financing if the outside groups' spending would not be controlled. This letter was sent to the Obama campaign by Common Cause and the League of Women Voters, among other groups, as soon as the campaign began hedging on its promise to stick with public financing made several months prior to his announcement.

February 15, 2008

Dear Senator Obama,

Our organizations are deeply concerned about recent statements by your campaign spokesperson, Bill Burton, regarding the commitment you made last year to participate in the public financing system in the presidential general election if nominated by your party and if your major party opponent also agrees to use public financing in the general election.

The purpose of the public financing system is to democratize the electoral process by making it possible for candidates who cannot self-finance to still be able to run. Presidential candidates are permitted access to public financing if they meet certain eligibility requirements and if they accept certain limits on their spending. The difficulty is that in recent years, groups that are unaffiliated with campaigns but are free to spend huge amounts of money on ad campaigns (the so-called 527 groups) have come to dominate the field in presidential elections. This means that if a campaign accepts public financing, the campaign is very likely to be outspent by the 527 groups. Moreover, the high costs of television advertising, travel, and so on have outpaced the level of public financing that is made available to candidates. These are among the reasons that Obama concluded that the system was broken.

The presidential public financing system was established to protect the integrity of the presidency and the interests of the American people. Every Democratic and Republican nominee for president since 1976 has used the public financing system for their general election campaigns.

243

According to *Politico* (February 14, 2008), Mr. Burton stated that the commitment you made last year is an "option," not a pledge.

Mr. Burton further said, "the only reason this is an option is because we pursued the decision from the FEC. As the Clinton campaign continues to remind you, Obama is not the nominee, but this is a question we will address when he is."

According to the *New York Times* (February 15, 2008), "'We will address that issue in the general election, when we're the nominee,' Mr. Burton said. 'We're just not entertaining hypotheticals right now.'"

These statements by Mr. Burton conflict with the commitment you made last year. There was nothing said in your commitment about public financing in the general election being an "option," or "a question we will address" at such time as you are the nominee.

Last year, on March 1, 2007, . . . Mr. Burton, stated: "If Senator Obama is the nominee, he will aggressively pursue an agreement with the Republican nominee to preserve a publicly financed general election," according to the *Associated Press*.

On the same day, Senator McCain's campaign issued a statement making the same kind of commitment. The statement said, "Should John McCain win the Republican nomination, we will agree to accept public financing in the general election, if the Democratic nominee agrees to do the same."

As it turned out, John McCain opted out of public financing for the Republican primary but did accept public financing in the general election, as he promised here.

Some nine months later you repeated the commitment in response to a questionnaire [from an alliance of 20 civic and public interest groups].

[. . .]

The following question was on the questionnaire:

If you are nominated for President in 2008 and your major opponents agree to forgo private funding in the general election campaign, will you participate in presidential public financing system?

You answered this question as follows:

OBAMA: Yes. I have been a long-time advocate for public financing of campaigns combined with free television and radio time as a way to reduce the influence of moneyed special interests. I introduced public financing legislation in the Illinois State Senate, and am the only 2008 candidate to have sponsored Senator Russ Feingold's (D-WI) bill to reform the presidential public financing system. In February 2007, I proposed a novel way to preserve the strength of the public financing system in the 2008 election. My plan requires both major party candidates to agree on a fundraising truce, return excess money from donors, and stay within the public financing system for the general election. My proposal followed announcements by some presidential candidates that they would forgo public financing so they could raise unlimited funds in the general election. The Federal Election Commission ruled the proposal legal, and Senator John McCain (R-AZ) has already pledged to accept this fundraising pledge. If I am the Democratic nominee, I will aggressively pursue an agreement with the Republican nominee to preserve a publicly financed general election.

The video that Obama released a few months later was hardly the resounding reaffirmation that Common Cause was looking for. McCain and other Republicans immediately pounced on Obama's change of heart. They derided him for flip-flopping on the issue and argued that such a switch revealed that he was actually not bringing a new kind of politics to Washington.

Given the uncertainty created by your campaign spokesman in the last two days about the status of the commitment you made, our organizations request that you reaffirm the commitment you made last year.

Our organizations strongly urge you to personally make clear to citizens that you remain committed to using the public financing system in the presidential general election if you are the Democratic nominee and if the Republican nominee also agrees to use the public financing system in the general election.

Campaign Legal Center
League of Women Voters

Common Cause

Public Citizen

Democracy 21

US Pirg

Source: "Common Cause Letters: Coalition Letter to Obama on Public Financing Pledge, February 15, 2008." Common Cause, http://www.commoncause.org/site/apps/nlnet/content2.aspx?c=dkLNK1MQIwG&b=4773617&ct=5075755.

Obama made the announcement that he would forego public financing via a video that was emailed to supporters. In the video, Obama made the argument that while he was committed to publicly financed campaigning on principle, his Republican opponent was not. To unilaterally disarm, Obama suggested, would be irresponsible. The following is the text of his video.

"Senator Barack Obama: It's not an easy decision, especially because I support a robust system of public financing of elections. But the public financing of presidential elections, as it exists today, is broken and we face opponents who've become masters of gaming this broken system. . . . John McCain's campaign and the Republican National Committee are fueled by contributions from Washington lobbyists and special interest PACs. We've already seen that he's not going to stop the smears and attacks from his allies running so-called 527 groups, who will spend millions and millions of dollars in unlimited donations."

By not accepting public funding, Obama would be free to spend in states unfettered by federal spending limits. He could blanket every media market. This forced McCain to spend in states that he had hoped to keep from being competitive.

It was a major decision that ran counter to Obama's well-established position on campaign finance. He was on the record supporting publicly financed campaigns and had voted for such measures as a senator. But when it came to campaign strategy, principle didn't compel him to limit his expenditures. A further irony was that McCain—who also opted out of public financing for the primary but not the general election—was himself a prominent champion of campaign finance reform as a Senator.

Obama would go on to trounce McCain in fund-raising, raising a total of almost $780 million—more than twice that of the McCain campaign.

Obama at the Democratic National Convention

**Barack Obama's Acceptance Speech
at the Democratic National Convention**

August 28, 2008

INTRODUCTION

It had already been a historic campaign. Not only would an African American receive a major party's presidential nomination, but Barack Obama had captured the victory after a hard-fought primary campaign against Hillary Rodham Clinton, who came closer to a major party presidential nomination than any woman before her. Campaign finance records were shattered, and a massive influx of voters, many of them young, had joined Obama's crusade. Now Obama would accept the nomination at the Democratic National Convention.

Thank you so much. Thank you very much. Thank you everybody.

> This is a standard line in nomination acceptance speeches, and it is always met with a sustained, robust applause.

To Chairman Dean, and my great friend, Dick Durbin, and to all my fellow citizens of this great nation, with profound gratitude and great humility—I accept your nomination for the presidency of the United States.

> As noted, it was a fierce, long battle for the Democratic nomination. Many voters continued to adore Clinton, so Obama's recognition of her early in the speech was a deft political move. It should also be noted that Obama would later benefit from a so-called gender gap in the general election.

Let me—Let me express—Let me express my thanks to the historic slate of candidates who accompanied me on this journey, and especially the one who traveled the farthest, a champion for working Americans and an inspiration to my daughters and yours: Hillary Rodham Clinton.

To President Clinton—To President Bill Clinton, who made last night the case for change as only he can make it, to Ted Kennedy, who embodies the spirit of service, and to the next Vice President of the United States, Joe Biden, I thank you. I am grateful to finish this journey with one of the finest statesmen of our time, a man at ease with everyone from world leaders to the conductors on the Amtrak train he still takes home every night, to the love of my life—the next First Lady, Michelle Obama; and to Malia and Sasha, I love you so much and I am so proud of you.

Four years ago, I stood before you and told you my story of the brief union between a young man from Kenya and a young woman from Kansas who weren't well-off or well-known, but shared a belief that in America, their son could achieve whatever he put his mind to.

It is that promise that's always set this country apart—that through hard work and sacrifice each of us can pursue our individual dreams but still come together as one American family, to ensure that the next generation can pursue their dreams as well.

It's why I stand here tonight. Because for two hundred and thirty two years, at each moment when that promise was in jeopardy, ordinary men and women, students and soldiers, farmers and teachers, nurses and janitors—found the courage to keep it alive.

We meet at one of those defining moments—a moment when our nation is at war, our economy is in turmoil, and the American promise has been threatened once more.

America was embroiled in wars in Iraq and Afghanistan, and later that year the housing and banking markets crashed, leading to a deep financial crisis. These two issues—wars in the Middle East and the Great Recession—would later define Obama's first term in office.

Tonight, more Americans are out of work and more are working harder for less. More of you have lost your homes and even more are watching your home values plummet. More of you have cars you can't afford to drive, credit cards, bills you can't afford to pay and tuition that's beyond your reach.

These challenges are not all of government's making. But the failure to respond is a direct result of a broken politics in Washington and the failed policies of George W. Bush.

Unlike some retiring presidents, George W. Bush was leaving office very unpopular—with approval ratings at roughly 30 percent. This was likely a play for independent voters, who would be the key to victory in November.

America, we are better than these last eight years. We are a better country than this. This country's more decent than one woman in Ohio on the brink of retirement finds herself one illness away from disaster after a lifetime of hard work.

We're a better country than one where a man in Indiana has to pack up the equipment that he's worked on for twenty years and watch as its shipped off to China, and then chokes up as he explains how he felt like a failure when he went home to tell his family the news.

We are more compassionate than a government that lets veterans sleep on our streets, and families slide into poverty; that sits—that sits on its hands while a major American city drowns before our eyes.

Tonight—Tonight I say to the people of America, to Democrats and Republicans and Independents across this great land: Enough!

This moment—This moment—this election is our chance to keep, in the 21st century, the American promise alive. Because next week, in Minnesota, the same Party that brought you two terms of George Bush and Dick Cheney will ask this country for a third. And we are here—we are here because we love this country too much to let the next four years look just like the last eight. On November 4th—On November 4th, we must stand up and say: "Eight is enough." . . .

I believe that, as hard as it will be, the change we need is coming, because I've seen it, because I've lived it. Because I've seen it in Illinois, when we provided health care to more children and moved more families from welfare to work. I've seen it in Washington, where we worked across party lines to open up government and hold lobbyists more accountable, to give better care for our veterans, and keep nuclear weapons out of the hands of terrorists.

Young voters were instrumental in capturing Obama's nomination, and they would play a key role in his victory in November. In the 2000 presidential election, just 35 percent of those under 30 years of age came to the polls. By 2008, that figure had reached 49 percent.

And I've seen it in this campaign, in the young people who voted for the first time and the young at heart, those who got involved again after a very long time; in the Republicans who never thought they'd pick up a Democratic ballot, but did. . . .

You know, this country of ours has more wealth than any nation, but that's not what makes us rich. We have the most powerful military on Earth, but that's not what makes us strong. Our universities and our culture are the envy of the world, but that's not what keeps the world coming to our shores.

Instead, it is that American spirit, that American promise, that pushes us forward even when the path is uncertain; that binds us together in spite of our differences; that makes us fix our eye not on what is seen, but what is unseen, that better place around the bend.

That promise is our greatest inheritance. It's a promise I make to my daughters when I tuck them in at night and a promise that you make to yours, a promise that has led immigrants to cross oceans and pioneers to travel west, a promise that led workers to picket lines and women to reach for the ballot.

And it is that promise that, 45 years ago today, brought Americans from every corner of this land to stand together on a Mall in Washington, before Lincoln's Memorial, and hear a young preacher from Georgia speak of his Dream. . . .

Obama was referencing perhaps the most notable phrase in the civil rights movement, from Martin Luther King Jr.'s August 1963 17-minute speech dubbed the "I Have a Dream" speech. King used that phrase eight times, each in reference to a more just society in America.

America, we cannot turn back, not with so much work to be done; not with so many children to educate, and so many veterans to care for; not with an economy to fix, and cities to rebuild, and farms to save; not with so many families to protect and so many lives to mend.

America, we cannot turn back. We cannot walk alone.

At this moment, in this election, we must pledge once more to march into the future. Let us keep that promise, that American promise, and in the words of Scripture hold firmly, without wavering, to the hope that we confess.

Thank you. God bless you. And God bless the United States of America.

Needless to say, the crowd at the convention loved the speech, and there is much evidence to suggest that it was very well received in kitchens, living rooms, and taverns across the country. Beyond persuading some voters to come to Obama's side, the speech is widely credited as being a powerful mobilizing speech. That is, Obama's address here and his words throughout the course of the autumn campaign pulled many voters into the electoral process. Turnout increased, likely due to the excitement of a dynamic candidate, and Obama was sent to the White House by a large margin.

Source: "Barack Obama: Address Accepting the Presidential Nomination at the Democratic National Convention in Denver, 'The American Promise,' August 28, 2008." The American Presidency Project, http://www.presidency.ucsb.edu/ws/?pid=78284.

McCain's "Fundamentals" Gaffe

Campaign Speech in Jacksonville, Florida

September 15, 2008

INTRODUCTION

Republican John McCain had to walk a tightrope on economic issues in the 2008 presidential campaign. His party, under the leadership of George W. Bush, had been at the helm for eight years, and at various points early in his run for the White House, McCain had suggested that the economy was in fine shape. Additionally, he had backed many of the economic policies that Bush had advanced. But as the election approached, an economic crisis seemed all too likely. Lehman Brothers, a massive global financial services firm, would collapse, setting off a major panic in the bank loan market. Housing prices declined quickly, and many investment and commercial banks suffered huge losses and faced bankruptcy. Clearly, the nation's economy was in trouble. McCain made the following statement on the campaign trail in Jacksonville, Florida, on the same day that Lehman Brothers made the largest bankruptcy filing in U.S. history.

This was a damaging statement, as most understood that there were deep problems in the economy. The Obama-Biden campaign would pick up on this comment and suggest to voters that McCain was either out of touch or in denial.

McCain's "fundamentals" comment was picked up by journalists and editorialists from across the nation, and a video copy of the speech spread across the Internet like wildfire. As with all campaign gaffes, it is hard to know the precise impact of McCain's "fundamentals" comment. Likely it merged into voter perceptions that he was less sure-footed on economic matters than on foreign policy concerns. We do know with certainty, however, that the state of the economy was the number one issue on the minds of voters that November, so it would make sense that McCain's floundering on this issue contributed to Barack Obama's massive win in November.

Sen. John McCain: Well, my friends, before I continue with too many of my remarks, you know that there's been tremendous turmoil in our financial markets and Wall Street, and it is—it's—people are frightened by these events. Our economy, I think, still—the fundamentals of our economy are strong. But these are very, very difficult time [*sic*]. And I promise you we will never put America in this position again. [Applause.] We will clean up Wall Street. We will reform government. And this is a failure.

We've got to take every action to build an environment of robust energy supplies, lower inflation, controlled health care costs, access to international markets, reduced taxes, and reduced burden of government to allow people to move forward toward a future of prosperity.

Source: "John McCain: Economy Fundamentally Sound, September 15, 2008." YouTube, http://www.youtube.com/watch?v=TBTVUHm1TJY.

The "Joe the Plumber" Exchange

Third Obama-McCain
Presidential Debate
October 15, 2008

INTRODUCTION

By the third 2008 presidential debate, the economy had taken center stage. The depth of the growing crisis was beginning to come into focus. Rising inflation, shrinking housing values, declining stock portfolios, the specter of new taxes, growing unemployment, and a host of related issues had become pressing concerns. Not surprisingly, the debate centered on these matters right from the beginning.

SCHIEFFER: Gentlemen, welcome. . . .

By now, we've heard all the talking points, so let's try to tell the people tonight some things that they—they haven't heard. Let's get to it.

Another very bad day on Wall Street, as both of you know. Both of you proposed new plans this week to address the economic crisis.

Senator McCain, you proposed a $52 billion plan that includes new tax cuts on capital gains, tax breaks for seniors, write-offs for stock losses, among other things.

Senator Obama, you proposed $60 billion in tax cuts for middle-income and lower-income people, more tax breaks to create jobs, new spending for public works projects to create jobs.

I will ask both of you: Why is your plan better than his?

Senator McCain, you go first.

McCAIN: Well, let—let me say, Bob, thank you. . . .

Americans are hurting right now, and they're angry. They're hurting, and they're angry. They're innocent victims of greed and excess on Wall Street and as well as Washington, D.C. And they're angry, and they have every reason to be angry.

The idea of suggesting a "new direction" surely made sense. The number of Americans who believed that the nation was on the wrong track had reached record heights. Americans wanted a change, to be sure. This often implies, however, bringing a new party into office—along with new personnel. For McCain this was problematic, given that his party had controlled the reins of government for the past eight years.

And they want this country to go in a new direction. And there are elements of my proposal that you just outlined which I won't repeat.

But we also have to have a short-term fix, in my view, and long-term fixes.

Let me just talk to you about one of the short-term fixes.

This is a disputed claim. Most economists would agree that these two lending institutions played a role in the crisis, but whether they caused the situation is debatable.

The catalyst for this housing crisis was the Fannie and Freddie Mae [*sic*] that caused subprime lending situation that now caused the housing market in America to collapse.

I am convinced that, until we reverse this continued decline in home ownership and put a floor under it, and so that people have not only the hope and belief they can stay in their homes and realize the American dream, but that value will come up.

Now, we have allocated $750 billion. Let's take 300 of that billion and go in and buy those home loan mortgages and negotiate with those people in their homes, 11 million homes or more, so that they can afford to pay the mortgage, stay in their home.

Now, I know the criticism of this.

Well, what about the citizen that stayed in their homes? That paid their mortgage payments? It doesn't help that person in their home if the next door neighbor's house is abandoned. And so we've got to reverse this. We ought to put the homeowners first. And I am disappointed that Secretary Paulson and others have not made that their first priority.

SCHIEFFER: All right. Senator Obama?

This issue—CEO compensation—angered many Americans. Government funds were being use to shore up huge financial institutions in order to avert a domino-like crisis, but there were media reports of bank executives continuing to get massive compensation packages.

OBAMA: . . . I think everybody understands at this point that we are experiencing the worst financial crisis since the Great Depression. And the financial rescue plan that Senator McCain and I supported is an important first step. And I pushed for some core principles: making sure that taxpayers can get their money back if they're putting money up. Making sure that CEOs are not enriching themselves through this process.

And I think that it's going to take some time to work itself out. But what we haven't yet seen is a rescue package for the middle class. Because the fundamentals of the economy were weak even before this latest crisis. So I've proposed four specific things that I think can help.

Obama's reference to the "fundamentals" was clearly designed to remind voters that one month before, at the dawn of the economic crisis, McCain had stated that the "fundamentals of our economy are strong." McCain would, of course, regret making that comment.

SCHIEFFER: All right. Would you like to ask him a question?

MCCAIN: No. I would like to mention that a couple days ago Senator Obama was out in Ohio and he had an encounter with a guy who's a plumber, his name is Joe Wurzelbacher.

Joe wants to buy the business that he has been in for all of these years, worked 10, 12 hours a day. And he wanted to buy the business but he looked at your tax plan and he saw that he was going to pay much higher taxes.

This was at a town hall campaign event. Wurzelbacher came up to one of the microphones to ask a question about his tax policies. Obama responded by suggesting that "when you spread the wealth around, it's good for everybody." This line was picked up and repeated by the McCain campaign. Was Obama advocating a radical redistribution of wealth?

You were going to put him in a higher tax bracket which was going to increase his taxes, which was going to cause him not to be able to employ people, which Joe was trying to realize the American dream.

Now Senator Obama talks about the very, very rich. Joe, I want to tell you, I'll not only help you buy that business that you worked your whole life for and be able—and I'll keep your taxes low and I'll provide available and affordable health care for you and your employees.

And I will not have—I will not stand for a tax increase on small business income. Fifty percent of small business income taxes are paid by small businesses. That's 16 million jobs in America. And what you want to do to Joe the plumber and millions more like him is have their taxes increased and not be able to realize the American dream of owning their own business.

All candidates understand the importance of small businesses in the nation's economy and the weight of small business owners on election day. McCain's argument was simple: tax hikes will hurt small businesses, such as the contracting business that Joe Wurzelbacher worked for.

SCHIEFFER: Is that what you want to do?

MCCAIN: That's what Joe believes.

OBAMA: He has been watching ads of Senator McCain's. Let me tell you what I'm actually going to do. I think tax policy is a major difference between Senator McCain and myself.

And we both want to cut taxes, the difference is who we want to cut taxes for.

Now, Senator McCain, the centerpiece of his economic proposal is to provide $200 billion in additional tax breaks to some of the wealthiest corporations in America. Exxon Mobil, and other oil companies, for example, would get an additional $4 billion in tax breaks.

What I've said is I want to provide a tax cut for 95 percent of working Americans, 95 percent. If you make more—if you make less than a quarter million dollars a year, then you will not see your income tax go up, your capital gains tax go up, your payroll tax. Not one dime. And 95 percent of working families, 95 percent of you out there, will get a tax cut. In fact, independent studies have looked at our respective plans and have concluded that I provide three times the amount of tax relief to middle-class families than Senator McCain does.

Now, the conversation I had with Joe the plumber, what I essentially said to him was, "Five years ago, when you weren't in a position to buy your business, you needed a tax cut then."

And what I want to do is to make sure that the plumber, the nurse, the firefighter, the teacher, the young entrepreneur who doesn't yet have money, I want to give them a tax break now. And that requires us to make some important choices.

The last point I'll make about small businesses. Not only do 98 percent of small businesses make less than $250,000, but I also want to give them additional tax breaks, because they are the drivers of the economy. They produce the most jobs.

McCAIN: You know, when Senator Obama ended up his conversation with Joe the plumber—we need to spread the wealth around. In other words, we're going to take Joe's money, give it to Senator Obama, and let him spread the wealth around.

I want Joe the plumber to spread that wealth around. You told him you wanted to spread the wealth around.

The whole premise behind Senator Obama's plans are class warfare, let's spread the wealth around. I want small businesses—and by the way, the small businesses that we're talking about would receive an increase in their taxes right now. . . .

OBAMA: OK. Can I. . . .

McCAIN: We're not going to do that in my administration.

OBAMA: If I can answer the question. Number one, I want to cut taxes for 95 percent of Americans. Now, it is true that my friend and supporter, Warren Buffett, for example, could afford to pay a little more in taxes in order

McCAIN: We're talking about Joe the plumber.

OBAMA: in order to give—in order to give additional tax cuts to Joe the plumber before he was at the point where he could make $250,000.

Then Exxon Mobil, which made $12 billion, record profits, over the last several quarters, they can afford to pay a little more so that ordinary families who are hurting out there— they're trying to figure out how they're going to afford food, how they're going to save for their kids' college education, they need a break.

So, look, nobody likes taxes. I would prefer that none of us had to pay taxes, including myself. But ultimately, we've got to pay for the core investments that make this economy strong and somebody's got to do it.

McCAIN: Nobody likes taxes. Let's not raise anybody's taxes. OK?

OBAMA: Well, I don't mind paying a little more.

McCAIN: The fact is that businesses in America today are paying the second highest tax rate of anywhere in the world. Our tax rate for business in America is 35 percent. Ireland, it's 11 percent.

Where are companies going to go where they can create jobs and where they can do best in business?

There are a number of differences between Democrats and Republicans, and one of them is the role of government. Democrats believe that government should be used to help cure many of the ills of society. It can be used to help individuals and groups do what they cannot do for themselves. As such, government revenues are needed, and the best way to get them is through a progressive tax system. Simply stated, if you make more, you should have to pay a larger proportion of your income to the government. Republicans, on the other hand, believe that government should be kept as small as possible—to the bare essentials of matters concerning safety and security. Taxes should be kept as low as possible, and all should pay the same rate. There is no right or wrong answer, of course, just differences in opinion. Stripped down, this basic difference was being played out in this exchange.

As it turns out, Wurzelbacher, who became widely known as "Joe the Plumber," was a strong Republican activist. After the debate, he started campaigning with John McCain and Sarah Palin. In 2012 he wrote a book on conservative principles, and he even ran for Congress in Ohio's 9th District.

We need to cut the business tax rate in America. We need to encourage business. . . .

Source: "Presidential Debates: Presidential Debate at Hofstra University in Hempstead, New York, October 15, 2008." The American Presidency Project, http://www.presidency.ucsb.edu/ws/?pid=84526.

Powell's Endorsement of Obama

Excerpt from Obama's Speech at Fayetteville, North Carolina

October 19, 2008

INTRODUCTION

Prior to Barack Obama's election, Colin Powell was arguably the most prominent and most popular African American political figure in the nation. Among many other posts, Powell had been national security adviser under Ronald Reagan, chairman of the Joint Chiefs of Staff under George H. W. Bush, and secretary of state under George W. Bush. Powell had also flirted briefly with a run for the presidency in 1992.

When Obama won the Democratic nomination in the summer of 2008, many pundits wondered if Powell would make an endorsement. Clearly Powell was pleased to watch an African American contending for the highest office in the world, but he was a lifelong Republican.

Before we begin, I'd like to acknowledge some news that we learned this morning. With so many brave men and women from Fayetteville serving in our military, this is a city and a state that knows something about great soldiers. And this morning, a great soldier, a great statesman, a great American has endorsed our campaign for change. I have been honored to have the benefit of his wisdom and counsel from time to time over the last few years, but today, I am beyond honored and deeply humbled to have the support of General Colin Powell.

Powell had been known as an ideological moderate. In his endorsement announcement on NBC's *Meet the Press,* he raised his "concerns about the direction that the party has taken in recent years. It has moved more to the right than I would like to see it, but that's a choice the party makes." Historically it was the Democratic Party that struggled with internal discord, but in recent years the division within the Republican Party had become pronounced. While Barack Obama already had the African American vote in the bag, Powell's endorsement likely made a big difference because Powell seemed to represent the voice of many moderate Republicans and independents. It surely was a boon for Obama's chances.

General Powell has defended this nation bravely, and he has embodied our highest ideals through his long and distinguished public service. He and his wife Alma have inspired millions of young people to serve in their communities and their country through their tireless commitment and trailblazing American story. And he knows, as we do, that this is a moment where we all need to come together as one nation—young and old, rich and poor, black, white, Hispanic, Asian, Native American, Republican and Democrat.

258

This is a moment to stand up and serve because this is a moment of great uncertainty for America. The economic crisis we face is the worst since the Great Depression. Businesses large and small are finding it impossible to get loans, which means they can't buy new equipment, or hire new workers, or even make payroll for the workers they have.

By the time of Colin Powell's endorsement, more and more evidence had emerged to suggest that the nation was headed for a deep recession. Yet McCain, at a campaign stop three weeks earlier, had commented that the "fundamentals of our economy are strong." In his endorsement of Obama, Powell raised questions about McCain's ability to judge this crisis: "In the case of Mr. McCain, I found that he was a little unsure as to how to deal with the economic problems that we were having and almost every day there was a different approach to the problem. And that concerned me, sensing that he didn't have a complete grasp of the economic problems that we had."

Seven hundred sixty thousand workers have lost their jobs this year. Wages are lower than they've been in a decade, at a time when the cost of health care and college have never been higher. It's getting harder and harder to make the mortgage, or fill up your gas tank, or even keep the electricity on at the end of the month. At this rate, the question isn't just "are you better off than you were four years ago?," it's "are you better off than you were four weeks ago?"

Source: "Barack Obama: Remarks in Fayetteville, North Carolina, October 19, 2008." The American Presidency Project, http://www.presidency.ucsb.edu/ws/?pid=84572.

Election of 2012

Rick Perry's "Oops Moment"

Republican Presidential Primary Debate, Rochester, Michigan

November 9, 2011

INTRODUCTION

To most observers, Barack Obama seemed vulnerable. He remained well liked by most voters, but the economy continued to lag throughout 2011, and there were growing questions about the direction of the nation. It was not surprising, then, that a host of Republicans would enter the contest to challenge the president. One of those candidates was Governor Rick Perry of Texas.

As Perry entered the race, he quickly jumped to the top of the pack. He was a popular governor from a large state—a state that seemed to weather the economic downturn rather well. He was also a prolific fund-raiser, quickly amassing a huge campaign war chest. But many pundits also wondered about his ability to run a national campaign and his agility in confronting a broad range of complex issues. Was he really prepared for the presidency?

The Republican candidates agreed to an unprecedented number of debates, beginning in May 2011. Governor Perry entered the race a bit later in the summer, and in his first debate, on September 7, he did modestly well. The exchange with fellow primary candidate Representative Ron Paul and moderators Maria Bartiromo and John Harwood is from a debate that took place two months later in Rochester, Michigan, and occurred near the end of the program.

MR. HARWOOD: Governor Perry, you play only home games in Texas. Do you give him points for winning on the road?

Perry was eager to talk about manufacturing in Texas.

GOV. PERRY: Listen, there is a reason that Caterpillar moved their hydraulics manufacturing and their engine manufacturing to the state of Texas. It didn't have anything to do with Republican versus Democrat. It had everything to do with creating a climate in our state where the job creators knew that they were going to have the opportunity to keep more of what they work for.

MR. HARWOOD: He's said he did.

One of the themes of the Republican contest in 2012 was creating a climate for business to grow, and this included drastic limits on government regulations—so much so that some conservatives even advocated dropping entire federal agencies.

GOV. PERRY: And that's what Americans are looking for. [Scattered applause.] They're looking for a tax plan that basically says you're going to be able to keep more

of what you work for. They're looking for a regulatory climate that doesn't strangle the life out of their businesses when they want to put those dollars out there to create the wealth.

That's what Americans are looking for.

I think we're getting all tangled up around an issue here about can you work with Democrats or can you work with Republicans. Yeah, we can all do that. But the fact of the matter is, we better have a plan in place that Americans can get their hands around, and that's the reason my flat tax is the only one of all the folks—these good folks on the stage. It balances the budget in 2020. It does the things for the regulatory climate that has to happen.

And I will tell you, it's three agencies of government, when I get there, that are gone: Commerce, Education and the—what's the third one there—let's see. [Laughter.]

REP. PAUL: You need five.

GOV. PERRY: Oh, five. OK.

It was now clear that Perry was stumbling, badly.

REP. PAUL: Make it five.

GOV. PERRY: OK. So Commerce, Education and— the—[pause]—

MR. ROMNEY: EPA?

GOV. PERRY: EPA. There you go. [Laughter.] [Applause.]

MS. BARTIROMO: Let's go—

MR: HARWOOD: Seriously? Is EPA the one you were talking about?

GOV. PERRY: No, sir. No, sir. We were talking about the agencies of government—EPA needs to be rebuilt. There's no doubt about that.

MR. HARWOOD: But you can't—but you can't name the third one?

Gov. Perry: The third agency of government.

Mr. Harwood: Yes.

Gov. Perry: I would do away with the Education, the Commerce and—let's see—I can't. The third one, I can't. Sorry. Oops.

The "Oops Moment" marked the beginning of the end for Perry's candidacy. Many public officials and average folks alike draw a blank on topics—sometimes topics that they know quite well. But this was different. Perry had come across as unprepared at many events, and, as they say in Texas, he seemed all hat. This gaffe, building on that narrative, seemed to cement the perception that Perry was not ready to lead the nation. Perhaps also, he was not particularly smart. His fund-raising slowed, and by early January he ended his candidacy for the White House.

Source: "Presidential Debates: Republican Candidates Debate in Rochester, Michigan, November 9, 2011." The American Presidency Project, http://www.presidency.ucsb.edu/ws/?pid=97022.

Bill Clinton at the Democratic Convention

Bill Clinton's Address to the Democratic National Convention, Charlotte, North Carolina

September 5, 2012

INTRODUCTION

The evolving popularity of Bill Clinton is, by itself, an interesting and long story. Given that he was caught up in a massive scandal and was one of only three presidents nearly removed from office by impeachment (he was acquitted by the Senate), many might have speculated that Clinton would have left office with his tail between his legs. But that's not Bill Clinton. In fact, after he left office at the end of his second term in 2000, his popularity had soared. By the time he addressed the crowd at the 2012 Democratic National Convention in support of Barack Obama, Clinton was one of the most popular politicians in America.

Thank you very much. Thank you. Thank you. [Sustained cheers, applause.] Thank you. Thank you. Thank you. Thank you.

Now, Mr. Mayor, fellow Democrats, we are here to nominate a president. [Cheers, applause.] And I've got one in mind. [Cheers, applause.]

I want to nominate a man whose own life has known its fair share of adversity and uncertainty. I want to nominate a man who ran for president to change the course of an already weak economy and then just six weeks before his election, saw it suffer the biggest collapse since the Great Depression; a man who stopped the slide into depression and put us on the long road to recovery, knowing all the while that no matter how many jobs that he saved or created, there'd still be millions more waiting, worried about feeding their own kids, trying to keep their hopes alive.

I want to nominate a man who's cool on the outside— [cheers, applause]—but who burns for America on the inside. [Cheers, applause.]

One of the mounting criticisms of Barack Obama was that he lacked passion, that he was too cool in the face of conservative opposition. Did he really have the fire in his gut to take on the Republicans? This line was intended to counter the idea that Obama did not. He "burns for America on the inside."

I want—I want a man who believes with no doubt that we can build a new American Dream economy, driven by innovation and creativity, by education and—yes—by cooperation. [Cheers.]

And by the way, after last night, I want a man who had the good sense to marry Michelle Obama. [Cheers, applause.] . . .

Now, folks, in Tampa a few days ago, we heard a lot of talk—[laughter]—all about how the president and the Democrats don't really believe in free enterprise and individual initiative, how we want everybody to be dependent on the government, how bad we are for the economy.

This Republican narrative—this alternative universe—[laughter, applause]—says that every one of us in this room who amounts to anything, we're all completely self-made. One of the greatest chairmen the Democratic Party ever had, Bob Strauss—[cheers, applause]—used to say that every politician wants every voter to believe he was born in a log cabin he built himself. [Laughter, applause.] But, as Strauss then admitted, it ain't so. [Laughter.]

We Democrats—we think the country works better with a strong middle class, with real opportunities for poor folks to work their way into it—[cheers, applause]—with a relentless focus on the future, with business and government actually working together to promote growth and broadly share prosperity. You see, we believe that "we're all in this together" is a far better philosophy than "you're on your own." [Cheers, applause.] It is.

So who's right? [Cheers.] Well, since 1961, for 52 years now, the Republicans have held the White House 28 years, the Democrats, 24. In those 52 years, our private economy has produced 66 million private sector jobs.

So what's the job score? Republicans, twenty-four million. Democrats, forty-two [million]. [Cheers, applause.] . . .

Michelle Obama had delivered a speech the evening before and did an excellent job. At this point in her husband's administration, she had an approval rating approaching 80 percent. In 2012, Democrats in particular loved the first lady!

And this is where Bill Clinton shined. Few politicians have been able to better explain complex issues to average Americans. Clinton—after the speech dubbed the "Explainer in Chief"—turned the issue into a simple, logical matter and by doing so made a powerful case for Obama's reelection.

Now, there's something I've noticed lately. You probably have too. And it's this. Maybe just because I grew up in a different time, but though I often disagree with Republicans, I actually never learned to hate them the way the far right that now controls their party seems to hate our president and a lot of other Democrats. I— [cheers, applause]—that would be impossible for me because President Eisenhower sent federal troops to my home state to integrate Little Rock Central High School. [Cheers, applause.] President Eisenhower built the interstate highway system.

When I was a governor, I worked with President Reagan and his White House on the first round of welfare reform and with President George H. W. Bush on national education goals.

[Cheers, applause.] I'm actually very grateful to—if you saw from the film what I do today, I have to be grateful, and you should be, too—that President George W. Bush supported PEPFAR. It saved the lives of millions of people in poor countries. [Cheers, applause.]

And I have been honored to work with both Presidents Bush on natural disasters in the aftermath of the South Asian tsunami, Hurricane Katrina, the horrible earthquake in Haiti. Through my foundation, both in America and around the world, I'm working all the time with Democrats, Republicans and independents. Sometimes I couldn't tell you for the life who I'm working with because we focus on solving problems and seizing opportunities and not fighting all the time. [Cheers, applause.]

And so here's what I want to say to you, and here's what I want the people at home to think about. When times are tough and people are frustrated and angry and hurting and uncertain, the politics of constant conflict may be good. But what is good politics does not necessarily work in the real world. What works in the real world is cooperation. [Cheers, applause.] What works in the real world is cooperation, business and government, foundations and universities. . . .

Much of this speech, and indeed much of Obama's 2012 campaign, was directed at independent voters. Surveys had shown that many moderate, less partisan voters yearned for compromise solutions. By painting a faction of the Republican Party as recalcitrant and unwilling to compromise, Clinton was suggesting that they were extremists. Clearly, that notion would not go over well with moderate voters in 2012. Clinton knew what button he was pushing.

Unfortunately, the faction that now dominates the Republican Party doesn't see it that way. They think government is always the enemy, they're always right, and compromise is weakness. [Boos.] Just in the last couple of elections, they defeated two distinguished Republican senators because they dared to cooperate with Democrats on issues important to the future of the country, even national security. [Applause.] . . .

Now, people ask me all the time how we got four surplus budgets in a row. What new ideas did we bring to Washington? I always give a one-word answer: Arithmetic. [Sustained cheers, applause.]

If—arithmetic! If—[applause]—if they stay with this $5 trillion tax cut plan in a debt reduction plan, the arithmetic tells us, no matter what they say, one of three things is about to happen. One, assuming they try to do what they say they'll do, get rid of—pay—cover it by deductions, cutting those deductions, one, they'll have to eliminate so many deductions, like the ones for home mortgages and charitable giving, that middle-class families will see their tax bills go up an average of $2,000 while anybody who makes $3 million or more will see their tax bill go down $250,000. [Boos.]

Or, two, they'll have to cut so much spending that they'll obliterate the budget for the national parks, for ensuring clean air, clean water, safe food, safe air travel. They'll cut way back on Pell Grants, college loans, early childhood education, child nutrition programs, all the programs that help to empower middle-class families and help poor kids. Oh, they'll cut back on investments in roads and bridges and science and technology and biomedical research.

That's what they'll do. They'll hurt the middle class and the poor and put the future on hold to give tax cuts to upper-income people who've been getting it all along.

Or three, in spite of all the rhetoric, they'll just do what they've been doing for more than 30 years. They'll go in and cut the taxes way more than they cut spending, especially with that big defense increase, and they'll just explode the debt and weaken the economy. And they'll destroy the federal government's ability to help you by letting interest gobble up all your tax payments.

Don't you ever forget when you hear them talking about this that Republican economic policies quadrupled the national debt before I took office, in the 12 years before I took office—[applause]—and doubled the debt in the eight years after I left, because it defied arithmetic. [Laughter, applause.] It was a highly inconvenient thing for them in our debates that I was just a country boy from Arkansas, and I came from a place where people still thought two and two was four. [Laughter, applause.] It's arithmetic. . . .

Source: "Bill Clinton's speech at the Democratic National Convention (Full Transcript)." *Washington Post,* http://articles.washingtonpost.com/2012-09-05/ politics/35497433_1_applause-transcript-laughter.

These lines about arithmetic were widely popular. Mitt Romney and the Republicans were being criticized by many in the media for offering economic policies that seemed to contradict studies done by nonpartisan organizations. In short, too many of their numbers did not seem to add up. So Clinton's line "two and two was four" was a clever, humorous way of saying that Romney and the Republican Party were not being honest with the American people.

Clinton's speech was clearly the most important address in Obama's efforts to win reelection in 2012 and may have been one of the best of Clinton's career. It was a simple, powerful statement on why Obama should be reelected. We will never know now many votes this speech might have won for Obama. But without a doubt, it was a big help at an important point in the campaign.

Mother Jones Releases Mitt Romney's "47%" Video

**Transcript of Video from Mitt Romney
Fund-raiser, Boca Raton,
Florida (May 17, 2012)**

September 17, 2012

INTRODUCTION

In 2012 after a crowded and contentious Republican primary, Mitt Romney—former governor of Massachusetts and son of George Romney, a 1968 presidential candidate—emerged as the party's nominee. His selection of a conservative member of Congress from Wisconsin, Paul Ryan, electrified the Republican base, which had yet to coalesce behind the relatively moderate Romney. With the selection of Ryan, a Tea Party star, the conservative activists within the party now had someone about whom they could be enthusiastic. But naming Ryan as his running mate cut both ways for Romney. Just as Ryan's selection was a boon to conservatives within the party, it also allowed Democrats to paint the center-right Romney as a far-right conservative.

Romney did not appear to fight that characterization either. During the Republican primary, he was forced to play a bit of that role in order to emerge from the crowded field where party activists dominate. In what appeared emblematic of this shift in Romney's perspectives, *Mother Jones,* a liberal magazine, released a story and an accompanying video of a comment that Romney made in May 2012 during the primaries at a $50,000 per plate campaign event in Florida. Here is the transcript of that video.

Audience member: . . . To what extent do people really understand that we're hurtling toward a cliff, and to what extent do people understand the severity of the fiscal situation we're in. Do people get it?

Romney: They don't. By and large people don't get it. People in our party, and part of—it's our fault because we've been talking about deficits and debt for about 25 or 30 years as a party, and so they've heard us say it and say it and say it. . . . Although the people who recognize that tend to be Republicans, and the people who don't recognize that tend to be Democrats. . . . I did the calculation for folks today. . . . [I]f you take the total national debt and the unfunded liabilities of Medicare, Social Security, and Medicaid, the amount of debt plus unfunded liabilities per household in America is $520,000. Per household.

Romney was long criticized for being out of touch with voters, although in this exceedingly wealthy crowd he was among other individuals who were similarly financially situated.

In his self-described "off the cuff remarks," Romney went on to suggest that roughly half of Americans don't pay taxes, are dependent on government, and will therefore support the incumbent President Obama no matter what tax plans the Republican nominee proposes.

Audience member: It's like 12 times their income, right?

Romney: At least. 10, 12 times their income. Even though we're not going to be writing the check for that amount per household, they're going to be paying the interest on that. You'll be paying the interest on that. [Audience laughs.] . . . But the Democrats, they talk about social issues, draw in the young people, and they vote on that issue. It's like, I mean, there won't be any houses like this if we stay on the road we're on.

[. . .]

Curiously enough, it was President Jimmy Carter's grandson who helped *Mother Jones* obtain the recording. There is simply no way to present this other than as a gift to the Obama campaign. This gaffe was consequential for a few reasons. First, it revealed a deep misunderstanding of who the beneficiaries are of governmental services and financial support. The 47 percent to which Romney referred consists of veterans, seniors, the working poor, and students. Moreover, among the 47 percent are core Republican voters as well as core Democratic voters. Second, to condemn half of Americans as freeloaders or moochers is never a good idea for a campaign for national office. And third, the image of Romney saying such derogatory things about people who struggle financially likely resonated with voters who already perceived him as being out of touch with the lives of the vast majority of Americans, an image he fought hard to overcome.

Clearly, the news of this remark left ample room for supporters of the Obama campaign to pile on. Although the Obama campaign was able to raise funds because of Romney's gaffe, the gaffe seemed to move the polls only slightly. In fact, during the first presidential debate that followed closely on the heels of the release of the video, Obama declined to mention the 47 percent remark, to the great consternation of his supporters. Perhaps the Obama campaign preferred to remain on the sidelines during a most inartful implosion of their adversary. But as polls tightened through October and the lead that Obama enjoyed disappeared, they began to use the image to reinforce the message that Romney was out of touch with the lives of average Americans.

Romney: There are 47 percent of the people who will vote for the president no matter what. All right, there are 47 percent who are with him, who are dependent upon government, who believe that they are victims, who believe the government has a responsibility to care for them, who believe that they are entitled to health care, to food, to housing, to you-name-it. That's an entitlement. And the government should give it to them. And they will vote for this president no matter what. . . . These are people who pay no income tax. . . . [M]y job is not to worry about those people. I'll never convince them they should take personal responsibility and care for their lives. . . .

Source: "Full Transcript of the Mitt Romney Secret Video." *Mother Jones,* September 19, 2012, http://www.motherjones.com/politics/2012/09/full- transcript -mitt-romney-secret-video#47percent.

An October Surprise: Hurricane Sandy

"FEMA and Federal Partners Continue Steadfast Support for Areas Affected by Superstorm"
Federal Emergency Management Agency Press Release
October 31, 2012

INTRODUCTION

An October surprise is an event or revelation of some kind that can generate an effect late in the campaign that shifts votes and therefore changes the outcome of the race. The occasion of Hurricane Sandy during the 2012 general election might fit that characterization. Certainly October surprises in the form of natural disasters cannot be staged in the same way that Ronald Reagan's negotiations with Iranian hostage takers or Henry Kissinger's declaration that "peace is at hand" in Vietnam can. But they can be used by campaigns to position a candidate to draw positive distinctions between that candidate and the opposing campaign. In the case of Hurricane Sandy, only the incumbent, President Barack Obama, was in a position to make such distinctions meaningful. His Republican rival, former Massachusetts governor Mitt Romney, was forced onto the sidelines.

WASHINGTON—Today, President Obama visited the Federal Emergency Management Agency's (FEMA) National Response Coordination Center in Washington, D.C. to participate in a briefing with several members of his cabinet.

The President directed the federal family during the briefing to continue to bring all federal resources to bear that are needed without delay as they lean forward to support states, tribes, and communities in their response. FEMA continues to coordinate the federal government's assistance to support the states in response and recovery of Hurricane Sandy.

As President, Obama had all the trappings of the office and also had the executive authority to oversee the federal emergency response to natural disasters. In that sense, it was a formal power of the office and an expected obligation of his authority for him to fly to New Jersey to meet with Republican governor Chris Christie, console survivors, and survey the damage.

Today, the President, Governor Chris Christie and FEMA Administrator Fugate toured the storm damaged New Jersey coast and met with disaster survivors and first-responders, and were briefed by state and local officials on response efforts.

The occasion privileged Obama in that it took the media attention away from the Romney campaign. Without any formal role to play in the recovery, Romney was forced to sit out several critically important days prior to the election. Without media attention on his campaign, the messaging that needed to happen in key swing states simply didn't occur.

It also mattered a great deal that Obama received the praise of New Jersey's Republican governor, who had until that point been a vocal critic of the Obama administration. This showed that partisanship can be put aside in the face of crisis and that the president had a formal role to play in alleviating the effects of the disaster.

Also, at the direction of the President, a power restoration working group has been established to cut through the red

tape, increase federal, state, tribal, local and private sector coordination and restore power to people as quickly as
possible. Led by FEMA Administrator Fugate, this working group includes representatives from private sector
utilities and includes government representatives from the
Department of Defense, Department of Transportation,
the Department of Energy, the U.S. Army Corps of Engi-
neers and representatives from local law enforcement,
among others.

More than 2,200 FEMA personnel are working to support
response operations, including search and rescue, situational awareness, communications and logistical support.
Nine federal urban search and rescue task forces are supporting local search and rescue operations and an additional
six teams are on alert should they be needed. Community
relations teams are on the ground in the hardest hit areas
of the Mid-Atlantic going door-to-door to inform disaster survivors about available services and resources and to
gather situational awareness. Mobile Emergency Response
Support (MERS) personnel and teams are located in storm-
affected states to provide secure and non-secure voice,
video, information services, operations and logistics support
to response efforts in affected states. 14 Incident Management Assistance Teams and 12 liaison officers, positioned in
affected states before the storm, continue to support response
activities and ensure there are no unmet needs.

"First responders and emergency crews on the ground have the
full support of the federal government," said FEMA Administrator Craig Fugate. "We are actively engaged with the entire
emergency management team—in and outside of government—to aggressively respond to the aftermath of this storm."

The President also signed federal emergency declarations for
Connecticut, Delaware, District of Columbia, Maryland, Massachusetts, New Hampshire, New Jersey, New York, Pennsylvania, Rhode Island, Virginia and West Virginia. This allows
FEMA to provide resources directly to state, tribal and local
government engaged in life-saving and sustaining activities.

The funding and personnel to complement state efforts that Governor Christie appreciated stood in stark contrast to remarks that Mitt Romney made in a Republican primary debate, where he suggested that FEMA ought not receive as much funding as it had been receiving. After Hurricane Sandy struck, the public was reminded of those comments, obliging Romney to explain and reframe his remarks. His argument was that states and localities are most able to respond to natural disasters but that where they cannot, the national government has an important role to play in assisting those states and localities. The difficulty, however, was that his initial comments seemed to frame increasing financial support for FEMA as immorally contributing to the national debt, saddling future generations with huge debt obligations. It was hard to defend such a perspective while so many struggled to put their lives back together. Romney was in a tough spot with very little time to recover, and indeed he did not. Obama would go on to win a decisive electoral college victory, 332 to 206, with a 3-point margin in the popular vote.

> **FEMA's mission is to support our citizens and first responders to ensure that as a nation we work together to build, sustain, and improve our capability to prepare for, protect against, respond to, recover from, and mitigate all hazards.**

Source: "FEMA and Federal Partners Continue Steadfast Support for Areas Affected by Superstorm." FEMA Press Release No. PR-12-128, October 31, 2012. Federal Emergency Management Agency, http://www.fema.gov/news-release/fema-and-federal-partners-continue-steadfast-support-areas-affected-superstorm.

Timeline

1948

On February 2, President Harry Truman delivers a special message to Congress on civil rights that becomes known as "Truman's 10-Point Civil Rights Program."

A civil rights plank is added to the Democratic Party platform, and southern delegates walk out of the national convention to form the States' Rights Party, or Dixiecrats. They nominate South Carolina governor Strom Thurmond for president on a strongly segregationist platform. In the end, the ticket carries only South Carolina, Mississippi, Alabama, and Louisiana.

On July 26, President Harry Truman issues Executive Order 9981, creating the President's Committee on Equality of Treatment and Opportunity in the Armed Forces, which quickly leads to integration of the armed services.

1952

At the July 7–11 Republican National Convention in Chicago, General Dwight D. Eisenhower receives the party's nomination for president. Senator Richard Nixon is his running mate.

1952

At the Republican National Convention on July 9, Wisconsin senator Joseph McCarthy delivers a speech in which he discusses the rise of communism—a central issue at the time—and accuses President Harry Truman of having "delivered nearly half of the world to Communist Russia."

General Dwight D. Eisenhower accepts the presidential nomination for the Republican Party on July 11 at the Republican National Convention. In his speech accepting the nomination, Eisenhower gives a nod to Richard Nixon, the party's vice presidential nominee, who had made a name for himself in 1948 as an outspoken member of the House Un-American Activities Committee.

At the July 7–26 Democratic National Convention in Chicago, Illinois governor Adlai Stevenson receives the party's nomination for president. Senator John Sparkman is his running mate.

With his place in the vice presidential slot of the 1952 Republican ticket at risk, Richard Nixon delivers a speech in September confronting the charges that he improperly used campaign funds. His "Checkers" speech proved to be an effective, tearful denial of wrongdoing that hindered efforts to force his resignation.

On election day, November 4, Republican Dwight D. Eisenhower is elected president with 55 percent of the popular vote to Democrat Adlai Stevenson's 44 percent. Voter turnout is 63.3 percent.

1953

Earl Warren, who had sought the Republican Party's presidential nomination in 1952, is appointed chief justice of the U.S. Supreme Court by the man who secured the nomination and went on to win the presidency: Eisenhower.

1956

As the Democratic Party faces division over the desegregation issue, the Republican Party begins to make inroads among African American voters in the North. President Dwight D. Eisenhower, who is running for reelection, remains silent on the issues of desegregation and passage of a civil rights act until speaking out in support of both issues is necessary to pull votes away from Democratic candidate Adlai Stevenson.

During the Suez Crisis, the Dwight D. Eisenhower administration insists that Great Britain, France, and Israel pull military forces out of the Suez Canal region. The policy risks alienating advocates of the State of Israel, whose support Eisenhower would need to win reelection.

At the August 13–17 Democratic National Convention in Chicago, Adlai Stevenson receives the party's presidential nomination. Senator Estes Kefauver is his running mate.

At the August 20–23 Republican National Convention in San Francisco, President Dwight D. Eisenhower again receives the party's nomination for president. Richard Nixon is again his running mate.

On election day, November 6, President Dwight D. Eisenhower is reelected with 57 percent of the popular vote to Democrat Adlai Stevenson's 41.9 percent. Voter turnout is 60.6 percent.

1960

In May, it is revealed that the United States had a long-standing program of intelligence-gathering high-altitude overflights in the Soviet Union. The revelation of the U.S. government's lies derails an upcoming summit with Soviet leader Nikita Khrushchev and tarnishes the ability of the United States to project legal and moral authority. Republican vice president Richard Nixon, who was then running for president, is forced to deal with a difficult situation that his administration is held responsible for.

At the July 11–15 Democratic National Convention in Los Angeles, Senator John F. Kennedy receives his party's presidential nomination. Senator Lyndon B. Johnson is his running mate.

At the July 25–28 Republican National Convention in Chicago, Vice President Richard Nixon receives his party's presidential nomination. Former senator Henry Cabot Lodge Jr. is his running mate.

In accepting the Republican presidential nomination on July 28 at the party's convention, Richard Nixon pledges to visit all 50 states during his campaign. The pledge costs him valuable campaign time in battleground states that was spent in states where the outcome was essentially already determined.

Democratic presidential candidate John F. Kennedy, who would be the first Catholic president if elected, faces concerns about the influence that the Catholic Church would have on him if he is elected president. In a September 12 speech before the Greater Houston Ministerial Association, Kennedy affirms his belief in separation of church and state and reassures the audience that if elected, he will not take instruction from the church. The speech puts the issue to rest, allowing Kennedy to focus on other issues.

On September 26, the first televised presidential debate is held. More than 70 million people watch the debate on television, while millions more listen on the radio. On television, Democratic nominee John F. Kennedy appears confident and energetic, while Republican nominee Richard Nixon appears uncomfortable, having been ill for several weeks prior and wearing an ill-fitting suit.

A television ad by the John F. Kennedy campaign attacking vice president and Republican presidential nominee Richard Nixon features clips of President Dwight D. Eisenhower saying at a press conference that he could not think of a major policy idea from Nixon that had been adopted. The ad undermines any claim that Nixon might have made that being vice president gave him experience that Senator Kennedy lacked.

On election day, November 8, Democrat John F. Kennedy is elected president with 49.7 percent of the popular vote to Vice President Richard Nixon's 49.6 percent. Voter turnout is 63.1 percent.

1964

At the July 13–16 Republican National Convention in San Francisco, Senator Barry Goldwater receives his party's presidential nomination. Representative William E. Miller is his running mate.

In a July 14 speech at the Republican National Convention, New York governor Nelson A. Rockefeller, a moderate, warns of the dangers presented by extremism within the Republican Party. In response and after securing the presidential nomination for the party, Barry Goldwater declares that "extremism in the defense of liberty is no vice. And . . . moderation in the pursuit of justice is no virtue."

At the August 24–27 Democratic National Convention in Atlantic City, President Lyndon B. Johnson, who ascended from the vice presidency upon the assassination of John F. Kennedy, receives his party's presidential nomination. Senator Hubert Humphrey is Johnson's running mate.

On September 7, the Lyndon B. Johnson presidential campaign airs its "Peace Little Girl" ad (also known as the "Daisy" ad), which plays on Americans' fears of nuclear war and seeks to remind them of Republican candidate Barry Goldwater's willingness to use nuclear weapons without actually mentioning Goldwater's name. Although the Johnson campaign only airs the ad once, it generates such controversy that network news programs rerun it for more than a week.

FACT magazine publishes "The Unconscious of a Conservative: A Special Issue on the Mind of Barry Goldwater," arguing that Republican presidential candidate

Goldwater is mentally unfit for office due to instability and paranoia. The article feeds into perceptions of Goldwater as an extremist, and although he wins a libel suit against the magazine, the suit is not brought until after the election.

On election day, November 3, President Lyndon B. Johnson is reelected with 61.1 percent of the popular vote to Republican Barry Goldwater's 38.5 percent. Voter turnout is 61.9 percent.

1967

An editorial by former vice president and current presidential hopeful Richard Nixon titled "What Has Happened to America?" is published in *Reader's Digest* in October. In the editorial, Nixon blames U.S. Supreme Court chief justice Earl Warren for "ours becoming a lawless society." Law and order as well as liberalism on the Supreme Court are the dominant themes in Nixon's campaign for the 1968 election.

On November 30, Senator Eugene McCarthy announces that he will challenge Democratic president Lyndon B. Johnson for the party's nomination in the 1968 election. During the election, McCarthy, who strongly opposes the Vietnam War, garners a wave of support from young voters.

1968

Former Alabama governor George Wallace announces on February 8 that he will run for president as the nominee for the American Independent Party. Wallace is a strong supporter of segregation, having said in his 1963 gubernatorial inaugural address "segregation now, segregation tomorrow, segregation forever."

Senator Eugene McCarthy wins 42 percent of the vote in the March 12 New Hampshire Democratic primary, signaling that President Lyndon B. Johnson, also a Democrat, is vulnerable.

U.S. senator Robert F. Kennedy, who had been attorney general during his brother John F. Kennedy's administration, announces on March 16 that he will seek the Democratic nomination for president. Robert Kennedy had long had a contentious relationship with the Democratic president, Lyndon B. Johnson, who had served as John Kennedy's vice president and would presumably be seeking reelection in 1968.

President Lyndon B. Johnson announces on March 31 that he will not seek reelection to the presidency. Over the course of his presidency, U.S. involvement in the Vietnam War led to Johnson being known as "the War President." Johnson believed—and polling data apparently confirmed—that he could not win reelection.

Civil rights leader Martin Luther King Jr. is assassinated in Memphis, Tennessee, on April 4. The assassination is followed by rioting across the nation. At a campaign stop, Senator Robert F. Kennedy tells the crowd of King's assassination, asking for prayers for King's family and calling for "love, and wisdom, and compassion toward one another, and a feeling of justice toward those who still suffer within our country."

Just after midnight on June 5, Robert F. Kennedy, who is seeking the Democratic nomination for president, is fatally shot after winning the California primary.

Edward M. Kennedy addresses the public memorial for his brother, Robert F. Kennedy, who had been assassinated on the campaign trail only days earlier. In his address, Edward Kennedy reads a speech that his brother gave to young South

Africans on their Day of Affirmation in 1966 and closes with words that Robert often repeated: "Some men see things as they are and say why. I dream things that never were and say why not."

At the August 5–8 Republican National Convention in Miami Beach, former vice president Richard Nixon receives his party's presidential nomination. Governor Sprio Agnew is his running mate.

At the August 26–29 Democratic National Convention in Chicago, Senator Hubert Humphrey receives his party's presidential nomination. Senator Edmund Muskie is his running mate.

Thousands of Vietnam War protesters converge on Chicago during the Democratic National Convention, resulting in mayhem and bloodshed and showing a nation divided and in disarray. Protesters and the police clash as police use clubs and mace against the crowds. Public opinion polls show most people siding with the police, but many protesters consider the police violence indicative of an oppressive society.

At the Democratic National Convention, Senator Abraham Ribicoff delivers a nomination speech for Senator George McGovern. In the August 28 speech, Ribicoff is critical of the Democratic Establishment for turning a deaf ear to the growing antiwar movement. He is also critical of the tactics used by the Chicago Police Department and Mayor Richard Daley in dealing with protesters at the convention.

On election day, November 5, Republican Richard Nixon is elected president with 43.4 percent of the popular vote to Democrat Hubert Humphrey's 42.7 percent. Voter turnout is 60.8 percent.

1971

The McGovern-Fraser Commission Report, commissioned in response to division in the Democratic Party during the 1968 election, leads the Democratic National Committee to adopt a binding primary and caucus system and proportional distribution of delegates for selecting the party's presidential candidates. The changes take power over the nominating process from local party bosses and allows for greater participation by all party members.

1972

In conjunction with the Richard Nixon campaign, right-wing newspaper publisher William Loeb publishes two editorials in February about Senator Edmund Muskie, Democratic candidate for president, one of which is a nasty attack on the senator's wife. When Muskie speaks to reporters in response he appears to have tears in his eyes, although it could have actually been melting snow. The incident, as covered by the press, contributes to the perception that Muskie was too sensitive and not fit to lead.

On May 15, Democratic presidential candidate George Wallace is shot in an assassination attempt. The attack leaves him paralyzed below the chest, and he is forced to withdraw from the campaign, in which he had been polling well.

Burglars are caught breaking into the Democratic National Committee's office in the Watergate building in Washington, D.C. The burglars, who have ties to President Richard Nixon's Committee to Re-Elect the President, are there as part of Nixon's plan to destabilize the Democratic Party.

At the July 10–13 Democratic National Convention in Miami, Senator George McGovern receives his party's presidential nomination. Senator Thomas Eagleton is chosen as his running mate.

On July 31 only weeks after Democratic presidential nominee George McGovern names Missouri senator Thomas Eagleton as his running mate, Eagleton is dropped from the ticket after it is revealed that he had been hospitalized for depression and received electroshock therapy. He is replaced by Sargent Shriver.

At the August 21–22 Republican National Convention in Miami Beach, President Richard Nixon again receives his party's presidential nomination. Vice President Spiro Agnew is again his running mate.

On election day, November 7, President Richard Nixon is reelected with 60.7 percent of the popular vote to Democrat George McGovern's 37.5 percent. Voter turnout is 55.2 percent.

1974

After the U.S. House of Representatives issues articles of impeachment against him in the wake of the Watergate Scandal, Richard Nixon announces on August 8 that he will resign the following day, becoming the first U.S. president ever to resign from the office. Nixon admits no wrongdoing related to Watergate.

President Gerald Ford, who as vice president succeeded Richard Nixon when he resigned the presidency, announces on September 8 that he is issuing Nixon a pardon that will shield him from any criminal charges. The pardon later becomes an issue in Ford's 1976 bid for reelection.

1976

Democratic presidential candidate Jimmy Carter's "Bio" campaign ad emphasizes integrity in government, religious values, and a kind of folksy humility that appeals to many voters, given the recent events surrounding the Watergate Scandal and the pardon of Richard Nixon by Gerald Ford.

Former California governor Ronald Reagan delivers a speech titled "To Restore America" at the Republican National Convention on March 31. In the speech, Reagan lays out his rationale for challenging sitting president Gerald Ford in seeking the Republican nomination for president.

At the July 12–15 Democratic National Convention in New York, Governor Jimmy Carter receives his party's presidential nomination. Senator Walter Mondale is his running mate.

At the August 16–19 Republican National Convention in Kansas City, President Gerald Ford again receives his party's presidential nomination. Senator Bob Dole is his running mate.

At the second presidential debate, held on October 6, Republican nominee President Gerald Ford mistakenly says that "there is no Soviet domination of Eastern Europe," although in fact Eastern Europe is the apex of Soviet domination in the 1970s. Ford does not back down from the statement for several days, and it becomes known as the gaffe heard around the world.

On election day, November 2, Democrat Jimmy Carter is elected president with 50.1 percent of the popular vote to President Gerald Ford's 48 percent. Voter turnout is 53.5 percent.

1979

On July 15 more than 10 days after he is scheduled to do so, President Jimmy Carter addresses the nation regarding the energy crisis. "This is not a message of happiness or reassurance," Carter says, "but it is the truth and it is a warning." Initially well received, the speech is later portrayed as pessimistic and defeatist and becomes known as the "Malaise" speech.

As support builds for Senator Edward M. Kennedy to challenge sitting president Jimmy Carter for the Democratic presidential nomination, Kennedy agrees to a live interview with CBS reporter Roger Mudd. When Mudd asks Kennedy why he wants to be president, he is unable to give the clear, powerfully articulated response that all candidates should have.

1980

President Jimmy Carter announces that a mission to rescue American hostages from the U.S. embassy in Tehran, Iran, has failed, resulting in the deaths of eight crewmen in two aircraft that collided.

At the July 14–17 Republican National Convention in Detroit, former governor Ronald Reagan receives his party's presidential nomination. Former representative and Central Intelligence Agency director George H. W. Bush is his running mate.

At the August 11–14 Democratic National Convention in New York, President Jimmy Carter again receives his party's presidential nomination. Vice President Walter Mondale is again his running mate.

Senator Edward M. Kennedy addresses the Democratic National Convention on August 12, conceding the party's presidential nomination to sitting president Jimmy Carter. In his speech, Kennedy congratulates Carter but does not heap praise on him as is usually done in such concession speeches. Kennedy concludes by saying that "For all those whose cares have been our concern, the work goes on, the cause endures, the hope still lives, and the dream shall never die."

At the second presidential debate, held on October 28, Republican nominee Ronald Reagan accuses Democratic nominee President Jimmy Carter of blaming the American people for the nation's economic problems, likely a callback to Carter's July 1979 "Malaise" speech in which the president suggested that many of the nation's problems were due to a "crisis of confidence." Reagan also delivers an effective blow to Carter's candidacy by asking the people "are you better off than you were four years ago?"

On election day, November 4, Republican Ronald Reagan is elected president with 50.8 percent of the popular vote to President Jimmy Carter's 41 percent. Voter turnout is 52.6 percent. Reagan is the first candidate to win more than 50 million votes.

1984

At the July 16–19 Democratic National Convention in San Francisco, Vice President Walter Mondale receives his party's presidential nomination. Representative Geraldine Ferraro, the first woman ever to appear on a major party ticket, is his running mate.

In accepting the Democratic nomination for president on July 19, former vice president Walter Mondale indicates that if elected he will control the national deficit by reducing spending and raising taxes, something that few candidates would come right out and say. He receives applause at the convention, but the reaction of average voters is surely less enthusiastic.

At the August 20–23 Republican National Convention in Dallas, President Ronald Reagan again receives his party's presidential nomination. Vice President George Bush is again his running mate.

The Ronald Reagan campaign issues its "Prouder, Stronger, Better" campaign ad, better known as the "Morning in America" ad. Using soft tones and images that evoke optimism, hope, patriotism, and prosperity, the ad draws distinctions between Reagan and Democratic challenger Walter Mondale by reminding voters of what the Reagan campaign saw as the failed policies of the Jimmy Carter administration, in which Mondale served as vice president.

In an October 21 foreign policy debate between Democratic presidential nominee Walter Mondale and Republican nominee President Ronald Reagan, Reagan effectively deflects questions about the effects that his age would have on his presidency by quipping that "I am not going to exploit, for political purposes, my opponent's youth and inexperience." Reagan is in his 70s, and Mondale is in his fifties.

On election day, November 6, President Ronald Reagan is reelected with 58.7 percent of the popular vote to Democrat Walter Mondale's 40.6 percent. Voter turnout is 53.1 percent.

1987

When allegations of womanizing are leveled against Democratic presidential front-runner Gary Hart, he dares reporters to follow him to prove that he's having an affair. The *Miami Herald* does just that and reports that a young woman spent the night at Hart's home while his wife was out of town. The following day, May 4, the *Washington Post* picks up the story, which the Hart campaign calls "character assassination" and refuses to "dignify it with a comment." This is the day that the line between reporting on the public and private lives of candidates is gone. Hart withdraws from the race on May 8.

1988

At the July 18–21 Democratic National Convention in Atlanta, Governor Michael Dukakis receives his party's presidential nomination. Senator Lloyd Bentsen is his running mate.

At the August 15–18 Republican National Convention in New Orleans, Vice President George H. W. Bush receives his party's presidential nomination. Senator Dan Quayle is his running mate.

During his campaign for the presidency, Vice President George H. W. Bush refuses to answer any questions about the Iran-Contra Affair, which saw more members of the Ronald Reagan administration (in which Bush served as vice president) indicted, convicted, or forced to resign than any other presidential administration in U.S. history. Bush denies having had any knowledge of the situation.

The George H. W. Bush campaign releases its "Tank Ride" ad in which opponent Michael Dukakis rides around in a tank in a staged event. The ad undermines Dukakis's credibility on foreign policy and defense issues, particularly since Bush had served as a fighter pilot in World War II, a member of Congress, an ambassador to China, and director of the Central Intelligence Agency.

A PAC claiming to operate independently of the George H. W. Bush campaign but later shown to have ties to the campaign releases the "Willie Horton" ad, which paints Democratic candidate Michael Dukakis as being soft on crime. The ad ties Dukakis to Willie Horton, who committed rape and assault while on furlough from prison in Massachusetts during Dukakis's tenure as governor of the state. The ad is misleading—Dukakis had inherited the furlough program—but is extremely effective.

At the Republican National Convention, Vice President George H. W. Bush accepts the party's presidential nomination on August 18 with the now-infamous declaration "Read my lips: no new taxes." As president, Bush will eventually raise taxes.

At a vice presidential debate between Republican candidate Dan Quayle and Democratic candidate Lloyd Bensten, Quayle compares the amount of experience he's had in Congress to John F. Kennedy's experience. Bensten responds, "I knew Jack Kennedy. . . . Senator, you are no Jack Kennedy."

At the second presidential debate between Incumbent George H. W. Bush and Democratic challenger Michael Dukakis on October 13, the anti–capital punishment Dukakis is asked whether, if his wife were raped and murdered, he would favor the death penalty for the killer. Dukakis matter-of-factly states that he would not instead of giving the expected emotional response. Dukakis is consistent with his principles, but many observers interpret his consistency as a lack of emotion.

On election day, November 8, Vice President George H. W. Bush is elected president with 53.4 percent of the popular vote to Democrat Michael Dukakis's 45.7 percent. Voter turnout is 50.2 percent.

1992

Two weeks before the first primary, in New Hampshire, Arkansas state employee Gennifer Flowers holds a press conference in which she details a 12-year affair between herself and Democratic candidate Bill Clinton. In response, Clinton and his wife, Hillary, appear live on *60 Minutes* on January 26. The Clintons present a united front and take the offensive; following the interview, the matter seems to fade away.

On February 2, a Vietnam War–era letter written by Democratic candidate Bill Clinton to the head of the University of Arkansas's Army Reserve program is made public. Clinton, who did not serve in the military, thanks the man for "saving" him from the draft. Instead of serving, Clinton went to Oxford as a Rhodes scholar.

Billionaire businessman Ross Perot announces on *Larry King Live* that "If you, the people, will on your own . . . register me in 50 states, I'll promise you this: between now and the convention we'll get both parties' heads straight."

At the July 13–16 Democratic National Convention in New York, Governor Bill Clinton receives his party's presidential nomination. Senator Al Gore is his running mate.

At the August 17–20 Republican National Convention in Houston, President George H. W. Bush again receives his party's presidential nomination. Vice President Dan Quayle is again his running mate.

At the Republican National Convention, Pat Buchanan, who sought to challenge President George H. W. Bush in his bid for reelection, says that the "Buchanan brigades are enlisted" to support Bush. However, Buchanan's dramatic speech seems to resonate more with hard-line conservatives than the moderates that the Republican Party will need to win the November election.

On election day, November 3, Democrat Bill Clinton is elected president with 43 percent of the popular vote to President George H. W. Bush's 37.5 percent. Independent candidate Ross Perot garners 18.9 percent of the popular vote. Voter turnout is 55.2 percent.

1995

After many weeks of intense attention by the national media, General Colin Powell announces at a November 8 press conference that he will not seek the Republican nomination for president, nor will he consider running as vice president. Although he had served his country in the military for more than 35 years, the difficulties of a political campaign in an era of increasing incivility and polarization weigh heavily on his decision.

1996

Senator Bob Dole, who is seeking the Republican nomination for president, resigns his Senate seat on June 11, after 27 years of service. In his resignation speech, Dole cites a long list of bipartisan legislative successes and emphasizes comity, civility, bipartisanship, and history, demonstrating that his ticket will not just be an extension of the Republican Party's conservative agenda and what the Bill Clinton campaign would portray as the excesses of the House Republicans' Contract with America.

At the August 12–15 Republican National Convention in San Diego, Senator Bob Dole receives his party's presidential nomination. Former representative and housing and urban development secretary Jack Kemp is his running mate.

At the August 26–29 Democratic National Convention in Chicago, President Bill Clinton again receives his party's presidential nomination. Vice President Al Gore is again his running mate.

On election day, November 5, President Bill Clinton is reelected with 49.2 percent of the popular vote to Republican Bob Dole's 40.7 percent. Voter turnout is 49 percent.

2000

In seeking the Democratic presidential nomination, Vice President Al Gore does not appear at campaign events with President Bill Clinton. Just a few years earlier, Clinton had denied allegations of an affair between himself and White House intern Monica Lewinsky. It was later discovered that Clinton perjured himself when testifying before Congress over the matter, and he is impeached by the House of Representatives. The Senate voted against conviction and removal of the president from office.

Soon after Senator John McCain wins the New Hampshire Republican primary, there are indications of a whisper campaign against him and reports of push polls asking whether respondents would "be more likely or less likely to vote for McCain for president if you knew he had fathered an illegitimate black child." The question is apparently an allusion to McCain's adopted daughter from Bangladesh. Rumors also emerge that McCain's wife, Cynthia, is a drug addict. The smear tactics are a heavy blow to the McCain campaign.

At the June 24–25 Green Party National Nominating Convention in Denver, consumer rights activist Ralph Nader receives the party's presidential nomination. Native American activist and environmentalist Winona LaDuke is his running mate.

Ralph Nader accepts the Green Party's presidential nomination on June 25. In his acceptance speech, Nader declares that the "will of the people has been thwarted" by a "worsening concentration of global corporate power over our government" that "has turned that government frequently against its own people, denying its people their sovereignty to shape their future."

At the July 31–August 3 Republican National Convention in Philadelphia, Governor George W. Bush receives his party's presidential nomination. Former representative and secretary of defense Dick Cheney is his running mate.

At the August 14–17 Democratic National Convention in Los Angeles, Vice President Al Gore receives his party's presidential nomination. Senator Joseph Lieberman is his running mate.

Democratic nominee Al Gore gives his wife, Tipper, a long, passionate kiss onstage at the Democratic National Convention. The media speculates as to whether the kiss was a calculated move to soften Gore's robotic image.

On election day, November 7, it is unclear whether Republican George W. Bush or Vice President Al Gore has won the election. Irregularities in the Florida election process sets off a monthlong legal battle that will ultimately be settled by the U.S. Supreme Court. In the end, Bush is elected president with 271 electoral votes to Gore's 266 electoral votes. While Bush wins the electoral college, he loses the popular vote, with 47.9 percent to Gore's 48.4 percent. Green Party candidate Ralph Nader receives 2.7 percent of the popular vote. Voter turnout is 50.4 percent.

The U.S. Supreme Court's 5 to 4 decision in *Bush v. Gore* halts the recount of ballots in Florida. The timing of the decision, released on December 12 just hours before the deadline for states to choose electors, leaves the legal team for Al Gore, who is behind in the Florida vote count, little room to maneuver. Gore concedes the election to George W. Bush the following day.

2004

In response to state action by courts, legislatures, and city administrators to permit same-sex couples to marry or establish civil unions, President George W. Bush, who is seeking reelection, calls for a constitutional amendment defining marriage as being between a man and a woman. With a dozen anti–gay marriage initiatives on state ballots, the issue will raise voter turnout in key battleground states.

The Associated Press reports on September 5 that the records released regarding George W. Bush's service in the Air National Guard during the Vietnam War are incomplete. Missing from the records are several documents that would explain gaps in Bush's service, and with the campaign centered on national security and military engagements, the candidates' records of their own military service gain a prominence that they hadn't had during Bush's campaign against Al Gore in 2000.

At the July 26–29 Democratic National Convention in Boston, Senator John Kerry receives his party's presidential nomination. Senator John Edwards is his running mate.

The 527 group Swift Boat Veterans for Truth, which objects to Democratic candidate John Kerry's accounts of his service in Vietnam, airs a series of ads saying that he is unfit to lead. The Kerry campaign brings in other Vietnam War veterans to counter the attacks, which draw Kerry's attention away from his most resonant critique of President George W. Bush's handling of the Iraq War and the threat from terrorism.

At the August 30–September 2 Republican National Convention in New York, President George W. Bush again receives his party's nomination. Vice President Dick Cheney is again his running mate.

On election day, November 2, President George W. Bush is reelected with 50.7 percent of the popular vote to Democrat John Kerry's 48.2 percent. Voter turnout is 56.2 percent.

2006

David Brooks, a long-standing conservative contributor to *The New York Times,* publishes an editorial in the paper urging Senator Barack Obama to consider running for president in 2008. Brooks argues that Obama represents something new, different, and necessary to cure the substantial ills of U.S. politics. Because Brooks is a prominent intellectual—particularly a prominent conservative intellectual— people take notice of his opinion.

2008

Following a win in the South Carolina primary, Democratic candidate Barack Obama appears on *ABC This Week with George Stephanopoulos.* In the January 27 interview, Obama addresses questions about the role that race is playing in the campaign as well as about comparisons made by former president Bill Clinton— husband of Democratic candidate Hillary Rodham Clinton—between Obama and Jesse Jackson. Jackson had won the South Carolina Democratic primaries in 1984 and 1988 but had not won the party's nomination. Prior to Obama's candidacy, Jackson had been the most successful African American primary candidate.

Democratic candidate Barack Obama faces severe criticism regarding the angry, racially tinged rhetoric of his longtime pastor and confidant, Reverend Jeremiah Wright. Obama has denounced Wright's words but continues to struggle to articulate his own view on race and distinguish that view from the anger and frustration felt by many in the black community—as evidenced by Wright's remarks. On March 18, Obama delivers a speech titled "A More Perfect Union" in which he reasserts his core principles, articulating a compelling view on issues of race and demonstrating a sensitivity to the issue of race that no public official had before exhibited.

In June, Democratic presidential candidate Barack Obama announces that should he receive the party's nomination, in the general campaign he will forego public financing—which would also exempt him from limits to expenditures. Obama, the first major party candidate ever to forego public financing in the general election, says that he believes in "a robust system of public financing of elections" but that the system for presidential elections is broken.

At the August 25–28 Democratic National Convention in Denver, Senator Barack Obama receives his party's presidential nomination. Senator Joseph Biden is his running mate.

At the Democratic National Convention on August 28, Barack Obama accepts the party's nomination for the presidency, becoming the first African American to head a presidential ticket among the two major parties. In his acceptance speech, Obama recognizes Senator Hillary Rodham Clinton, a Democratic primary opponent who came closer to a major party presidential nomination than any woman before her.

At the September 1–4 Republican National Convention in St. Paul, Senator John McCain receives his party's presidential nomination. Governor Sarah Palin is his running mate, the first woman ever to appear on the Republican ticket.

In the midst of a serious economic crisis, Republican candidate John McCain says that the fundamentals of the U.S. economy are strong. McCain quickly back-pedals, indicating that he was referring to American workers, whom he considers the backbone of the economy. He also describes the economic situation as being in "a total crisis" in an effort to realign with voters who consider the economy the most important issue in the election.

The third presidential debate, held on October 14, is dominated by economic issues. In discussing small businesses, Republican candidate John McCain brings up Joe Wurzelbacher—later known as "Joe the Plumber"—who had questioned Democratic candidate Barack Obama about tax policy at a campaign stop. In his response to Wurzelbacher, Obama had commented that "when you spread the wealth around, it's good for everybody." The line was picked up by the McCain campaign, which questioned whether Obama was advocating a radical redistribution of wealth.

In an interview on *Meet the Press,* Colin Powell, former secretary of state and chair of the Joint Chiefs of Staff, lifelong Republican, and one of the most prominent African Americans in U.S. politics, endorses Democrat Barack Obama's campaign for the presidency.

On election day, November 4, Democrat Barack Obama is elected president with 52.9 percent of the popular vote to Republican John McCain's 45.6 percent. Voter turnout is 58.2 percent.

2011

On November 9 in an early debate among Republican primary presidential candidate, Texas governor Rick Perry, viewed as a major contender for the nomination, makes a major campaign gaffe when he says that he will cut three government agencies to reduce government regulation but can ultimately only name two—the Department of Commerce and the Department of Education.

2012

On August 11, presumptive Republican presidential nominee Mitt Romney announces that his vice presidential running mate will be Representative Paul Ryan, the Tea Party–backed congressman representing Wisconsin's 1st District and chairman of the House Budget Committee. Ryan is closely associated with the drafting and promotion of the Republican Party's controversial federal budget proposal, often called simply "the Ryan Plan."

At the August 27–30 Republican National Convention in Tampa, Florida, Mitt Romney formally receives and accepts the Republican Party's 2012 presidential nomination. Among the convention's most-discussed events is an impromptu address by actor and director Clint Eastwood in which he mockingly speaks to an empty chair as if it is President Obama.

At the September 4–6 Democratic National Convention in Charlotte, North Carolina, Barack Obama formally receives and accepts the Democratic Party's 2012 presidential nomination. Former president Bill Clinton gives one of the most significant speeches of the campaign season, endorsing President Obama and questioning the arithmetic of Republican budget proposals. Obama later calls Clinton his "Explainer in Chief."

On September 17, the magazine *Mother Jones* releases a leaked video from May 17, 2012, of Republican presidential candidate Mitt Romney at a private $50,000-per-plate fund-raising dinner. Romney's comments that 47 percent of Americans who pay no income tax "believe that they are victims" and that his job as a prospective president is "not to worry about those people" will be used by the Obama campaign to paint Romney as a plutocrat out of touch with the struggles of poor and middle-class Americans.

On October 3 in the first of three presidential debates, Mitt Romney performs strongly against President Barack Obama, controlling the debate and directing moderator Jim Lehrer. Postdebate polls reveal that most of the public views Romney to be the debate winner and that Obama had appeared to be the less powerful potential leader. Polls also reveal that Romney had regained ground on President Obama, showing the two candidates to be nearly tied and in some cases showing Romney ahead after the first debate.

On October 31 just after Hurricane Sandy makes landfall, leaving major East Coast cities flooded and without power, President Obama meets with the prominent Republican governor of New Jersey, Chris Christie, and FEMA officials to tour the ravaged New Jersey coastline. The nature of the disaster forces Republican presidential candidate Mitt Romney to suspend his campaign only days before the election, while Obama continues to receive significant news coverage for his handling of the disaster and earns praise from the high-profile Christie.

On November 7, President Barack Obama wins reelection with 50.6 percent of the popular vote, while Republican Mitt Romney receives 47.8 percent of the vote. The electoral college tilts heavily to Obama, who receives 332 electoral college votes to Romney's 206.

Sources

ABC-CLIO. *American Government.* 2012. http://americangovernment.abc-clio.com.

Biographical Directory of the United States Congress, 1774–Present. http://bioguide.congress.gov.

National Governor's Association. http://www.nga.org.

Ragsdale, Lyn. *Vital Statistics on the Presidency: Washington to Clinton.* Washington, DC: Congressional Quarterly, 1996.

Troy, Gil, Arthur M. Schlesinger Jr., and Fred L. Israel, eds. *History of American Presidential Elections, 1789–2008,* Vol. 3, *1944–2008.* 4th ed. New York: Facts on File, 2012.

Further Reading

Presidential Election of 1952

Asher, Herbert. *Presidential Elections & American Politics: Voters, Candidates & Campaigns since 1952.* Boston: Harcourt, 1997.

Blumberg, Nathan B. *One-Party Press? Coverage of the 1952 Presidential Campaign in 35 Daily Newspapers.* Lincoln: University of Nebraska Press, 1954.

Charles, James C. *Meaning of the 1952 Presidential Election.* Philadelphia: American Academy of Political and Social Science, 1952.

Cohn, Ronald, and Jesse Russell. *United States Presidential Election, 1952.* Paris: VSD, 2012.

David, Paul Theodore. *Presidential Nominating Politics in 1952.* Baltimore: Johns Hopkins University Press, 1954.

Donaldson, Gary A. *The 1952 Presidential Election.* Lanham, MD: Rowman and Littlefield, 2012.

Dreier, Alex. *Presidential Election Preview 1952: Eisenhower and Nixon versus Stevenson and Sparkman.* Arlington, VA: Skelly, 1952.

Greene, John Robert. *The Crusade: The Presidential Election of 1952.* Lanham, MD: University Press of America, 1985.

Janowitz, Morris, and Dwaine Marvick. *Competitive Pressure and Democratic Consent: An Interpretation of the 1952 Presidential Election.* Westport, CT: Greenwood, 1976.

Mattson, Kevin. *Just Plain Dick: Richard Nixon's Checkers Speech and the Mad Election of 1952.* New York: Bloomsbury USA, 2012.

Miller, Warren E., Teresa E. Levitin. *Leadership and Change: Presidential Election from 1952–1976.* New York: Little, Brown, 1976.

Strong, Donald S. *The 1952 Presidential Election in the South.* Birmingham: Bureau of Public Administration, University of Alabama, 1955.

Presidential Election of 1956

Bartley, Numan V. *The Rise of Massive Resistance: Race and Politics in the South During the 1950s.* Baton Rouge: Louisiana State University Press, 1999.

Divine, Robert A. *Foreign Policy and United States Presidential Elections, 1952–60*. West Sussex, UK: Littlehampton Book Service, 1974.

Nichols, David A. *Eisenhower 1956: The President's Year of Crisis; Suez and the Brink of War*. New York: Simon and Schuster, 2011.

1956 Presidential Handbook. Saint Paul, MN: Brown and Bigelow, 1956.

Ra, Jong Oh. *Labor at the Polls: Union Voting in Presidential Election, 1952–1976*. Amherst: University of Massachusetts Press, 1977.

Thomson, Charles A. H., and Frances M. Shattuck. *The 1956 Presidential Campaign*. Westport, CT: Greenwood, 1974.

United States Presidential Election 1956: United States Presidential Candidates, 1956, Dwight D. Eisenhower. Memphis, TN: General Books, 2010.

Presidential Election 1960

Buell, Emmett H., Jr., and Lee Sigelman. *Attack Politics: Negativity in Presidential Campaigns since 1960*. Lawrence: University Press of Kansas, 2009.

Casey, Shaun A. *The Making of a Catholic President: Kennedy vs. Nixon, 1960*. New York: Oxford University Press, 2009.

Donaldson, Gary A. *The First Modern Campaign: Kennedy, Nixon, and the Election of 1960*. Lanham, MD: Rowman and Littlefield, 2007.

Gifford, Laura. *The Center Cannot Hold: The 1960 Presidential Election and the Rise of Modern Conservatism*. DeKalb: Northern Illinois University Press, 2009.

Kallina, Edmund F., Jr. *Kennedy v. Nixon: The Presidential Election of 1960*. Gainesville: University Press of Florida, 2011.

Menendez, Albert J. *The Religious Factor in the 1960 Presidential Election: An Analysis of the Kennedy Victory over Anti-Catholic Prejudice*. Jefferson, NC: McFarland, 2011.

Pietrusza, David. *1960—LBJ vs. JFK vs. Nixon: The Epic Campaign That Forged Three Presidencies*. New York: Union Square, 2010.

Robb, David L. *The Gumshoe and the Shrink: Guenther Reinhardt, Dr. Arnold Hutschnecker, and the Secret History of the 1960 Kennedy/Nixon Election*. Chicago: Santa Monica Press, 2012.

Rorabaugh, W. J. *The Real Making of the President: Kennedy, Nixon, and the 1960 Election*. Lawrence: University Press of Kansas, 2009.

Scott, Thomas G. *A New World to Be Won: John Kennedy, Richard Nixon, and the Tumultuous Year of 1960*. Westport, CT: Praeger, 2011.

United States Presidential Candidates, 1960: Richard Nixon, United States Presidential Election. Memphis, TN: General Books, 2010.

White, Theodore H. *The Making of the President, 1960*. Rev. ed. New York: Harper Perennial, 2009.

Presidential Election of 1964

Donaldson, Gary. *Liberalism's Last Hurrah: The Presidential Campaign of 1964*. Armonk, NY: M. E. Sharpe, 2003.

Grofman, Bernard. *Legacies of the 1964 Civil Rights Act*. Charlottesville: University of Virginia Press, 2000.

Johnson, Robert David. *All the Way with LBJ: The 1964 Presidential Election*. Cambridge: Cambridge University Press, 2009.

Lamb, Karl A. *Campaign Decision-Making: The Presidential Election of 1964.* Belmont, CA: Wadsworth, 1968.

Myers, David Samuel. *Foreign Affairs and the 1964 Presidential Election in the United States.* Delhi, India: Sadhana Prakashan, 1972.

New York Herald Tribune. *1964 Presidential Election Guide.* Las Vegas, NV: Whitney Communications, Book Division, 1964.

United States Presidential Election 1964: United States Presidential Candidates, 1964; United States Presidential Primaries 1964. Memphis, TN: General Books, 2010.

White, Theodore H. *The Making of the President, 1964.* New York: Harper Perennial, 2010.

Presidential Election of 1968

Boomhower, Ray E. *Robert F. Kennedy and the 1968 Indiana Primary.* Bloomington: Indiana University Press, 2008.

Gould, Lewis L. *1968: The Election That Changed America.*

2nd ed. Lanham, MD: Ivan R. Dee, 2010.

Kurlansky, Mark. *1968: The Year That Rocked the World.* New York: Random House Trade Paperbacks, 2005.

LaFeber, Walter. *The Deadly Bet: LBJ, Vietnam, and the 1968 Election.* Lanham, MD: Rowman and Littlefield, 2005.

McCarthy, Eugene, and Christopher Hitchens. *1968: War & Democracy.* Petersham, MA: Lone Oak, 2000.

Richardson, Darcy. *A Nation Divided: The 1968 Presidential Campaign.* Bloomington, IN: iUniverse, 2002.

Schlesinger, Arthur Meier, Jr., Fred L. Israel, and David J. Frent. *The Election of 1968 and the Administration of Richard Nixon.* Broomall, PA: Mason Crest, 2002.

United States Presidential Election, 1968: 1968 Democratic National Convention, 1968; Democratic National Convention Protest Activity. Memphis, TN: General Books, 2010.

Wainstock, Dennis. *The Turning Point: The 1968 United States Presidential Campaign.* Jefferson, NC: Mcfarland, 1988.

White, Theodore H. *The Making of the President, 1968.* New York: Harper Perennial, 2010.

Presidential Election of 1972

French, Tom. *The 1972 Presidential Campaign in Buttons: An Illustrated Guide of Nearly 2,000 Different Campaign Items of the 1972 Election, with Short Campaign Summaries for Each Candidate.* Temperance, MI: Political Collector, 1973.

Garza, Hedda. *The Watergate Investigation Index: Senate Select Committee Hearings and Reports on Presidential Campaign Activities.* New York: Scholarly Resources, 1982.

Nelson, Candice J. *Grant Park: The Democratization of Presidential Elections, 1968–2008.* Washington, DC: Brookings Institution Press, 2011.

Select Committee on Presidential Campaign Activities. *Presidential Campaign Activities of 1972, Senate Resolution 60: Watergate and Related Activities.* Ann Arbor: University of Michigan Library, 1973.

Sullivan, Denis, Jeffrey Pressman, Benjamin Page, and John Lyons. *The Politics of Representation: The Democratic Convention, 1972.* New York: St. Martin's, 1974.

Steck, Joan Orr. *Press Commentary and the 1972 Presidential Election: An Analysis of Selected Columnists,* Vol. 2. Madison: University of Wisconsin–Madison Press, 1980.

Thompson, Hunter S. *Fear and Loathing on the Campaign Trail '72.* New York: Simon and Schuster, 2012.

United States Presidential Election, 1972: George McGovern Presidential Campaign, 1972; United States Presidential Election in California, 1972. Memphis, TN: General Books, 2010.

White, Theodore H. *The Making of the President, 1972.* New York: Harper Perennial, 2010.

Witcover, Jules. *Marathon: The Pursuit of the Presidency, 1972–1976.* Springfield, VA: Outlet, 1980.

Presidential Election of 1976

Anderson, Patrick *Electing Jimmy Carter: The Campaign of 1976.* Baton Rouge: Louisiana State University Press, 1994.

Blackman, Paul H. *Presidential Primaries and the 1976 Election.* Washington, DC: Heritage Foundation, 1975.

Gilroy, Jane H. *A Shared Vision: The 1976 Ellen McCormack Presidential Campaign.* Parker, CO: Outskirts, 2010.

Miller, E. Willard, and Ruby M. Miller. *The Presidential Elections, 1976: A Bibliography.* Monticello, IL: Vance Bibliographies, 1987.

Osborn, George Coleman. *The Role of the British Press in the 1976 American Presidential Election.* Pompano Beach: Exposition Press of Florida, 1981.

Schlesinger, Arthur Meier, Jr., Fred L. Israel, and David J. Frent. *The Election of 1976 and the Administration of Jimmy Carter.* Broomall, PA: Mason Crest, 2002.

Seifert, Erica J. *Politics of Authenticity in Presidential Campaigns, 1976–2008.* Jefferson, NC: Mcfarland, 2012.

Stewart, William Histaspas. *Alabama and the 1976 Presidential Election.* Birmingham: Bureau of Public Administration, University of Alabama, 1977.

United States Presidential Election, 1976: United States Presidential Election in California, 1976; 1976 Republican National Convention. Memphis, TN: General Books, 2010.

Presidential Election of 1980

Adams, William C. *Television Coverage of the 1980 Presidential Campaign.* New York: Ablex, 1983.

Busch, Andrew E. *Reagan's Victory: The Presidential Election of 1980 and the Rise of the Right.* Lawrence: University Press of Kansas, 2005.

David, Paul T., and David H. Everson. *The Presidential Election and Transition, 1980–1981.* Carbondale: Southern Illinois University Press, 1983.

Drew, Elizabeth. *Portrait of an Election: The 1980 Presidential Campaign.* New York: Simon and Schuster, 1981.

Ferguson, Thomas. *The Hidden Election: Politics and Economics in the 1980 Presidential Campaign.* New York: Pantheon, 1981.

Howison, Jeffrey. *The 1980 Presidential Election: Ronald Reagan and the American Conservative Movement.* Florence, KT: Routledge, 2013.

Mason, Jim. *No Holding Back: The 1980 John B. Anderson Presidential Campaign.* Lanham, MD: University Press of America, 2011.

Schlesinger, Arthur Meier, Jr., Fred L. Israel, and David J. Frent. *The Election of 1980 and the Administration of Ronald Reagan.* Broomall, PA: Mason Crest, 2002.

United States Presidential Election, 1980: United States Presidential Candidates, 1980; United States Presidential Primaries, 1980. Memphis, TN: General Books, 2010.

Wattenberg, Martin P. *The Rise of Candidate-Centered Politics: Presidential Elections of the 1980s.* Cambridge, MA: Harvard University Press, 1992.

Presidential Election of 1984

Barker, Lucius J. *Our Time Has Come: A Delegate's Diary of Jesse Jackson's 1984 Presidential Campaign.* Champaign: University of Illinois Press, 1988.

Blume, Keith. *Presidential Election Show: Nightly News Coverage of the 1984 Campaign.* Westport CT: Bergin and Garvey, 1985.

Forest, John. *Warriors of the Political Arena: The Presidential Election of 1984.* Orlando, FL: Vantage, 1986.

Germond, Jack W., and Jules Witcover. *Wake Us When It's Over: Presidential Politics of 1984.* New York: Macmillan, 1985.

Green, Rodney, and Lorenzo Morris. *The Social and Political Implications of the 1984 Jesse Jackson Presidential Campaign.* Westport, CT: Praeger, 1990.

Moore, Jonathan. *Campaign for President: The Managers Look at '84.* Towson, MD: Auburn House, 1986.

Scammon, Richard M., and Alice V. McGillivray. *America at the Polls 2: A Handbook of Presidential Election Statistics, 1968–1984.* Washington, DC: CQ Press, 1988.

Steed Robert P., Laurence W. Moreland, and Tod A. Baker. *The 1984 Presidential Election in the South: Patterns of Southern Party Politics.* Westport, CT: Praeger, 1985.

United States Presidential Election, 1984: United States Presidential Candidates, 1984; United States Presidential Primaries, 1984. Memphis, TN: General Books, 2010.

Watson, Richard A. *The Presidential Contest: With a Guide to the 1984 Race.* Hoboken, NJ: Wiley, 1984.

Presidential Election of 1988

Edwards, Janis L. *Political Cartoons in the 1988 Presidential Campaign: Image, Metaphor, and Narrative.* Florence, KY: Routledge, 1997.

Farnsworth, Stephen J., and Robert S. Lichter. *The Nightly News Nightmare: Media Coverage of U.S. Presidential Elections, 1988–2008.* Lanham, MD: Rowman and Littlefield, 2010.

Goldstein, Micheal L. *Guide to the 1988 Presidential Election.* Washington, DC: CQ Press, 1988.

Kimball, Penn. *"Keep Hope Alive!": Super Tuesday and Jesse Jackson's 1988 Campaign for the Presidency.* Lanham, MD: University Press of America, 1991.

Moreland, Laurence W., Robert P. Steed, and Tod A. Baker. *The 1988 Presidential Election in the South: Continuity Amidst Change in Southern Party Politics.* Westport, CT: Praeger, 1991.

Simon, Paul. *Winners and Losers: The 1988 Race for the Presidency; One Candidate's Perspective.* New York: Continuum, 1989.

Swerdlow, Joel L. *Presidential Debates: 1988 and Beyond.* Washington, DC: CQ Press, 1987.

United States Presidential Election 1988: Read My Lips. Memphis, TN: General Books, 2010.

Presidential Election of 1992

Alderton, Steven A. *The American Presidential Election of 1992: A Change in the Electoral Order? Applying Shafer's Electoral Order Model to the 1992 Presidential Election.* Victoria, Australia: University of Melbourne, 1994.

Alexander, Herbert E., and Anthony Corrado. *Financing the 1992 Election.* Armonk, NY: M. E. Sharpe, 1995.

Baker, Tod A., Laurence W. Moreland, and Robert P. Steed. *The 1992 Presidential Election in the South.* Westport, CT: Praeger, 1994.

Benoit, William L., and William T. Wells. *Candidates in Conflict: Persuasive Attack and Defense in the 1992 Presidential Debates.* Tuscaloosa: University of Alabama Press, 1996.

Ceaser, James, and Andrew Busch. *Upside Down and Inside Out: The 1992 Elections and American Politics.* Lanham, MD: Rowman and Littlefield, 1993.

Goldman, Peter, Thomas M. DeFrank, Mark Miller, Andrew Murr, and Tom Matthews. *Quest for the Presidency 1992.* College Station: Texas A&M University Press, 1994.

Loevy, Robert D. *The Flawed Path to the Presidency 1992: Unfairness and Inequality in the Presidential Selection Process.* Albany: State University of New York Press, 1994.

McGillivray, Alice V. *Presidential Primaries and Caucuses, 1992: A Handbook of Election Statistics.* Washington, DC: CQ Press, 1992.

Pomper, Gerald M., F. Christopher Arterton, and Ross K. Baker. *The Election of 1992: Reports and Interpretations.* London: Chatham House, 1993.

Presidential Election of 1996

Denton, Robert E., Jr. *The 1996 Presidential Campaign: A Communication Perspective.* Westport, CT: Praeger, 1998.

Dover, E. D. *The Presidential Election of 1996: Clinton's Incumbency and Television.* Westport, CT: Praeger, 1998.

Gree, John Clifford. *Financing the 1996 Election.* Armonk, NY: M. E. Sharpe, 1999.

Kaid, Lynda Lee, Mitchell S. McKinney, and John C. Tedesco. *Civic Dialogue in the 1996 Presidential Campaign: Candidate, Media, and Public Voices.* New York: Hampton, 2001.

Moreland, Laurence W., and Robert P. Steed. *The 1996 Presidential Election in the South: Southern Party Systems in the 1990s.* Westport, CT: Praeger, 1997.

Pika, Joseph August, and Richard A. Watson. *The Presidential Contest: With a Guide to the 1996 Presidential Race.* Washington, DC: CQ Press, 1995.

United States Presidential Election, 1996: United States Presidential Election in California, 1996. Memphis, TN: General Books, 2010.

Wayne, Stephen J. *The Road to the White House, 1996: The Politics of Presidential Election; Post-Election Edition.* New York: St. Martin's, 1997.

Presidential Election of 2000

Ceaser, James W., and Andrew E. Busch. *The Perfect Tie: The True Story of the 2000 Presidential Election.* Lanham, MD: Rowman and Littlefield, 2001.

Dover, E. D. *The Disputed Presidential Election of 2000: A History and Reference Guide.* Westport, CT: Greenwood, 2003.

Franklin, John. *Blue Moon over Miami: An Adult Fairytale about the 2000 Presidential Election Miscounts.* Concord, MA: Infinity, 2000.

Gillman, Howard. *The Votes That Counted: How the Court Decided the 2000 Presidential Election.* Chicago: University of Chicago Press, 2003.

Issacharoff, Samuel, Pamela S. Karlan, and Richard H. Pildes. *When Elections Go Bad: The Law of Democracy and the Presidential Election of 2000.* La Habra, CA: Foundation Press, 2001.

Johnson, Richard, Michael G. Hagen, and Kathleen Hall Jamieson. *The 2000 Presidential Election and the Foundations of Party Politics.* Cambridge: Cambridge University Press, 2004.

New York Times. *36 Days: The Complete Chronicle of the 2000 Presidential Election Crisis.* With an Introduction by Douglas Brinkley. New York: Holt, 2001.

Rakove, Jack N. *The Unfinished Election of 2000.* New York: Basic Books, 2002.

Steed, Robert P., and Laurence W. Moreland. *The 2000 Presidential Election in the South: Partisanship and Southern Party.* Westport, CT: Praeger, 2002.

Toobin, Jeffrey. *Too Close to Call: The Thirty-Six-Day Battle to Decide the 2000 Election.* New York: Random House Trade Paperbacks, 2002.

United States Presidential Election, 2000, By State: United States Presidential Election in Virginia, 2000. Memphis, TN: General Books, 2010.

Weisberg, Herbert, and Clyde Wilcox. *Models of Voting in Presidential Elections: The 2000 U.S. Election.* Stanford, CA: Stanford Law and Politics, 2003.

Presidential Election of 2004

Campbell, David E. *A Matter of Faith: Religion in the 2004 Presidential Election.* Washington, DC: Brookings Institution Press, 2007.

Conyers, John, Anita Miller, and Gore Vidal. *What Went Wrong In Ohio? The Conyers Report on the 2004 Presidential Election.* Chicago: Academy Chicago, 2005.

Denton, Robert E., Jr. *The 2004 Presidential Campaign: A Communication Perspective.* Lanham, MD: Rowman and Littlefield, 2005.

Freeman, Steven F., Joel Bleifuss, and John Conyers Jr. *Was the 2004 Presidential Election Stolen? Exit Polls, Election Fraud, and the Official Count.* New York: Seven Stories, 2006.

Goldstein, K. *Presidential Election, 2004.* Princeton, NJ: Princeton University Press, 2007.

Goldstein, Michael L. *Guide to the 2004 Presidential Election.* Washington, DC: CQ Press, 2003.

Miller, Mark Crispin. *Loser Take All: Election Fraud and the Subversion of Democracy, 2000–2008.* Brooklyn, NY: Ig, 2008.

North, David. *The Crisis of American Democracy: The Presidential Elections of 2000 and 2004.* Oak Park, MI: Mehring Books, 2004.

Thomas, Evan, Eleanor Clift, and the Staff of Newsweek. *Election 2004: How Bush Won and What You Can Expect in the Future.* Boston: PublicAffairs, 2004.

United States Presidential Election, 2004: United States Presidential Election, 2004; Timeline, Swift Vets and POWs for Truth. Memphis, TN: General Books, 2010.

Presidential Election of 2008

Heilemann, John, and Mark Halperin. *Game Change: Obama and the Clintons, McCain and Palin, and the Race of a Lifetime.* New York: Harper, 2010.

Institute of Politics, John F. Kennedy School of Government. *Campaign for President: The Managers Look at 2008.* Lanham, MD: Rowman and Littlefield, 2009.

Johnson, Haynes, and Dan Balz. *The Battle for America 2008: The Story of an Extraordinary Election.* New York: Viking Adult, 2009.

Jones, Erik, and Salvatore Vassallo. *The 2008 Presidential Elections: A Story in Four Acts.* Basingstoke, UK: Palgrave Macmillan, 2009.

Kapeluck, Branwell DuBose, Laurence W. Moreland, and Robert P. Steed. *A Paler Shade of Red: The 2008 Presidential Election in the South.* Fayetteville: University of Arkansas Press, 2009.

Kenski, Kate, Bruce W. Hardy, and Kathleen Hall Jamieson. *The Obama Victory: How Media, Money, and Message Shaped the 2008 Election.* New York: Oxford University Press, 2010.

Maass, Matthias. *The World Views of the U.S. Presidential Election, 2008.* Basingstoke, UK: Palgrave Macmillan, 2009.

Smidt, Corwin, Kevin Den Dulk, Bryan Froehle, James Penning, Stephen Monsma, and Douglas Koopman. *The Disappearing God Gap? Religion in the 2008 Presidential Election.* New York: Oxford University Press, 2010.

Smith, Mark W. *The Official Handbook of the Vast Right-Wing Conspiracy: The 2008 Presidential Election Edition.* Washington, DC: Regnery, 2008.

Starks, Glenn L. *The Galvanization of the Young Vote in the 2008 Presidential Election: Lessons Learned from the Phenomenon.* Lanham, MD: University Press of America, 2009.

Todd, Chuck, and Sheldon Gawiser. *How Barack Obama Won: A State-by-State Guide to the Historic 2008 Presidential Election.* New York: Vintage, 2009.

Trillin, Calvin. *Deciding the Next Decider: The 2008 Presidential Race in Rhyme.* New York: Random House, 2008.

United States Presidential Election, 2008: International Reaction to the United States Presidential Election, 2008. Memphis, TN: General Books, 2010.

Presidential Election of 2012

Blatz, Daniel. *Obama vs. Romney: "The Take" on Election 2012.* Washington, DC: Diversion Books, 2012.

Nelson, Michael, ed. *The Election of 2012.* Washington: Congressional Quarterly, 2013.

Sabato, Larry. *Barack Obama and the New America: The 2012 Election and the Changing Face of Politics.* Lanham, MD: Rowman and Littlefield, 2013.

Thrush, Glenn. *The End of the Line: Romney vs. Obama; The 34 Days That Decided the Election.* New York: Random House, 2012.

Index

About the Authors

Daniel M. Shea, PhD, is a professor of government and the director of the Gold-farb Center for Public Affairs and Civic Engagement at Colby College, Waterville, Maine. He is widely published in the areas of party politics, legislative dynamics, campaign management, and youth political engagement. Also with Praeger, Shea has written *Campaign Craft: The Strategies, Tactics, and Art of Political Campaign Management,* now in its fourth edition.

Brian M. Harward, PhD, is an associate professor of political science and the director of the Center for Political Participation at Allegheny College in Meadville, Pennsylvania. He received his doctorate in political science from the School of Public and International Affairs at the University of Georgia. His recent publications explore issues related to federalism, executive power, the U.S. Senate, and congressional oversight.